Rita Risser

STAY OUT OF COURT

THE MANAGER'S GUIDE TO PREVENTING EMPLOYEE LAWSUITS

PRENTICE HALL
Englewood Cliffs, New Jersey 07632

Prentice-Hall International (UK) Limited, *London*
Prentice-Hall of Australia Pty. Limited, *Sydney*
Prentice-Hall Canada, Inc., *Toronto*
Prentice-Hall Hispanoamericana, S.A., *Mexico*
Prentice-Hall of India Private Limited, *New Delhi*
Prentice-Hall of Japan, Inc., *Tokyo*
Simon & Schuster Asia Pte. Ltd., *Singapore*
Editora Prentice-Hall do Brasil, Ltda., *Rio de Janeiro*

10 9 8 7 6 5 4 3 2 1

This publication is sold with the understanding that the author and publisher are not engaged in rendering legal or other professional services. The publisher disclaims any liability, loss or risk incurred as a consequence, directly or indirectly, of the use and application of any of the contents of this publication. The information in this publication is not a substitute for the advice of a competent legal or other professional person.

Library of Congress Cataloging-in-Publication Data

Risser, Rita.
    Stay out of court! : the manager's guide to preventing employee lawsuits /
by Rita Risser.
        p. cm.
    Includes index.
    ISBN 0-13-845561-9. — ISBN 0-13-845553-8
    1. Labor laws and legislation—United States. 2. Personnel management—
United States. I. Title.
    KF3457.Z9R57 1993
    344.73′01—dc20   93-6799
    [347.3041]   CIP

ISBN 0-13-845553-8
ISBN 0-13 845561-9 (PBK)

PRENTICE HALL
Career & Personal Development
Englewood Cliffs, NJ 07632
Simon & Schuster, A Paramount Communications Company

Printed in the United States of America

for my father
Joseph A. Risser
in memory

About the Author

*R*ita Risser is an attorney who has specialized in discrimination and employment law since 1979. She is a graduate of Boalt Hall, the University of California, Berkeley, School of Law.

After 10 years of practice, she now is a professional speaker, consultant, and author. Her speeches and seminars are sponsored by companies and associations around the country. Her newsletter, *Just Management*, gives business leaders quarterly updates on the law.

For information about her speaking, newsletter and tapes, contact:

Rita Risser, J.D.
Stay Out of Court
P.O. Box 2146
Santa Cruz, CA 95063
408-458-0500
fax 408-458-0181

A Word from the Author

*A*fter 10 years of practicing employment law, I still remember the first time I represented a company. I remember, because we lost.

My clients were a husband and wife. They owned a manufacturing shop with 27 employees—technicians, assemblers, shipping, and office clerks.

A disgruntled former employee filed a claim with the Equal Employment Opportunity Commission, the government agency in charge of investigating sex discrimination complaints.

We resolved that claim quickly and cheaply. The employee dropped the case.

But the EEOC decided to audit my clients' general hiring practices. The agency wanted copies of

- All my clients' help-wanted ads for the last two years

- The names and sex of the people who were hired

- The names and sex of the unsuccessful applicants

- The job applications of the employees and applicants

My clients didn't have all this. They didn't know they were supposed to keep old applications. They thought it was *illegal* to note the sex of applicants. Now the government was saying they were supposed to keep track of it!

Despite my clients' ignorance (or maybe because of it), the EEOC said they were liable for $75,000. No, not millions. But this company's net profit the year before had been $10,000. And by now, they had spent most of that on me.

My clients were shocked. They always had tried to treat their employees fairly. They had a culturally diverse work force. They had women in management.

They couldn't believe the EEOC found against them. When the wife heard about it, she burst into tears. A few months later, they sold out at a low price. They moved to the mountains, to be alone. They left defeated.

This could have been avoided if my clients had hired an attorney before they got sued. But like most business owners and managers, they thought it was too expensive.

They were right. It *is* too expensive to hire a lawyer. That's why you need this book.

This book reflects my personality and perspective, so you should know my biases up front. I got my law degree at the University of California, Berkeley. Since 1979, my specialty has been discrimination and employment law.

After I graduated, I represented only employees. After all, that's why I went to law school—to help people.

In 1981, I started my law firm and learned the necessity of having paying clients. That's one of the problems with representing the employee side—they're all unemployed. So I began representing managers and companies. I used to joke that we'd represent anybody, for money.

By 1990, Employment Rights Attorneys had grown to seven employees, and I learned to be a manager. I hired. I fired. I met a payroll month after month. And I came to the conclusion that being a manager is the toughest job around.

Along the way, I violated various employment laws. In this book, I'll share my experiences so you can learn from my mistakes. You also will learn, as I have, from the experiences of my clients.

In addition to practicing law, I've spent over 10 years training managers around the country on how to manage within the law. They taught me early on to keep a sense of humor, and that's here, too.

Like the anecdote earlier, I'll be using these experiences to make points. In about half the stories, I've changed the type of business, the gender of the people involved, or some of the facts to disguise the source. I've simplified them to make a point. But every story I tell is essentially true and illustrates sound legal principles.

A Word About Words

One area where our biases show is in language. I would like to be politically correct, but I also want to be legally correct and understandable.

For example, throughout this book the following terms will be used: "black" for African-Americans and others of African heritage; "Hispanic" for people originally from Central and South America and the Iberian Peninsula; "Asian" to describe the people of the Far East, including China, Japan, India, and the Pacific Islands such as Samoa and the Philippines; "American Indian" for the native peoples of the North American continent; and "white" for people of European descent. Although other terms may be preferred by some groups, these are used to be consistent with those most commonly found in the laws, regulations, and cases.

I also use the word "minorities" even though when taken together, minorities are the majority. I use it because these groups historically have been the minority among people in power.

Outside of the stories, I avoided using either he or she. Where necessary to use a pronoun, I tried to use one or the other on a rotating basis.

Especially when discussing sexual harassment, the word "victim" is controversial; some people prefer "target." To me, target implies that harassment is intentional. Usually it's not. To compromise, I use both words.

The words "manager" and "supervisor" are used interchangeably to mean a person who has the authority to affect the employment of employees. Where there is a legal difference between the two, I will note the distinction in the text.

Human resources professionals will be surprised to see I use the term "personnel" throughout this book. Most managers still call it personnel. As does George Tansill of *The Personnel News*, I'd rather communicate in their language.

I've written this book for someone for whom legalese is a foreign tongue. I imagine attorneys cringing at some of my words. This is not as precise as a legal brief. But I do give you citations to the laws and cases so you easily can look up the specifics.

My hope is that, in reading this book, you will first be scared, then enlightened, and finally challenged to implement the suggestions. For I believe that in following the law, we create fair working environments for all employees, including ourselves.

Rita Risser
Santa Cruz, California
January, 1993

Acknowledgments

I would like to thank the clients who gave me the experiences in this book. The managers and employees who have taken my classes since 1982 have given me their insights, humor, and values. Without them, this book would not be what it is.

All the people associated through the years with my law firm, Employment Rights Attorneys, gave me the opportunity to learn how to be a manager. They were the victims of my many mistakes, but tolerated me with good humor.

Many people read parts of this book as it evolved. I particularly thank Arlyne June, the executive director of Project Match, a nonprofit housing agency, and Chuck Dolci, corporate counsel for Sun Microsystems, Inc. I am grateful to Dian Emerson, Virgil King, Ann Monroe, and Bob Morales for reading it in its final stages. I implemented many of their suggestions. Sometimes I rejected their advice, so I take sole responsibility for what follows.

Thanks also to Kathleen Morgan-Martinez, the law clerk who made this book as accurate as possible, and my business manager, Jo-Ann Birch, who contributed by reading, typing, and offering her unique perspective. The people of the University of California at Santa Cruz have been instrumental in expanding my horizons. They hired me early on as a lecturer in the extension program and as a speaker for Student Employment Services. The Employment Development Department also encouraged my development as a speaker.

Many human resources professionals in the Bay Area have encouraged me to grow. I'd especially like to thank Jan Peterson for always challenging me.

My friends and mentors in National Speakers Association pushed me to dream and then believe that I could achieve.

My ex-husband, Ray Swartz, supported and encouraged me. He has been my professional role model from the beginning. He opened me to the possibilities.

How This Book Will Help You

*T*his book is for executives, managers, supervisors, and business owners. If you hire, manage, and fire employees, you can get an overview of the danger zones by reading straight through. You'll find legal explanations in plain English, stories, case examples, and practical tips on how to implement the law step by step.

You'll also find sample forms, policies, checklists, charts, tables, glossary, footnotes, and an index, so you can keep it at your desk for guidance when questions come up.

There are six major areas of law every manager should know to prevent employee lawsuits:

Discrimination law (Chapter 2) prohibits treating employees differently because of their sex, age, race, national origin, religion, pregnancy, citizenship, or disability. Only six states protect sexual orientation.

The law today deals not only with outright bias, but also with the unspoken assumptions and prejudices we all have that lead to subtle discrimination.

Companies with U.S. government contracts and subcontracts, and local, state, and federal government agencies, are required to have Affirmative Action plans to ensure that their employees mirror the diversity of the work force.

Wrongful termination law (Chapter 3) is a departure from the days of old England. Then, employment was "at will," meaning an employee could be terminated at any time, for any reason, or for no reason. Recent cases have changed all that. Today in many states, there are three exceptions to employment at will. These can be expressed as three rules for preventing wrongful termination lawsuits:

1. Keep your promises.
2. Treat employees fairly.
3. Don't fire whistleblowers.

Layoffs due to reorganization, lack of business, or plant closing rarely lead to wrongful termination lawsuits. But you can be sued for discrimination if the layoff impacts one group more than others, for example, if mostly older workers are picked for layoff. Also, adequate warning must be given to employees under the Worker Adjustment and Retraining Notification (WARN) Act.

Privacy law (Chapter 4) protects employees at home and at work. As a result, employers cannot unreasonably invade the personal lives of employees. At the same time, employers have the right to protect themselves if employees' personal lives affect their ability to work.

Substance abuse at work is a problem. Many companies have tried drug testing programs to stop it. However, drug testing is illegal in many states because it invades employee privacy.

When your employees call in sick or go out on medical leave, you learn information about their medical condition. In many states, medical information is private and can't be revealed to others.

Hiring laws (Chapter 5) are part of the discrimination, wrongful termination, and privacy areas. These three areas are brought together to show you how to write a job description, advertise the opening, post the job internally, contact recruiting agencies, ensure application forms are legal, accept resumes, screen applicants, write out interview questions, conduct interviews, give necessary tests, perform background checks, call references, write the offer letter, contact rejected applicants, and train the new employee.

Sexual harassment (Chapter 6) is illegal, as is any harassment of employees because of their sex, race, age, national origin, religion, citizenship, or disability.

There are four factors necessary to prove a harassment case. Examples of harassment range from gross to subtle, including the problems of affairs between supervisors and subordinates.

A company is required by law to take all steps necessary to prevent harassment. These include posting a policy, training managers, and establishing a grievance procedure.

Safety laws (Chapter 7) require companies to provide safe and healthy environments. When they are injured, employees get worker's compensation benefits.

The fastest-growing type of claim today is workplace stress. In one case, a court ruled that a woman was not harassed, but since she felt she was harassed, she was entitled to worker's compensation for stress.

Other critical issues in workplace safety today are repetitive strain injuries (like carpal tunnel syndrome), injuries from using computers, AIDS in the workplace, serving alcohol at work, secondhand cigarette smoke, indoor air pollution, and constructive discharge.

In addition to these six major areas, the following topics are addressed in the last two chapters.

Whether an employee is paid hourly or is salaried, and thus whether an employee is required to be paid for *overtime*, depends on whether the employee is "exempt" or "nonexempt" from the wage and hour laws of the U.S. Department of Labor. There also are state laws.

Beginning in 1991, the Internal Revenue Service announced it would crack down on the illegal use of *independent contractors* to avoid federal withholding requirements. Many states have their own, sometimes conflicting, requirements for a worker to be called an independent contractor.

Former employees are entitled to *unemployment benefits* if they are fired without good cause or if they quit with good cause. You can represent the company in unemployment hearings and win.

Giving employees *severance pay* is subject to the provisions of the Employee Retirement Income Security Act (ERISA). This law also covers pensions and benefits. The Consolidated Omnibus Budget Reconciliation Act (COBRA) allows employees to continue their medical benefits after termination.

If you are in a *union* environment, the collective bargaining agreement must be followed. If you don't have a union and want to keep them out, there are restrictions on what you can do.

Government employees have Constitutional rights in their jobs. Some of those rights are covered here.

Employee responsibilities include the duties to show up on time, do a competent job, get along with others, and follow orders. And you have *manager's rights*, which will be covered in Chapter 9.

In all these areas, this book gives you systems and procedures for preventing lawsuits and complying with government audits. At the same time, these systems and procedures also are just good management.

Table of Contents

Table of Charts, Policies, and Forms

Chapter 1

MANAGING IN A MINE FIELD

The Growing Threat of Employee Lawsuits

One of the risks of being a manager today is getting sued. The number of employee lawsuits has been doubling every year since the mid-1980s.[1] In the late 1970s, only 200 wrongful termination lawsuits were pending nationwide. In 1988, that number had grown to over 25,000.[2]

The costs are enormous. According to a nationwide study, the average jury verdict in wrongful termination cases is over $600,000, and companies lose 64% of the cases.[3] Moreover, these numbers do not include discrimination or other employment cases, and the averages are based on cases from the mid-1980's.

Today the trend is toward multi-million-dollar verdicts. For example, in the first six months of 1992, there were two verdicts in sex discrimination cases, one in New York, the other in Los Angeles. Both women were denied promotions into management. Both said they were victims of a "glass ceiling," because there were few women above them in the company. One was awarded $7 million, the other $20 million.[4]

HOW MONEY DAMAGES ARE AWARDED

Actual Damages

People sometimes wonder how a denial of promotion could be worth millions of dollars The law requires juries to award certain types of money damages. For example, if employees win, in almost all cases they must receive *back pay*. Back pay is the amount they would have received if they had not been treated illegally, minus what they actually made in other jobs, up until the date of trial.

Employees who win sometimes also are awarded *front pay*. That's the salary they would have received (including reasonable future pay increases and promotions) from the date of trial until some date in the future. For older employees, say, after 50, it's not unusual for front pay calculations to go out to retirement age. Since it is often difficult for employees this age to get comparable jobs, they may be awarded full salary for 10 or 15 years.

Back pay and front pay together are referred to as *actual damages*. Actual damages also include other out-of-pocket expenses such as medical bills, costs due to forced sale of income property, and other reasonably foreseeable losses.

In discrimination, privacy, and some wrongful termination cases, employees also can win *compensatory damages* for emotional distress. These are designed to compensate the person for pain and suffering, humiliation, and embarrassment. In some states, the emotional distress damages must be somewhat comparable to the actual damages. For example, they might be 2 times or 10 times the amount of actual damages. In other states, the jury can pick any number they think is appropriate.

Punitive Damages

If the jury is allowed to award emotional distress damages, they probably also are allowed to assess *punitive damages*. Punitive damages are designed to punish the company for intentional wrongdoing. They usually are a percentage of the company's net worth, annual income, or some other financial measure. The percentage may be set by law, or it may be up to the jury to decide.

Punitive damages are what sent the verdicts into the millions in those two glass ceiling cases. By definition, a glass ceiling means intentional discrimination has occurred, not only against the employees suing but also against many others before them.

These two cases were brought under state laws that have no caps on punitive damages. In discrimination cases brought under the U.S. law prohibiting discrimination, there are limits on compensatory and punitive damages. The limits are

$50,000 for employers with 15 to 100 employees

$100,000 for employers with 101 to 200 employees

$200,000 for employers with 201 to 500 employees

$300,000 for employers with more than 500 employees.[5]

In discrimination and some other cases, employees who win also get attorney's fees to pay their lawyers a reasonable hourly rate. Depending on the size of the case, you could pay hundreds of thousands more in attorney's fees to the employee's attorney.

When you add all these damages together, you can see how verdicts can be so high.

CRIMINAL LIABILITY

If lawsuits aren't scary enough, every company is subject to random audits and inspections by government entities such as the Occupational Safety and Health Administration (OSHA), the Department of Labor (DOL), the Equal Employment Opportunity Commission (EEOC), or state agencies. Violations can lead to fines, shutdowns, or imprisonment.

Managers of corporations can be found guilty of crimes under many U.S. and state laws. There is criminal liability for environmental crimes, securities violations, and federal contract fraud. Corporations have been held criminally liable for acts by employees that were contrary to "longstanding, well-known and strictly enforced" company policies.[6]

Criminal penalties can be $500,000 per offense, and can go into the multimillions. Fighting the government can be much more costly than defending a case brought by one employee.

HIDDEN COSTS OF LAWSUITS

Whether or not a company wins a lawsuit, there are internal costs when it's sued:

- Lost productivity of the people involved: managers, employee-witnesses, and top executives

- Lost time of in-house lawyers, personnel department, payroll, benefits, and accounting clerks

- Poor reputation with investors, customers, vendors, competitors, business associates, and applicants for employment

- Poor morale and gossip among current employees

Managers also can be sued personally. Some potential costs to you are:

- Personal attorneys fees
- Lost time, productivity, and focus from work
- Stress resulting in medical conditions and doctor's bills
- Strain on marriage and family
- Negative career growth
- Being fired
- Paying fines
- Going to jail

If you are named personally in a lawsuit, your state's law may require your company to defend you if you were acting in the course and scope of your employment. For example, as a manager, firing people is part of your job. If you are sued for wrongful termination, the company could be required to represent you.

Sexual harassment, on the other hand, is not part of your job. If you're accused of that, your company might have the right to refuse to defend you.

In addition to acting within the course and scope of your employment, you must be able to show you acted reasonably and in good faith. Even if you made a mistake, if you were just doing your job and tried to do the right thing, the company may be required to represent you.

But if the company finds you acted maliciously, out of personal animosity or hatred, not only does it not have the duty to represent you, but it also could terminate your employment, name you as a cross-defendant, or sue you for violation of your duties as an employee.

If a judgment is brought against you, in some cases the company may be able to pay it for you. But if the verdict specifies you are liable individually, you must pay out of your own pocket.

Your homeowner's, umbrella, or general liability insurance policies may cover you in some of these cases. But I don't recommend extra insurance. The best insurance is knowledge of the law.

WHY COMPANIES WOULD RATHER SETTLE THAN FIGHT

Most lawsuits don't go to trial. Over 95% of all cases settle out of court. State Farm Insurance Company settled a class action sex discrimination suit in 1992 for $157 million.[7] That was a record at this writing.

Since settlements usually are confidential, it's hard to say how most cases settle. Among the attorneys I know, whether they represent employees or companies, six-figure settlements are rare and come "on the courthouse steps" right before trial starts. Disputes that settle after just a letter from a lawyer usually involve a few months' pay.

If you are sued, but you were completely reasonable and acted within the law—you were right—your company still may choose to settle the case. The company must weigh business factors in addition to legal costs in evaluating whether settlement is less costly than litigation.

According to the Rand Corporation, the average amount spent by companies in defending wrongful termination lawsuits from 1980 to 1986 was about $100,000 per case. That was only the cost of attorneys fees, and didn't include hidden costs. If employees are willing to settle for $25,000, it may make economic sense to pay them off.

Another reason to settle is that the law may change significantly. What was completely legal at the time it was done might be declared illegal later by a court in a similar case. Then it's prudent to settle rather than risk losing.

Finally, companies settle to prevent bad publicity. If a case has caught the attention of the media, the industry, your customers, your investors, or other key groups, the loss of reputation can be devastating. Even if you win, what most people will remember is that you were sued. For this reason, it sometimes is desirable to settle a case quickly and quietly.

If a case does settle, and you learn about the settlement because it's a necessary part of your job, it is your responsibility to keep the information confidential. In the vast majority of cases, the company agrees to keep the settlement confidential. If you violate that promise, the company can be sued again by the same person.

More important, if news of a settlement gets out, other employees will be encouraged to sue. The snowball effect of one leaked settlement can impact the company for many years afterward.

HOW WE GOT INTO THIS MESS

It wasn't always this way. In the past, companies didn't fear lawsuits. Managers didn't worry about being sued. In fact, the idea of the law intervening in the employment relationship is relatively new.

Historically, employees evolved from slaves and serfs. No government told lords and masters how to treat their property. This attitude continued into the Industrial Revolution.

The first inroad on employer's rights in the United States was a child labor law passed in Massachusetts in 1842. This was highly controversial and was fought vigorously by business. It took a Civil War to abolish slavery in 1865.

In 1926 the first law was passed recognizing the rights of employees to join labor unions. The federal minimum wage law was passed in 1938. After World War II a law was passed that guaranteed veterans their rights to reemployment.[8]

For 20 years, there was virtually no activity for employee rights.

A turning point came in 1964. That was the year the Civil Rights Act was adopted prohibiting race and sex discrimination. In the next 15 years the floodgates opened. Laws and regulations were passed on age discrimination, rights for Vietnam-era veterans, occupational safety and health, affirmative action, sexual harassment, and more.

In the 1980s, legislative activity lessened, but the courts got more involved. Not only did the courts give expansive readings to these new laws, but they virtually invented the concept of wrongful termination and greatly expanded the right of privacy. For the first time, they allowed employees to claim damages for stress.

In the 1990s Congress became active again, passing two major pieces of legislation: the Americans with Disabilities Act and the Civil Rights Act of 1991.

Before 1980, "employment law" did not exist. Today it's the specialty of thousands of lawyers. For employers, the 1990s promise more legislation and more litigation. After all, we lawyers have to make money too!

THE FOUR KEY CONCEPTS OF EMPLOYMENT LAW

There are four key concepts that transcend the topics covered in the rest of this book. These concepts will help you avoid all types of employment lawsuits. They also are good guidelines for other business dealings.

Four Key Concepts

1. Be consistent.
2. Have a legitimate business reason for every decision.
3. Document events.
4. When in doubt, call an expert.

---

1. Be Consistent

Be consistent in the way you treat your employees. You can't discriminate on the basis of sex, race, or other classifications. Even if people are the same sex and race, you still must treat them the same. That's because in wrongful termination cases the courts say employers have a duty of good faith and fair dealing. In other words, you must treat all employees fairly. The easiest way to prove you treated people fairly is to show you treated all of them the same.

The idea of consistency is taken quite far by the courts. For example, you must be consistent in documenting events to support your decision to fire an employee. You must document everyone's actions in order to prove that one person should be disciplined.

Let's say you have salaried employees working for you. They don't use time cards. You are aware of who is coming in when, but as long as nobody abuses it, you don't care if people are a few minutes late. You have a little flexibility.

Imagine you've hired a new employee and you notice he is always late—30 minutes to an hour. This is taking flexibility too far. You decide to document the late arrivals. After two weeks, you call the personnel department and say you want to discipline the employee. The personnel rep is impressed with your documentation. Then she asks, "What time did everybody else get in?" You say, "Everybody else was on time." She says, "Prove it."

You can't prove it because you didn't keep consistent documentation. If you fire this person for tardiness, he will argue what every tardy employee has argued throughout history: everybody else was late, too. Whenever a tardy employee made this argument to me, I always wondered, "How do they know?" I used to represent a lot of tardy employees, but I stopped. They were always late for their appointments.

If you single out employees for documentation or discipline, you are not treating them fairly, and you have violated your duty of good faith and fair dealing.

There is a practical reason to treat people consistently: it will stop you from discriminating unintentionally. I once represented a woman who was the first female hired in a plant of 3,000 men. After a few months, she was fired for producing only 68% of quota. She wanted me to represent her because she said it was sex discrimination. She said the men produced less than she did.

Frankly, I didn't believe her. I figured she was lazy and just looking for an excuse. But when we got the production records, we discovered she was one of the highest producers in the shop. The average production was less than half of quota!

When we questioned her supervisor, he said he pulled her production records because he noticed she wasn't working. He didn't pull the men's records because he didn't notice them not working. That oversight cost the company millions of dollars, because she filed a class action sex discrimination case that eventually covered over 10,000 female employees and applicants at her former company.

Be consistent to avoid this type of unintentional result.

2. Have a Legitimate Business Reason for Every Decision

The second key concept is to have a legitimate business reason for everything you do. It is perfectly legal for you to treat people differently if you have a legitimate business reason for doing so.

For example, when you are hiring, you might receive 20 or 200 applications for the job. You have to pick one person. By picking one, you are discriminating, in the larger sense of the word. But it is not illegal to discriminate as long as the person you hire is the most qualified for the job. You can always hire the most qualified person, as long as you define qualifications consistently.

Legitimate business reasons are directly related to work. *Performance* is a legitimate business reason for giving one person a higher merit increase than another. *Company rules* sometimes allow you to treat people inconsistently. For example, it's common for employees not to receive vacation their first year of employment.

Business conditions also allow you to treat people inconsistently. Let's say you have two secretaries who have the same general job description. But one is responsible for answering the phone, and the other isn't. You've told your customers, whether internal or external, that your phone is answered from 8 to 5. You have a legitimate business reason for requiring the one secretary to be at work on time and not to care if the other secretary is a few minutes late.

Whenever you make decisions about who will be hired, promoted, trained, and fired, you should be able to articulate a legitimate business reason.

3. Document Events

The third key concept is to document events. As a manager, you need to write down what happens with your employees on a day-to-day basis. A case could take up to five years to get to trial. You could be gone by then. If there's no documentation from you, the company won't know how to defend it. They won't know what was on your mind when you made your decisions.

Even if you aren't gone, you can forget what happened five years ago. And even if you have a crystal clear memory, you still need documentation because if you don't, the attorney for the employee will try to make you out to be a liar.

If the attorney for the employee gets you on the witness stand, he or she will do something like this:

> "You testified that you had a legitimate business reason for terminating the employee, isn't that right?"
>
> "Yes."
>
> "But you didn't write a memo to anyone about that, did you?"
>
> "No."
>
> "And you didn't make any notation in the personnel file?"
>
> "No."
>
> "You didn't keep any personal notes, did you?"
>
> "No."
>
> "Now before you came to testify here, you met with your lawyer, didn't you?"
>
> "Yes."
>
> "How many times did you meet?"
>
> "Three or four times."
>
> "How long each time did you meet?"
>
> "Two or three hours."
>
> "Isn't it true that during that time you and your lawyer concocted a story to tell the jury because you knew there was no documentation to contradict you?"

At this point, there will be an objection. You can't be asked about confidential conversations with your lawyer. But what has the lawyer done? Planted a seed in the minds of the jury. The jury will think you've made up your story.

Don't give an employee's lawyer this type of leverage on you. Document what you did and why you did it.

Even if you don't write it down immediately, you can go back later and document it. Put the date you wrote the notes on the top, and then in the body of the memo, write down the date it occurred. The attorney for the employee still will jump on you about the delay, but you are in a much stronger position with late documentation than with no documentation at all.

I was talking about the importance of documentation in class one day when a manager became so agitated he broke his pencil in half. He said, "Do you really believe this?" I asked, "Believe what?" He said, "Do you really believe that documenting wins cases? Everyone knows people lie on the stand, make up documents, and do whatever else it takes to win!"

Obviously, that's illegal. More important, I don't think it's true. In my experience representing hundreds of employees, only one ever claimed a document was forged.

If the authenticity of a document is questioned, expert document examiners can test it. The state of the technology today is such that they can determine the age of paper, ink, typing, and printing.

When to Document

Documenting is simple. Use your calendar, notebook system, or engineering log to keep track of informal warnings. This can be done manually or on computer. Whenever an employee makes a mistake, make a note on that date. Write just a sentence or two. If it turns out it was just a minor problem—everyone makes mistakes—you never need to use that information.

But if you see a consistent pattern of the same kinds of mistakes, you can put it in a warning or review. When you do that, make a copy of your informal documentation and put it in the official personnel file.

Save message slips, work orders, or reports that show employees' mistakes. In some states, you must save these in the official personnel file. In other states, including California, a manager can keep a separate working file of documents, as long as they aren't used to judge employees.

Many times, you don't know if you are going to use an incident in the employee's performance appraisal. It depends on how the employee acts in the future. So keep the note for a while. If the employee shows no other signs of a problem, throw it away. If, instead, the employee's performance deteriorates, you can show the first time it occurred. Attach this evidence to the performance appraisal or warning as backup documentation.

The Official Personnel File

In many states, employees have the right to see their own personnel files. You may be able to put reasonable limits on when, where and how often employees may review their files. Your state may require you to give employees copies of their file or at least copies of documents they've signed. You also may be required to show employees documents before you put them in the file.

As a practical matter, it's best to get employees' signatures on all warnings, performance appraisals, and other important documents.

I once was cross-examining a manager who had fired my client. He had produced a performance appraisal which my client said she'd never seen before. The manager insisted he had given it to her. But her signature was not on the form.

The manager testified he had "forgotten" to ask her to sign the form. I was trying to show that he knew how important it was to get a signature. I said:

"You had my client sign her 1981 appraisal, didn't you?"

"Yes."

"You had her sign the one in 1982, right?"

"Yes."

"You had her sign 1983?"

"Yes."

"And 1984?"

"Yes."

"You had her sign them because you *knew* documentation was important, didn't you?"

"Well, I don't know if I did then, but I sure do now!"

How to Document

Follow these simple rules whenever you give a written document to an employee:

Assume a judge is going to see your disciplinary memo, so write a memo you want a judge to see. It should look professional. Type it, or write neatly. There is nothing more frustrating than having good documentation that no one can read.

I once represented a technical writer who was fired for poor grammar and spelling errors. The final warning he received was riddled with grammatical and spelling mistakes. The company settled that case quickly.

Don't give conclusions without facts to back you up.

Never say, "You have a bad attitude." That's a conclusion. You can't prove a person's attitude. You can only prove behavior. You don't care what an employee's attitude is, as long as the behavior is satisfactory. List the objective, verifiable facts that led you to the conclusion that there was a bad attitude. For example:

"Two times on May 15, Terry asked you to help out and you refused. On May 16 and 17, you slammed down the phone, swore in a loud voice, and stomped away from your desk six different times."

That's objective. Its verifiable. It's not "bad attitude," it's "unprofessional behavior."

Don't say "frequently" there is a problem. That's not objective or verifiable. Instead, say how many times. Or better still, "On (this date) at (this time) you (did this)."

Don't use subjective words such as common sense, good judgment, ambitious, loyal. In order for employees to improve, they must know exactly what to do. They won't know how unless you outline objective, verifiable behavior.

Use clear, precise language. Don't use big words that people may not understand. Consider translating services for employees whose second language is English.

Avoid extremes. Never say never, always avoid always. See below for more examples.

Use Clear Precise Language

Poor Wording	*Better Wording*
You frequently are tardy.	You were more than 15 minutes late on three occasions.
You don't concentrate on your work.	You made 29 typing errors on the letter of May 2.
You do not get along with co-workers.	You yelled at Chris Smith twice.
You are irritable and refuse to communicate.	You locked yourself in your office and refused to answer.
You abused sick leave.	You have exceeded accrued sick leave.
You make too many personal phone calls.	You make 30% more personal phone calls than others.
Your performance is substandard.	Production quota is 30 per hour. Your output is 15.

4. *When in Doubt, Call an Expert*

The fourth key concept is this: when in doubt, call an expert—either your company's personnel or legal department or an outside lawyer. Experts should be consulted early on, before there is a problem. It's always easier (and cheaper!) for an expert to give advice at the beginning of a problem than at the end.

Call whenever one of the following events occurs:

- You receive a complaint about sexual harassment, discrimination, overtime pay, or other legal claim.

- You hear from a former employee threatening to sue or asking for a copy of the personnel file.

- You want to terminate an employee who is over 40, minority, female, or with longevity in the company.

- You want to terminate a highly paid executive or key player (especially employees with knowledge of trade secrets, customer lists, or other confidential information).

- You want to terminate an employee who has complained recently about a real or perceived legal violation by the company (e.g., safety hazard, discrimination).

- You want to terminate an employee on the spot, without prior warning.

Of course, this list is not exhaustive.

If your company has a personnel department, it's important to call them. The law changes. It changes rapidly. Something in this book probably will be wrong by the time it sees print. Your personnel department is supposed to keep current on the law and can let you know of any major changes.

You also should contact your personnel department so that you can benefit from their experience and ensure that you are acting consistently with company policy and practice.

If you contact personnel, they tell you what to do, you follow their instructions, and then there is a lawsuit—you can blame them. And the company is far more likely to back your decision if you've had their independent professional perspective.

Most of the personnel people I've met are wonderful. But some people in personnel are ignorant and gutless. I've had personnel "professionals" in major corporations tell me they advised their managers to do the exact opposite of what the law required. I've seen entire human resources departments staffed by personnel representatives who didn't take any continuing education courses.

If you get advice from a representative in personnel that you don't believe is right, go up the chain of command or call an employment lawyer.

How to Work with Lawyers

Working with lawyers is an occupational hazard for managers. It's a sad commentary on today's world that you must have one on call.

Most executives know when they have to call their lawyers, but they hate doing it. Lawyers never return phone calls. Once they do, they talk too long and charge too much. They don't give "yes" or "no" answers. They say, "It depends."

I know, because I'm guilty of all those and worse. I hate dealing with lawyers, too. But as costly as we are, lawyers are a great bargain when compared to the cost of defending just one lawsuit.

What will an employment lawyer do for you? A lawyer will ask questions to see what you have done so far. We have a checklist, either on paper or in our minds, of how to handle each problem. We will walk you through that list, step by step.

Some clients have asked for my checklist so they don't have to call me every time. But they still call. The law is concerned not only with what you do, but how you do it. An attorney brings an outside perspective to your problem. For example, you may have given a warning, but after questioning, a lawyer might decide you didn't give an adequate warning.

A lawyer may or may not give you "the answer." It depends on the situation. Many times, you have to choose among several options, all of them legal. You need to make a management decision. We merely make sure it's an informed one.

For example, the office manager of a small company called me one day. She said, "We hired a new technician three weeks ago. He asked one of the women out for a date a couple of times. She complained, and we told him that wasn't appropriate behavior. Now we've got a complaint that he is talking about his sex life to other guys in front of the women. Should we fire him?"

"Is he otherwise a good employee?"

"Yes, he's great. I just can't believe he didn't get it after the first time I talked to him."

"Did you tell him he could be fired?"

"I don't know if I put it in so many words, but sexual harassment is listed as a terminable offense in our employee handbook, and he's read that."

"It's up to you. You can fire him, since he's a new employee, he's been warned once, and you have good cause anyway. Or you can give him a final written warning. One more time, he's out."

"Won't I get in trouble for sexual harassment if I don't fire him?"

"No. Giving a final warning will still protect you from a sexual harassment suit. This is low-level harassment. You've taken immediate corrective action. That's all you're required to do."

She decided to give him one more chance, because he was a good tech. Before she talked to me, she was so worried about a sexual harassment charge, she was going to fire him immediately.

By talking to a lawyer, the office manager saw that there were a number of options open to her. Other times, a lawyer will narrow your options. Either way, a good lawyer with a practical approach can be helpful in your decision-making process.

How to Pick a Lawyer

What should a lawyer cost? Preventative advice from an attorney can range in price from $20 (yes, twenty dollars) to $1,000 and up, depending upon the complexity of the matter.

It's important to understand how attorneys charge before doing business with them. If we work on an hourly basis, we usually charge a minimum fee for each contact with you. For example, I charged 0.1 hour (one-tenth of an hour, or six minutes) for my telephone conversation with the office manager. That's my minimum. Other lawyers charge two-tenths. A few bill in minimum increments of a quarter hour or a half hour.

When comparing lawyers of equal experience, a rule of thumb is the lower the hourly rate, the higher the minimum increment for billing. So always ask about both.

Until recently, attorneys refused to give clients a total estimate on the cost of representing them. But more and more clients are demanding that we make estimates and stick to them. You can and should manage your attorneys just as any other employees, giving them deadlines and budgets to meet.

How should you pick a lawyer? The most important factor is how you feel about the lawyer as a person. You want a comfortable, long-term relationship. If it sounds like marriage or partnership, it is. You want your lawyer to become intimately familiar with your company's practices and philosophy. Advice must be given in the special context of your company.

Since you are paying by the hour, find an attorney who listens more than talks. You want a lawyer who can ask insightful questions, make a succinct analysis of the law, and give you practical advice for making your decision, in the least amount of time.

Never pick a law firm just because it has a thick carpet, expensive furniture, and terrific view. Who do you think pays for all that?

Whether you consult your personnel department or a lawyer, you can help them help you by following a few simple steps. Before you call, study the personnel file of the individual involved. Read the applicable sections in your employee handbook and procedures manual. Talk to all the people who witnessed or participated, including the employee, to get every side of the story.

Tell your lawyer the truth, the whole truth, and nothing but the truth. Sometimes it's embarrassing to admit how you or your company fouled up. But it's better to tell them right away so they can make a complete and accurate assessment of any potential case against you.

A Success Story

A woman got a job as an administrative assistant. She and her boss got along great from the first time they met. They immediately began teasing, joking, and bantering with each other. But after a while, she felt he had crossed a line.

She filed a complaint of sexual harassment with the personnel department. They investigated by talking to the boss and to the other workers in the area. They determined sexual harassment had not occurred, because she had welcomed the sexual teasing.

She didn't agree with the decision, so she filed a lawsuit against him in federal court. She continued working for him. But after a while, she felt uncomfortable working for someone she was suing. So she went to a doctor. He put her out on stress disability leave. After two years, the case was still going on, and her doctor cleared her to return to work.

She went back and was given another administrative assistant job, at the same grade level, reporting to the same boss. After two weeks she quit and filed another lawsuit claiming retaliation. She said the tasks she was given to do were not as good as before. She was denied management training classes. And she claimed her boss wouldn't talk to her about anything except work.

The sexual harassment and retaliation cases were consolidated for trial.

At trial, the judge found she had not been sexually harassed. But that did not dispose of her retaliation claim. Even if she was not harassed, she still might have been retaliated against.

On the retaliation claim, the judge found that the jobs she was given were not as good as the jobs she'd been given before. She was denied management training. And he found that the manager wouldn't talk to her socially.

But the manager and the company won the lawsuit. And they won it because they followed the four key concepts.

1. The manager was *consistent*. The jobs he gave her to do were the same type of jobs he gave other administrative assistants.

2. He had a *legitimate business reason* for not giving her management training—she wasn't a manager and she wasn't on a management track. And he had a legitimate business reason for not talking with her socially, since he was scared to death he would get sued again.

3. He *documented* everything: the jobs he gave her, the jobs he gave other assistants, and why he denied her management training.

4. He *called an expert*. He had the personnel department involved every step of the way, for an independent and professional perspective on his decisions.

If you follow the four key concepts, I can't guarantee that you won't get sued. As a practical matter, you can be sued at any time by anybody for anything. But if you follow the four key concepts, your likelihood of being sued is greatly decreased, and your likelihood of winning is greatly increased.

More important, if you follow these four key concepts you will treat employees fairly. Fairness is the spirit of employment law. As speaker Mark Sanborn says, "The great leaders act on the basis of commitment, not compliance. [They see the law] not as oppressive obligation, but as a creative opportunity to do something worthwhile."[9]

Chapter 2

THE VALUE OF DIVERSITY

Discrimination Law and Affirmative Action

*O*ne of the first employees I hired was for the position of receptionist in my law firm. The job required screening phone calls. We got about 100 calls a month from potential new clients. They usually were hysterical. They had just lost their jobs and wanted to talk to a lawyer *now*.

The receptionist's job was to calm them down, quickly find out the facts, and decide whether or not to make an appointment.

The best person for this job, I decided, was someone with a legal assistant background, who could screen the callers. More important, I wanted someone who was empathetic, who could get the story out. But the receptionist also needed to be direct, to cut the caller off when necessary, and get on to the next one.

I decided the best person for this job would be a mother type. Someone who had a lot of experience with 2-year-olds would be the perfect person, I thought, to handle my hysterical clients.

I put an ad in the paper for a "Legal Assistant/Receptionist." I received a bunch of resumes from women. The last day, I got a resume from a man. I looked at the man's name on the top of the page and thought to myself, "Typical male! He didn't even read the ad. It said right in the ad the job involved heavy phones. No man wants to be a receptionist." I started to put his resume in the reject pile.

Then I noticed he had a legal assistant certificate. He had worked at another law firm as a receptionist, screening callers. On paper, he was the most qualified applicant.

I started thinking, "Maybe he's qualified, but he wouldn't feel comfortable here. We're an all-woman office. He won't fit in." Again I started to put away the resume.

Then it struck me, "That's discrimination! I can't do that. What if I got caught?" One of my worst fears was a newspaper headline that said, "Discrimination Lawyer Sued for Discriminating." I decided I should at least interview the guy to make it look good. Then I wouldn't hire him.

As it turned out, he interviewed well, I hired him, and he was a great receptionist.

In that situation, my assumptions, biases, and prejudices almost led me to discriminate. The law recognizes we all are biased in some way. That's fine. You can have prejudices—as long as you don't act on them. In fact, you should be aware of your biases so that you make a conscious decision not to discriminate unconsciously.

EQUAL EMPLOYMENT OPPORTUNITY LAW

Congress and most states have passed laws that require equal employment opportunity (EEO) by prohibiting discrimination. Most of the discrimination laws apply to companies with 15 or more employees. The age discrimination law applies to companies of 20 or more employees. Both apply to U.S. citizens working abroad for U.S.-owned or -controlled companies.[1] Most states also have discrimination laws. Some apply to companies with as few as one employee.

Equal employment opportunity means giving people a chance to succeed. It's a law that codifies the fundamental principle of fairness.

HOW TO TELL IF YOU'RE GUILTY OF DISCRIMINATING

"Discrimination" means people in one group are treated worse than people from a different group. In Chapter 6, we'll look at discriminatory harassment. Here, we will concentrate on discrimination that affects a person's job opportunities.

Whenever you choose between two or more people, you literally are discriminating. But not all discrimination is illegal. Discrimination is illegal only if members of *different* groups are treated differently. For example, if a person who is black complains of race discrimination because he wasn't promoted, he must show that a nonblack got the job. If another African-American was hired, that's not race discrimination.

You sometimes hear people say, "It's illegal to discriminate against women," or "It's illegal to discriminate against minorities." That's true, but it's not the whole truth. It is illegal to discriminate on the basis of sex. It's just as illegal to discriminate against men as it is against women. It is illegal to discriminate on the basis of race. It's just as illegal to discriminate against whites as it is against people of color. Sometimes, the idea that whites are protected is referred to as "reverse discrimination," but in fact all races are fully protected by the law.

EEO means equal treatment. It doesn't require you to give favorable treatment to anyone. It allows you to hire, promote and pay the best people you can find—as long as "best" is not defined in a discriminatory way.

EEO is sound business practice. By definition, "discrimination" means you are not hiring or promoting people who are the best qualified. That doesn't make sense.

Two Ways Employees Can Prove Discrimination

There are two types of discrimination employees can prove.

The first type is called "disparate treatment" or intentional discrimination, because you appear to be intentionally treating one group worse than another. For example, if you ask applicants, "What is your religion?" and then refuse to hire anyone who says Jewish, you are discriminating on the basis of religion. Compared to other religious groups, such as Christians, Jews are being excluded.

Even if no illegal questions are asked, intentional discrimination still can be proven. You don't have to ask someone's race, you can see it. If people of color apply but aren't hired, it appears you are discriminating on the basis of race, unless you can prove that every time minorities applied, you hired nonminorities who were more qualified.

Disparate treatment cases involve all aspects of the employment process. If you treat people differently whenever you make any of these decisions there is a potential discrimination case:

Hiring applicants

Paying employees

Choosing subordinates for training programs

Evaluating employees' performance

Disciplining employees

Making job assignments

Deciding who to promote

Picking employees for layoff

Terminating employees

A person who is prejudiced will try to use any of these decisions as opportunities to discriminate.

Unintentional Discrimination is Illegal, Too

The second way discrimination is proven is through disparate impact—even though all your employment criteria are non-discriminatory, the impact of your employment practices excludes one group as compared to others. This type of discrimination is more subtle and is illegal even if it is unintentional.

An example of disparate impact is a job requirement that on its face is not discriminatory, but which has the effect of excluding certain groups. For example, if you will not hire people under 5'6", that requirement has the effect of excluding women, Hispanics and Asians, who tend to be shorter than black and white males.

Employees don't have to prove much to get to trial in disparate impact cases. All they have to prove is that, statistically, one group is worse off than another. Then the company must prove it had a *job-related reason consistent with business necessity* for the decision that led to the result.

For example an airline might be hiring only people over 5'6" as flight attendants, because they must be able to reach emergencye quipment stowed in overhead bins.

Standardized, multiple-choice tests, such as civil service exams and pre-employment screening tests, frequently have a disparate impact on minorities. As a result, Uniform Guidelines on Employee Selection Procedures were adopted by the federal government covering virtually every type of test.[2] See Chapter 5 for a complete discussion on tests.

In this chapter, we will apply these general concepts to the specifics of discrimination based on race and color, national origin, citizenship, religion, sex, age, and disability. Then Affirmative Action is addressed.

Some states, counties, and cities prohibit discrimination on other grounds. It is illegal under the laws of some states to discriminate against married, single, divorced, and widowed persons because of their marital status. An example is a layoff where a single woman is chosen for layoff rather than a man with a family to support.

A few states, including Wisconsin, protect people from height and weight discrimination. People who are obese due to eating disorders, glandular conditions, or other medical reasons may be covered under the disability laws. Some statex protect groups "historically underrepresented in the workforce."

Six states and the District of Columbia prohibit discrimination against gay men, lesbians, bisexuals, and heterosexuals on the basis of sexual orientation. These laws are covered in Chapter 4 under privacy.

DISCRIMINATION LAW: EIGHT AREAS OF PROTECTION FOR EMPLOYEES AND APPLICANTS

1. Race and Color Discrimination

Sometimes we forget why certain laws were passed. The first Civil Rights Act (also known as Title VII)[3] originally was proposed by President Kennedy in 1963. That year, black activist Medgar Evers was murdered, and four young girls died in the bombing of a Birmingham church. That was the year of Martin Luther King, Jr.'s "I have a dream" speech at the March on Washington.

In 1963, discrimination against blacks and other minorities was rampant. They did not have equal education. When they did, they were not hired equally. When they were hired, they were not paid equally, they were not promoted equally, and they were harassed.

The law was introduced in Congress in 1963, but it languished there amid political debate. Then on November 22, 1963, President Kennedy was assassinated. Five days later, Lyndon Johnson gave his first address as president before both houses of Congress. He challenged Congress to pass the law as a "living memorial" to President Kennedy. It passed within a few months, to become the Civil Rights Act of 1964.[4]

The law attempts to achieve equal employment opportunity for all by prohibiting discrimination.

All races are covered by the law. Whites, blacks, Asians, and American Indians (including Native Alaskans) are protected. Asians include natives of India, Pakistan, and the Pacific Islands such as Guam, Samoa, and the Philippines.

It's been almost 30 years since the law passed, but discrimination against racial minorities still exists today. In 1990, a manager told me the reason more blacks and Hispanics aren't in management is because "they're lazy."[5]

That's his opinion. As long as he keeps it to himself he can think whatever he wants. If a particular person doesn't work hard enough, he or she can be terminated because of that. But if the manager assumes his opinion is true, and acts on that assumption without facts to back him up, that's illegal discrimination.

Race discrimination cases today often reflect much more subtle forms of bias. A 1990 case illustrates this. A black woman was the top-ranked contract analyst at Texaco. Over time, however, her performance deteriorated. Her supervisor did not criticize her because he was afraid she would charge him with discrimination. He did give criticism to white employees who performed poorly.

During this time he filled out two performance appraisals for her. In both, he rated her "satisfactory." In fact, he was not satisfied with her performance, but he gave her these reviews because he didn't want to go through the trouble of putting her on a performance improvement plan, as required by company policy.

Eventually, she became the lowest-ranked analyst. Then Texaco had a reduction in force. She was picked for layoff because of her poor performance. She sued for race discrimination and won. The court of appeals found that because she was not given accurate feedback on her performance, she was denied the opportunity to improve.[6]

Another example is a case decided by the U.S. Supreme Court in 1988.[7] Clara Watson, who is black, was hired by the bank in 1973. After three years, she was promoted to drive-in teller. Four years later, she applied for the job of supervisor of lobby tellers. A white male was promoted instead. Then she applied for supervisor of drive-in tellers, but a white female got the job.

For the next year, Ms. Watson worked informally as the assistant to the new supervisor of lobby tellers. When he left, she applied for his job. It was given to the woman who had been drive-in teller supervisor.

She applied for the drive-in job. It was given to another white male. She sued for race discrimination.

The U.S. Supreme Court ruled in her favor. The court noted the company did not have *any* precise or formal criteria to back up these decisions. Instead, the managers relied on their subjective judgment of who would do a better job. This not only is illegal, but also doesn't make much business sense.

Racism was rampant at the time the law was passed. Since then, great strides have been made in eliminating discrimination. In the 1990s, more companies are going beyond just complying with the law. Instead, they value the cultural diversity of their work forces.

2. *National Origin Discrimination*

It is illegal to discriminate because of national origin, the country where someone themselves, or their ancestors are from. Persians (Iranians) and Hispanics who are of the white race are covered under the national origin classification, as are people from Russia, South Africa, and every other country. Telling Polish and Italian jokes, for example, can be national origin harassment.[8]

One day at the end of an EEO class, a manager came up to me with a worried look on his face. He said, "I just realized that I don't like to hire Hispanics." I said, "Why not?" He said, "When I drive home from work, I see Hispanics working in the fields. To me, a Hispanic is a farmworker, not an engineer."

I said, "How has this affected your decisions?" He said, "I'm sure I've been rejecting resumes from Hispanics, just as you nearly rejected that man who wanted to be your receptionist." His unconscious stereotype may have prevented him from hiring the best.

National origin discrimination claims also are caused by problems of communicating across cultures. For example, a manager called me one day to say that his subordinate, a native Japanese, was "deliberately ignoring" his requests. The manager said, "I tell him what to do, he says he'll do it, and the next day I find out he did the opposite." I said, "That sounds like insubordination to me. That's a terminable offense." I explained how to document the incident, warn the employee, and ultimately fire him.

The manager followed my instructions. A few weeks later, the employee was fired. He filed a complaint of national origin discrimination. But we showed our documentation and won with the government agency.

We won, but it didn't feel like a win. A year later, I realized what had happened. I was reading an article that claimed it is not uncommon for native Japanese people to say "yes" and appear to agree with verbal instructions when in fact they don't understand them. What we had here was a failure to communicate.

While the company won the case, they lost, because an employee with valuable skills was fired. It's possible that with the right lawyer, the employee would have won the case. As the courts become more sophisticated about cross-cultural communication, they will expect businesses to do so as well.

Communication: An Essential Part of Every Healthy Business

Communication is an essential requirement for a healthy business. In a few cases, you may have a legitimate business reason for not hiring someone with a very heavy accent.[9] For example, in a customer service or receptionist position, you want someone who is able to be understood by everybody.

For the vast majority of jobs, you can't discriminate against people with accents, unless you absolutely can't understand them. As a manager, you do have the right to be able to communicate with your employees. But document the communication problems. In fact, have another manager or personnel representative as a witness.

If you inherit employees you can't understand, there are some steps you can take. First, discuss it privately with the individual employees. Tell them, "I have a very difficult time understanding you. I am going to do all I can to try to understand you. I'd like to ask you to do everything you can to make it easier for me." Suggest they take their time when talking so you can understand them. Encourage them to enroll in accent reduction classes. These courses are taught at local colleges and in adult education programs.

Communicate in writing to prevent misunderstanding. Ask for help from other employees who are bilingual. You could take a course in their language, although it's not required by law. If after all this you still can't communicate, maybe you can transfer to another area where you won't have this problem.

Can employees be transferred because they can't learn to communicate with you, the manager? If they won't have losses in pay, benefits, or career growth, it is safe to transfer them.

Demoting or terminating employees who can't communicate with you is probably justified. I once was asked to represent an employee who was dismissed after taking accent reduction classes for a year without improving. I didn't take the case—I couldn't understand him! In cases like this, there are no easy answers.

English-only rules discriminate on the basis of national origin and generally are illegal. There is rarely a business necessity for not allowing employees to speak among themselves in their own languages while working or during breaks.

All of us have a national origin. We are all proud of our roots. The national heritage of others should be respected.

3. Citizenship Discrimination

You can't discriminate against qualified applicants because they are not citizens if they are authorized to work in this country.[10] A "green card" (they aren't even green these days) is one type of valid work permit. There are other classifications that allow people who are immigrants to work in the United States. See Chapter 8 for the technical requirements.

Your employment application should ask, "Are you legally entitled to work in this country?" This question must be asked of all applicants, even if they don't appear foreign. Otherwise, you are discriminating on the basis of national origin.

One of my corporate clients found out how tricky this area can be. One of their managers was an immigrant himself. He was interviewing an applicant who also was an immigrant. In the rapport-building part of the interview, the manager said, "I've had a lot of problems with the Immigration Service. Have you?" The applicant said he had, too. They commiserated with each other for a while and then went on with the interview.

The applicant wasn't hired. He filed a claim for citizenship discrimination. After all, they talked about his citizenship status almost as much as about his qualifications.

The only time you can refuse to hire a noncitizen is if the job requires a government security clearance. The federal government doesn't give security clearances to noncitizens. That's discrimination, but it's not illegal. This law doesn't apply to the government.

Some applicants are not legally entitled to work in the United States, but they could become authorized if your company assisted them. They must prove their skills are so unique that there are no U.S. citizens who can do the job. You are not required to hire such applicants, but you may choose to do so because in fact they are unique.

The United States is fortunate to attract the best people from countries all over the world. Equal treatment for immigrants benefits us all.

4. Religion Discrimination

People of every religion, including pagans and atheists, are protected from discrimination because of their beliefs.[11] You can't refuse to hire or promote employees because of their religion, or do as one manager did, hire all your employees at your church.

Religious expression by employees raises complicated issues. Tastefully displaying a religious item at one's workstation may be permitted. Proselytizing fellow employees, reading holy books aloud, or denouncing other's religions are not acceptable behavior.

Religious devotees also must be reasonably accommodated in order to practice their religion. This is one of the exceptions to the rule about treating employees consistently. Reasonable accommodation means that you treat some people better than others because of their religion, unless it would cause "undue hardship" on the company.

For example, you can't require an employee to take off a turban in order to meet your dress code. Turbans are required to be worn at all times by members of the Sikh religion, in the same way that yarmulkes are worn by Orthodox Jews.

You must allow employees reasonable time off to follow religious observances, beyond their accrued personal time off. The leave may be with or without pay, as long as you are consistent with other employees who are given time off for personal reasons. You also must reasonably accommodate the schedules of employees who can't work on Saturdays or Sundays for religious reasons.

If you have never required employees to work on weekends, you can't list that as a job requirement. It is not a true requirement, and it tends to discriminate against people on the basis of religion.

What happens if suddenly you need employees to work Saturdays for a month or two? You have several employees whose religion prohibits work on Saturdays. They can't work other days because there is no supervision. Can you fire them? Probably not.

If the Saturday work is required for only a limited time, reasonable accommodation means you will just have to allow them to be exempt from the requirement. If Saturday work will be required from now on, then you should be able to justify terminating them or transferring them into another department. But there is no guarantee that you won't get sued.

You can, however, refuse to hire new employees who can't work on Saturdays if it will be required for the foreseeable future.

Other employees may complain you are giving religious employees favorable treatment. The answer is you are, and you will treat them the same way as soon as they convert.

The United States was founded on religious freedom. Today, there is strong support in the law for freedom of religion at work.

5. Sex Discrimination

Men and women must be treated equally.[12]

"Equal pay for equal work" has been the law of the land since the Equal Pay Act of 1963.[13] The purpose of the law is for women and men to be paid the same for doing the same job.

Although it sounds simple, equal pay is not always easy to put into practice. The biggest issue is how to define the same job. The law says for women and men to receive equal pay, their jobs must be of equal skill, effort, and responsibility. The jobs do not need to be identical, but they must be substantially similar.

You are allowed to pay more to a man who is doing the same job as a woman if you have a bona fide seniority plan. In other words, if it is your policy to give annual raises, naturally employees with more seniority will be paid more.

You also can pay extra for experience when hiring a new employee. If you hire two new employees at the same time, it is expected you will pay more to the one with more experience, male or female, because they bring more to the job.

You can't pay based solely on the applicants salary history.[14] Some companies won't pay applicants more than 15% over their last salary. This approach discriminates against women. That's because as of 1989, women make 68% of what men do.[15] Women doctors, women architects, and women lawyers all make less than 80% of what men make, holding constant for type of job, age, experience and education. Setting salaries based on salary history or salary expectations perpetuates this discrimination.

I once shared office space with a lawyer who hired only women lawyers. Yet he constantly made sexist comments, expected them to clean up after him, and bring him coffee. One day, in my diplomatic way, I asked him, "Why do you hire only women lawyers when you're such a male chauvinist pig?" He said, "I found out I can hire two women for the price of one man!" It was true. He asked them what salary they wanted, and the women always wanted far less than the men.

As long as he hired only women, he couldn't be accused of sex discrimination. But the day he hired a male lawyer, and paid him as much as the most experienced woman, he was in trouble.

Measuring the Value of a Job: The Concept of Comparable Worth

Since the Equal Pay Act applies only when men and women are performing the same jobs, it affects very few women. Most women work in female-dominated professions like nursing, teaching, and clerical. There are few men in these fields to compare to women.

The concept of comparable worth was designed to address this problem. Its purpose is equal pay, not for equal jobs, but for jobs of comparable value.

The value to the company of every job can be measured. These values are computed by compensation specialists, industrial engineers, and industrial psychologists. These values then can be compared.

In one study, the value to the employer of a secretary's job was equal to a painter's, yet (male) painters were paid 37% more than (female) secretaries.[16] To establish comparable worth, the secretaries would receive higher and more frequent salary increases until they were equal to painters.

Comparable worth is a concept that has been adopted by only a few local governments for their own employees, but it is not required by law. Employees have argued that the EEO laws should be interpreted to require comparable worth. As of this writing, the courts have not agreed.

The Danger of Stereotyping

Once you hire women (or minorities), you might have some preconceived ideas about them. Almost everyone has some preconceptions about one group or another. Our stereotypes probably are unconscious; they even may be well meaning. But stereotyping is a subtle form of discrimination. It is so subtle, in fact, that for years it was not recognized as the basis for a discrimination lawsuit.

That changed in 1989, when the U.S. Supreme Court decided the case of *Price Waterhouse* v. *Hopkins*.[17] Ann Hopkins was one of 88 candidates for partnership in the Big Eight accounting firm. She brought more business to the firm than any other candidate. But she was not chosen for partner. The firm said she needed to "walk more femininely, talk more femininely, dress more femininely, wear make-up, have your hair styled, and wear jewelry." The partners complained she used too much profanity for a lady. One said she needed a course in charm school.

The Supreme Court said these comments showed that stereotyped views of women were being used as criteria for partnership. This was illegal, since by all legitimate business standards, she was an excellent employee.

If stereotyped comments have been made, they will be used to prove your intent to discriminate. Even good-natured joking or teasing can be used as evidence. For example, calling the women in the office honey or girls is not enough for a discrimination lawsuit. But if a woman is denied a promotion, these comments prove women were not treated the same as men.

Stereotyping also affects training opportunities. One company offered two in-house training programs for its clerical staff. One was blueprint reading. It was a prerequisite for becoming a technician and led to an engineering career path. The other class was time management for secretaries. It led to a dead-end, secretarial job.

The manager of the mailroom let only men take the blueprint reading course and only women take the time management course. The company was sued for sex discrimination and lost.

Perhaps less obvious is the "glass ceiling" that prevents women and minorities from entering top management. According to a 1991 U.S. Labor Department report, women aren't given the same opportunities as men. As speaker Nido Qubein puts it, "In our society we have a double standard: we judge men on the basis of potential and women on the basis of performance."

The Labor Department has threatened to yank the contracts of federal contractors and subcontractors if they don't give women and minorities the training and experience needed for advancement.[18]

Sex discrimination was added to the original Civil Rights Act in 1964 by a southern congressman who was trying to kill the bill. No one, he thought, would support a bill that gave equal rights to *women*.

Much to his surprise, the five women representatives adopted his idea as their own and quickly forced its passage. Despite this inauspicious start, John Naisbitt and Patricia Aburdene in *Megatrends 2000* listed women in the work force as 1 of the 10 most influential trends of the twenty-first Century.[19]

6. *Pregnancy Discrimination*

A special form of illegal sex stereotyping is pregnancy discrimination. This is prohibited by U.S. law,[20] as well as by some state laws.[21]

You can't discriminate against pregnant women. If a pregnant applicant or employee is the most qualified for the job, you must hire or promote her. You cannot assume she will take a leave of absence, and you can't ask whether she intends to take one.

I remember saying this in class in Philadelphia one day and a manager exploded. He said, "I'm not going to hire someone who's pregnant, I don't care what the law says. What is Congress trying to do, put America out of business?" A woman spoke up. "Germany has some of the best maternity laws in the world. It hasn't hurt them!"

The only time you might be able to refuse to hire a pregnant employee is if the job is a temporary one that must be completed within a relatively short period of time, say, six months. In that case, you should ask all applicants about their ability to work for that period of time.

If your company allows short-term medical or disability leaves for other reasons, they must be offered to pregnant employees. For example, if you allow up to six months leave for employees who hurt themselves away from work, you must give women who are disabled as a result of pregnancy or childbirth up to six months leave, too.

This leave is only for the time they are in fact disabled; U.S. law does not require maternity leave for bonding or child care (although bills to require companies to give parental leave have been introduced repeatedly in Congress).

Some states, including California, Connecticut, Maine, Minnesota, New Jersey, Oregon, Rhode Island, Washington, and Wisconsin, require companies to give parental leave to both parents in the event of a birth or adoption.

Just like other people who are disabled, pregnant employees must be reasonably accommodated if they request light duty. Light duty might include changing working hours during the early part of the pregnancy in order to accommodate morning sickness and allowing an employee to sit rather than stand to ease foot swelling and backaches.

Fetal Protection Policies

You might be tempted to prohibit pregnant women from working in hazardous jobs or force them to take light duty. This is illegal pregnancy discrimination according to a 1991 decision by the U.S. Supreme Court.[22]

The case involved a company that makes batteries using lead. Lead is a known carcinogen. It is particularly toxic to fetuses and ovulating women, and there is some evidence it injures the sperm of men. As a result, the company refused to allow women of childbearing years to work in the area where the batteries were made, unless the women could prove they'd been sterilized.

Some of the employees brought suit claiming this was illegal pregnancy discrimination. The Supreme Court agreed. It said you cannot prohibit women from jobs because they are pregnant, even if they might have a miscarriage or a child with birth defects. The Court said some women, for economic or other reasons, are willing to take the risk. They are allowed to make that decision for themselves. You can't make it for them.

From a human standpoint, this seems like a terrible decision. How would you feel if you allowed one of your employees to work with hazardous substances and her child was born with a severe birth defect?

From a legal perspective, it's almost worse. If a child is born with birth defects, can you be sued? The Court *assumed* you couldn't be, if you follow the procedures outlined shortly. But there is no guarantee. In fact, many lawyers believe this Supreme Court case will cause numerous suits in the future.

Even if you aren't sued directly for injuring the unborn child, you could be dragged into a lawsuit. For example, let's say a pregnant employee insists on working with hazardous chemicals. Let's also assume that, while she's pregnant, she and her husband divorce. The child is born with a birth defect. The husband could sue the wife, on behalf of the child, for child endangerment. Your records could be subpoenaed, and you would be asked to testify.

Or what if the police decided to charge the mother with criminal endangerment of her child? This approach has been taken against the mothers of crack babies. Again, you would be involved in the case.

Last, the Supreme Court seemed to say that if employers followed all Occupational Safety and Health Administration (OSHA) regulations,[23] they couldn't be sued. Most experts disagree. But in any event, it certainly is true that if you *don't* follow OSHA rules, you will be sued and you definitely will lose.

> *practical pointers:* You can't prevent pregnant employees from working in dangerous areas. But you can take a number of steps to decrease the likelihood of a lawsuit.
>
> You can offer an alternative to the pregnant employee. If she accepts, that solves the problem. For example, you can make arrangements to have other employees (even you) take over the hazardous functions. You can transfer her, if there is no loss of pay, benefits, or career growth. In fact, if the employee's doctor demands she not be exposed to these conditions, you are required to reasonably accommodate her.
>
> If a pregnant employee wants to work in a dangerous area, you may be able to require her to sign a waiver and indemnification. This waiver notifies her of the danger that her unborn child could be affected, and says she has been advised by you not to work in the area. She also agrees to indemnify you if you are sued, and she herself agrees not to sue for injuries to her child. (She would be entitled to worker's compensation for any injury to herself.)
>
> Waivers may not be binding. You are asking the mother to waive the rights of her child. Legally, she may not be able to do that. However, a waiver may discourage her from suing.

As a practical matter, you should require all employees to sign such a form, not just pregnant ones, because that may be considered pregnancy discrimination. Also, sometimes women become pregnant without knowing. And some toxics are equally hazardous to men's reproductive capabilities. You should have every employee, male and female, sign one.

The bottom line is that employers, more than ever, must be extremely careful about maintaining a safe and healthy workplace, not only for employees, but also for their unborn children.

The unborn children of pregnant employees are our future. Treating mothers with respect and due regard for their dignity is only right.

7. Age Discrimination

People age 40 or over can't be discriminated against in favor of younger people.[24] Federal law doesn't prohibit age discrimination against people under 40, but some states do.

Age discrimination cases are popular with employees' lawyers. The reason: big money damages are awarded in age cases. Why? Most judges and jurors are over the age of 40. They can relate to an older person who claims discrimination. Older people generally make more money, so their losses are higher. And their front pay often will be awarded until they reach retirement age.

Age discrimination is different from sex and race discrimination in one important way. In race and sex cases, you must compare how one person was treated to someone in a different group (e.g., males versus females). But in age cases, you can compare people of the same group (over 40) as long as one is significantly older than the other.

Let's say two people apply for a job. One applicant is 41, the other is 49. The 49-year-old is more qualified, but the 41-year-old gets the job. That's age discrimination, even though they both are in the same group (over 40).

Now assume a 42-year-old applies for the job and has the best qualifications, but the 41-year-old still gets the job. Is that age discrimination?

Where do you draw the line? According to the regulations,[25] there should be at least five year's difference between the person who gets the job (or other favorable treatment) and the person who doesn't. But there may be exceptions to this rule.[26]

Managers say, "How do we know the ages of applicants? It's not on the application." Usually the difference in age is obvious. Most cases involve people in their 50s and 60s replaced by people in their 20s or 30s.

What It Really Means When "You're Overqualified"

A complaint frequently made by older workers in the job market is being told, "You're overqualified." This statement, when made in an interview, could be grounds for an age discrimination lawsuit. Courts have said overqualified is a code word for "too old."[27]

Consider the process you go through before you interview an applicant. You receive applications and resumes. You eliminate the candidates who, on paper, do not appear qualified for the job. Then you call in the rest for interviews.

You know the qualifications of every person before you see them in the interviews. If some are in fact "overqualified," you would not have asked them for interviews in the first place. The interviews are the first time you see the applicants and how old they are. If at that point you say the applicant is overqualified, it sounds like an excuse.

Being overqualified also does not sound like a legitimate business reason for not hiring an applicant. Don't you want the best qualified person for the job? If you get them at a bargain, so much the better.

Some managers argue that an applicant who is clearly overqualified for the job would not be happy in a lesser position. Maybe so, but let the applicant make that decision. If you describe the duties, responsibilities, working conditions, and pay, and the applicant still is interested, you should hire him or her as the most qualified person.

A friend was a technical writer for many years. He loved his work. Then one day he was promoted to manager. After a month he went to his boss and said, "I hate being a manager. All I do is listen to people's problems. I haven't accomplished anything constructive since my promotion. I want to go back to being a writer."

The boss said, "Remember our company policy? Once a manager, always a manager. We can't let you go back."

My friend decided to leave and get a job elsewhere as a writer. But everywhere he went, employers said, "You're overqualified to be a writer. You should be manager." It took him almost a year to find a company willing to "risk" hiring him. Yet he probably had far more skill, ability, and experience than the younger writers who were hired instead of him.

Don't Make Assumptions

Another bogus requirement that discriminates against older applicants is the college degree. Every job description, advertisement, and posting should read "degree or equivalent experience." Every resume and application should be carefully reviewed to see if the candidate has equivalent experience.

A manager hired a young woman in her 20s, with a B.A. degree, instead of a man in his 50s with 30 years of experience. The manager said that the younger person's knowledge was more current. That is a legitimate business reason for picking her if current knowledge is a significant requirement of the job. But in this case, the job involved maintaining old technology. The young woman had never even taken a class in it. That looks like age discrimination.

When it comes to training programs, you must consider an older worker just as you would a younger one: on the basis of legitimate business reasons. You can't assume the older worker will retire soon. Your *assumption* about how long your employees will stay is not a legitimate business reason. For all you know, it is more likely that a younger worker will leave before an older one. On the other hand, if employees tell you they're planning to leave soon, you don't have to put them in training programs. Base your decisions on facts, not assumptions.

Older workers often are victims of layoff when companies cut jobs. If the company's only criterion for picking people for layoff is high salary, that tends to impact older workers, since salary goes up with seniority. For that reason, courts have said that you can't pick employees for layoff solely because their salaries are high.[28]

Even if layoff criteria are legitimate, if they aren't applied consistently, there may be age discrimination.

Preserving Employment

When employees are older and have worked for your company for many years, you may be required to preserve their employment. This does not mean they're entitled to the same job for life, but you should make reasonable efforts to keep them employed.

In one case, a man was hired at the age of 49 as a director. During the next 10 years, his staff grew to 10 people. Beginning when he was 60, the company began reorganizing his department. Over the next seven years, his job responsibilities were taken away and given to younger people. Two of his job duties were spun off to subsidiaries, at a savings of almost $1 million a year.

By the time he was 67, he had no staff and no job duties. The company laid him off. He sued for age discrimination and won. The court noted that the company did not make any attempt to put him into any of the other jobs created during his last 7 years of work.[29]

Contrast that to a case where a 57-year-old vice president was demoted, paid 40% less, and assigned to work for a much younger employee whom he had trained. When the vice president quit, the court held he could claim constructive discharge.[30] That is, a reasonable person under the circumstances would have considered this age discrimination and would feel forced to quit.[31]

From these cases, you see this area is a dangerous one. On the one hand, you can't restructure employees out of their jobs. On the other, you can't demote them into lesser jobs.

> *practical pointer:* Perhaps the best approach is to include employees in the decision-making process. If they see their positions being phased out, they can apply for transfers or look elsewhere. They also should be offered opportunities to take lesser positions voluntarily.

Early Retirement: How to Prove It's Voluntary

There is no mandatory retirement age in the United States. With exceptions for airline pilots, top executives, and tenured professors, it is illegal to require employees to retire.[32] If employees want to work until they're 100, that's up to them. They are entitled to work as long as they can.

If they can't perform, you can dismiss them. But as long as they perform, you have to consider them for promotion, training, and pay increases just like anyone else.

Companies sometimes offer early retirement programs in order to trim budgets and avoid layoffs. Early retirement programs are legal and do not discriminate on the basis of age, if they are voluntary. To prove a program is voluntary, you must show that:

1. The employee had a true choice between early retirement or keeping the job. Of course, you can't guarantee an employee won't ever be laid off or terminated. But saying to employees, "Take early retirement or you'll be fired," is not giving them the opportunity to make voluntary decisions.

2. The employee was not discriminated against in other ways. If an employee is frequently asked about retirement plans, called senile, or often referred to as the old man, he can claim the early retirement program was used to get rid of him.

3. The employee was not required to make a quick decision. Employees considering early retirement should be allowed to con-

sult with their attorneys, financial advisers, and families. It can take
weeks to get all the information necessary to make a truly informed,
voluntary decision.

There are additional technical requirements.[33] See a lawyer before offering
early retirement.

As the baby boom becomes the age wave,[34] fewer young people and
more older ones will be in the work force. In *The Age of Unreason*,[35] Charles
Handy forecasts that few people will fully retire in the future. He believes
many of us will work part time for life.

The future is here. Now is the time to value employees who are older
for their experience and wisdom.

8. Disability Discrimination

The Americans with Disabilities Act (ADA) was passed by Congress in
1990.[36] It covers companies with 25 or more employees as of July 1992.
Beginning in July 1994, employers with 15 or more employees are covered.
Some states have laws prohibiting disability discrimination by smaller
companies. Since this is a new law, it will be explained here in some depth.

The law protects people who suffer from a permanent impairment of
a major life function, like walking, seeing, or breathing. It does not cover
minor or temporary disabilities, like broken legs.

The ADA covers virtually every type of disability:

physical disabilities, including people in wheelchairs, blind, and
deaf

Medical conditions, such as cancer, AIDS, diabetes, chronic fatigue
syndrome, and disabling stress

Mental illnesses, like schizophrenia, bipolar disease, and manic
depression

Developmental disabilities such as learning disorders, dyslexia,
retardation, and Down's syndrome

Rehabilitated alcoholics and drug addicts

The law also applies to people who have a history of being disabled.
For example, a woman manager who had breast cancer returned to work
with the disease in remission. She was not disabled. But her boss said she
would never get anywhere in the company because she was "weak." This
is discrimination based on her history of disability.

People who are mistakenly perceived as being disabled are also protected. For example, an employer might assume that people who are heavy can't keep up the pace. This is an assumption based on stereotypical perceptions. If an employer discriminates on this basis, it probably is illegal under the ADA.

Similarly, if an employer believes an employee is using drugs, but in fact the employee is not, that employee is perceived as disabled and is protected under the ADA. Accusing an employee of taking drugs puts the employee in a protected category.

Finally, people who are care givers for people with disabilities are covered. For example, I once couldn't decide whether to hire an attorney who was engaged to a man who recently had become a paraplegic. I worried she wouldn't be able to work the overtime required. As it turned out, she never missed work. Making that assumption today would be a violation of the ADA.

Not Disabled, Not Protected

People who are homosexuals, bisexuals, or transvestites are not protected from discrimination under the ADA because they are not considered disabled.

Other people may be disabled, but are not protected anyway:

Current users of alcohol or drugs

Food handlers with communicable diseases

Gamblers, kleptomaniacs, and pyromaniacs

Also not protected are people who pose a danger to others. For example, people with contagious diseases are not required to be employed if they will infect others.

Courts look at two factors in judging whether an employee poses a danger to others. First, how is the disease transmitted? In the case of autoimmune deficiency syndrome (AIDS), it is communicable only through the exchange of bodily fluids. In most workplaces, bodily fluids are not exchanged. The disease can't be transmitted to coworkers. Tuberculosis, on the other hand, is communicable through the air after many months of exposure to an infected person. The likelihood of infecting coworkers is much greater.

The second issue is: How long is the carrier infectious? In the case of tuberculosis, it's communicable for a relatively short period of time. It might be reasonable to give the infected employee time off on medical leave. On the other hand, a person who is positive for the human immunovirus (HIV) always is infectious. If the job is one in which the virus could be transmitted, the person with AIDS can be transferred or demoted. An employee who is terminated because he or she can't work should be entitled to disability insurance.

If there is a reasonable probability someone else at work will become infected, you can refuse employment. If there is no such probability, but only fear based on misinformation, you can't discriminate.

Self-injury Not Preventable

It is not unusual for employers to refuse to hire people with disabilities out of fear they will injure themselves on the job. That, too, may be illegal.

One company refused to hire a woman truck driver who had a birth defect of the lower back.[37] Nine years before applying for the job, she had a partial laminectomy. Since then, she had no more back problems.

Truck drivers climb, crawl, bend, pull open hoods weighing over 100 pounds, and drag hoses weighing up to 60 pounds. Based on this job description, the company's doctor could not say for certain whether the woman would injure her back. Nevertheless, he gave his opinion that she could not safely work as a truck driver.

She sued for disability discrimination and won. The judge said the company can refuse to hire her only if it could show there was a reasonable probability of substantial harm. In other words, what are the odds this employee will hurt herself on the job?

"Reasonable probability" means that a doctor (not you) can *swear*, based on the employee's work experience and medical history, that this particular person has a 50% chance of injuring himself or herself in the future. It is not enough to say that people with similar disabilities tend to injure themselves. "Substantial harm" means the potential future injury must be significant. A pulled muscle that twinges a bit is not substantial harm.

The key question, according to the judge, is whether applicants are capable of performing the job at the time they apply. If so, they must be hired.

While her case was going through the courts, this woman was hired at another trucking company. By the time of trial, she had worked several years there and never hurt her back.

That's why this law makes sense. If the company had hired her instead of assuming she couldn't do the job, it would have had the benefit of her services.

Don't Assume—Ask

The spirit of the ADA says don't make assumptions about what a person with a disability can or can't do. Instead, *ask.*

My first job out of law school was with the Disability Law Center in Campbell, California. One of our coworkers was a young man in a wheelchair. He was handsome and vigorous, played wheelchair basketball, and had a wry sense of humor.

One day, he went to lunch with another woman and me. At the entrance, we saw the stairs went straight up to the door, while the wheelchair ramp was off to the side. Rather than walking up the stairs, we turned and followed him up the ramp.

When it was time to leave, he led the way out. But rather than turning down the ramp, he gave his chair a push and flew out over the steps.

She and I gasped in unison and looked at each other in disbelief. Oh no! This poor, befuddled, disabled person had forgotten to go down the ramp! We turned back, expecting to see him crash below. Instead, he bounced off the sidewalk, popped a wheelie, made a 180 degree turn, thrust his fists into the air in victory and shouted, "Yes!"

Despite the fact that she and I worked with and for disabled people, we had fallen into the old stereotype. What he was saying was, "Yes! Look at me! I'm a person, too!" And it must have worked, because she later married him.

Don't judge people until you know them. In interviews, you can ask people who are disabled only about their ability to do the job. If they say they can do the job, don't assume they can't. Take them at their word, test them, or hire them on a temporary basis.

Why Job Descriptions Are Essential

You must hire a person with a disability only if he or she is the most qualified and can perform the essential functions of the job.

The "essential functions" are the tasks the employee who holds the position *must* be able to perform. If the position exists in order to perform the function (a typist, for example), then it is essential. If the task makes up a large portion of the job, it is essential.

There are some functions that an employee may never perform, but they are still essential. For example, firefighters must be able to carry adults out of burning buildings. They are the only people in our society hired to do this, so it's an essential function. Yet a firefighter may never actually have to do it.

practical pointer: Rewrite all job descriptions (or write job descriptions for the first time) so they indicate the essential functions of each job. The law states that job descriptions written before advertising job openings will help you win discrimination claims. See Chapter 5 for more information on functional job descriptions.

If you don't write job descriptions, an employee's performance appraisal may be presumed to show all the essential functions.

By writing accurate job descriptions and using them in the hiring process, you will protect yourself from a discrimination suit. You also will make a better hiring decision no matter who you pick.

How to Offer a Reasonable Accommodation

Employees who are disabled also must be reasonably accommodated. A reasonable accommodation is a change you make in a job's requirements so a person with a disability can do it.

You should offer a reasonable accommodation as soon as you realize an employee is disabled and needs help to perform the job. You are responsible for suggesting an accommodation, not the employee. But you should ask the employee for suggestions.

According to the government regulations, the manager should "initiate an informal, interactive process" with the person who is disabled in order to learn what accommodation is appropriate. In other words, ask. It all comes back to not making assumptions.

Reasonable Accommodation
Six ways you may be required to reasonably accommodate people with disabilities:

1. Buy equipment.
2. Modify structures.
3. Restructure jobs.
4. Schedule part-time work.
5. Rewrite tests.
6. Provide readers and interpreters.

This list is not exhaustive, but only illustrative of the lengths Congress expects of employers to hire people with disabilities.

People in wheelchairs can be accommodated by building ramps over stairs. A person who is blind can be given an optical character reader to scan printed materials. An employee who is deaf can use networks and TTY (teletypewriter) telephones. Indeed, due to rapid advances in technology, many physical limitations can be overcome at work.

Jobs must be restructured so people with disabilities can perform them. But you don't have to restructure out the essential functions of the job. For example, let's say you have two shipping and receiving clerk positions in the warehouse. The jobs are identical. The clerks are required to open the doors when a shipment arrives, open and unpack boxes, check the items against the packing list and purchase order, inventory the items in the computer, and stock the shelves by driving a forklift and lifting up to 50 pounds to a height of 6 feet.

A person in a wheelchair might be able to do all these functions except lifting over 4 feet. A reasonable accommodation would be to restructure these two jobs, so that an applicant in a wheelchair could do one of them.

Giving employees part-time work schedules also may be required by reasonable accommodation. But you also can pay them part-time wages. In contrast, if you hire a reader or interpreter for employees who are deaf or blind, that cost can't be deducted from their pay.

Reasonable accommodation of other disabilities takes different forms. A person with cancer may require chemotherapy, and a person with kidney disease must undergo dialysis. They are able to work most of the time. Reasonable accommodation might require they be given off one day a week for treatment.

When employees have AIDS, reasonable accommodation might require you to give them some leeway in taking their disability leaves in bits of time rather than all at once. That's because they can become ill frequently with colds, pneumonia, bronchitis, and other infections. They might be at work for three weeks, then out for a week. They should be allowed to use their sick days and disability leave for those weeks as they come up.

Although not required by law, some companies allow employees to bank their accrued sick leave and donate it to coworkers who need it.

If disabled employees don't accept accommodation, they are no longer protected by the law. For example, one of my corporate clients had an employee who was hard of hearing, but she refused to wear a hearing aid. As a result, she couldn't perform all her job duties. She could be dismissed.

Recovering alcoholics and rehabilitating drug addicts also must be reasonably accommodated. If they need to attend a treatment program, the company must allow reasonable time off. But their addictions should not be accommodated. Current abusers aren't covered. If they can't do the job, don't show up for work, or are frequently tardy, you can fire them the same as other nonperformers.

One morning I was sitting in the office of the president of a small company located in an industrial mall. He was telling me and the personnel director how proud he was of a new director he had hired. The new director had worked for the company right across the parking lot. He knew the area. He had a good reference from the president next door. He was really going to clean up some chronic problems.

At that moment, the vice president of operations burst in. "That new Director we hired! I just ran into a friend of mine from next door. He said they fired that guy for drinking on the job!"

The president turned red. He wanted to fire him immediately. You know what I told him. "Alcoholism is a disability. We can't discriminate against him because of that. If he doesn't do the job, we can offer one shot at rehabilitation. If he doesn't make it, fire him."

Two years later, the director is still there, doing a great job. That's why recovering alcoholics and rehabilitating drug addicts should be reasonably accommodated.

Determining What Makes an Undue Hardship

You are not required to reasonably accommodate any disability if it would be an undue hardship. According to one company's lawyer, "As far as the government is concerned, spending money is never an undue hardship!" Buying equipment is almost always considered reasonable.

An undue hardship causes significant difficulty or creates a significant expense for the company site (not just for you or your department). You look at the net cost after tax credits.[38]

When the ADA passed, Congress recognized that hiring people with disabilities could cost companies more. Congress explicitly made the decision to shift the cost of supporting people with disabilities from the taxpayers, who pay the cost of a nonworking disabled population, to employers who will get the benefit of the work they perform.

Congress was asked to put a $10,000 limit on the amount an employer could be required to spend. This was defeated, so you could be required to spend more. However, according to a report from the Office of Vocational Rehabilitation, over half the employers who accommodated people with disabilities had no extra costs, and another 30% spent less than $500.

The same report found 91% of the disabled workers had average or better productivity on the job than nondisabled employees, and 75% had better safety records. And *non-disabled* workers' turnover rate was 11:1 compared to people with disabilities. Most important to the issue of reasonable accommodation, 55% of the people with disabilities had better attendance than did able-bodied workers, and only 5% had worse records.

If an employee with a disability needs it, how much time off do you have to give before it's an undue hardship? It depends on the answers to these questions:

- Is temporary help available?

- How essential are the job functions?

- How will work delays impact the company?

- How much time off is requested?

- Is the employee otherwise satisfactory?

My guideline in deciding whether or not to give time off is the "CEO test." If the chief executive officer of your company became disabled and needed this time off, would the company be able to accommodate him or her? If so, the company probably can accommodate anyone else.

If this is a critical job and temporary help is not available, you might justify a termination. But this is a very dangerous area. There's nothing like a newspaper headline that says, "Fired Cancer Victim Sues Your Company." The decision not to accommodate a person with a disability should be made together with a lawyer.

Tips on Working with Employees Who Have Special Needs

Once hired, employees who are disabled must be treated the same as nondisabled employees whenever you make decisions about pay increases, transfers, training, overtime, promotions, and terminations.

Just as important, you should support them after they are on the job. That means including them in casual conversation, giving them visibility as a representative of your area, and preparing them for promotion in the organization.

Don't allow yourself or others to blame employees errors on their disabilities. Everyone makes mistakes. On the other hand, Don't be overly solicitous of employees who are disabled. Don't make the assumption that people with disabilities need help unless they ask for it.

W Mitchell, a professional speaker who uses a wheelchair, tells of the time a well-meaning person tried to help him when he wasn't expecting it. He almost fell over the edge of the stairs. Mitchell advises always to ask people in wheelchairs if they want help before giving it. Otherwise, just act naturally.

Here are some tips to keep in mind when interviewing or working with people who are disabled:

1. Sit when talking for a long time to people in wheelchairs and people who are short.

2. For people whose hearing is impaired, get their attention before you begin speaking; don't put your hands in front of your face, don't chew gum, and learn a little sign language.

3. People who are blind should not be touched without warning; allow them to hold your arm while walking; let them know what's coming ("step up").

4. Don't worry about using common phrases such as (to a person who is blind), "Do you see what I mean?"

The ADA was passed because Congress perceived the value of the 43 million of "differently abled" people among us. If you treat them fairly, they will make great contributions to your company.

How the Equal Employment Opportunity Commission Operates

The U.S. Equal Employment Opportunity Commission (EEOC) enforces the federal laws against discrimination. State laws are enforced in a similar manner by state fair employment agencies.

The EEOC gets involved when one of your employees makes an appointment. The employee must file a complaint with the agency before suing. The employee has 180, 240, or 300 days to file a complaint, depending on your state. Federal government employees have only 30 days to file.

Once the employee files, the investigator sends out a "Request for Information." The company must respond to every allegation made by the employee and provide more general information. For example, if a woman claims she wasn't promoted, the company may be asked about promotions denied to other women in other jobs.

The company usually is given 30 days to respond. After the company responds, in most cases the complaint goes to the bottom of the stack to await processing. It's not unusual for a case to sit for a year before the investigation begins.

Eventually, the investigator will talk to witnesses for both the employer and the employee, review the manager's documents about the event, and read the company's response to the Request for Information. Investigators are required to be impartial. They do not work for either side, even though they hear the employee's side of the case first.

The investigator finishes fact-finding, and then decides whether there is reasonable cause to believe the employee suffered discrimination. If there is no cause to find discrimination, the EEOC issues a "Right to Sue Letter." With this letter, the employee has the right to file a lawsuit in federal court within 90 days. Once it's filed, the company should receive notice of the lawsuit within 120 days.

If the EEOC finds there is cause to believe discrimination occurred, the EEOC lawyers will represent the employee in any suit against the employer. At that point, many companies believe it is wise to settle out of court.

THREE REQUIREMENTS OF AFFIRMATIVE ACTION

Remember the political turmoil that led to the passage of the Civil Rights Act in 1964? During the next year, the civil rights movement continued gaining strength. President Johnson decided more action was needed—affirmative action. He wanted companies to do more than not discriminate. He wanted them to go out and recruit minority and female employees.

He issued a presidential edict, called an Executive Order.[39] It required Affirmative Action. This Executive Order can be revoked at any time by any president. But not one president since Johnson has tried to stop Affirmative Action. Affirmative Action also has been upheld by the so-called Reagan (U.S. Supreme) Court. In 1989, the Court approved an Affirmative Action plan implemented by an employer as required by the Executive Order.[40]

Affirmative Action has this kind of broad-based support because it does not require quotas. It does require making a few changes in the way we think about hiring, promoting, and firing.

Affirmative Action applies only to federal government contractors and subcontractors and public agencies with at least 50 employees.[41] It applies only to women, certain defined minorities, Vietnam-era veterans, and people with disabilities. It does not apply to employees over 40 or religious groups.

Companies that have Affirmative Action plans are required to keep data about the race, sex, disability, and veteran status of all applicants. Questions that are otherwise illegal can be asked in order to compile this applicant flow data. The company is required to ask for the information, but it is voluntary for the applicant to give it.

The data are used by the U.S. Office of Federal Contract Compliance Programs (OFCCP) to audit the company's success. If the company doesn't meet the requirements, it can be debarred or prevented from receiving federal funds.

So what is Affirmative Action? There are three requirements:

1. Have an Affirmative Action plan.

2. Recruit targeted groups.

3. Hire the best.

1. The Affirmative Action Plan

The Affirmative Action plan (AAP) is simply a statistical check on the company's hiring, promotion, and termination practices. It can take one person several months to put together an AAP. For big companies, it takes up a thick binder.

The AAP has five parts: the work force, availability and underutilization analyses, goals, and timetables. (See the appendix for a complete explanation of the mechanics.)

The work force analysis shows the number of women and minorities currently working at the company in every job classification. This is a statistical snapshot of the work force on one day.

The next step is the availability analysis, the number of women and minority employees outside the company who are qualified and available for employment. Eight different factors are evaluated to calculate these numbers.

For example, it is not fair to require a company to have 50% female engineers just because half of the people in the local community are women. Half of all engineers are not women. Indeed, only 15% of 1987 engineering school graduates were female.[42]

So the company looks at the numbers of women graduating from engineering schools, those currently working, and those in-house who are on an engineering track to get a picture of the number of women in the local area available as engineers. This same process is followed for every job group and for each minority group.

The third step in the AAP process is simple: compare the number of employees in the work force with the number available to see if the company has "utilized" as many women and minorities as expected.

Then the company sets goals and timetables for curing areas of under-utilization. You decide, based on your own business plans, the job market, and other factors, how quickly you can reach your goals. The government does not expect it to be done overnight.

What's the difference between a goal and a quota? Quotas are court ordered. If you don't meet a quota, you're in trouble. Goals are enforced by the OFCCP. If you don't meet a goal, it will not automatically shut you down. Instead, you will be asked why you didn't meet the goal.

There are many nondiscriminatory reasons why you might not meet your goals. If you just had a major layoff, it will be difficult to hold on to the gains you've made, much less achieve new ones. Hiring and promotion freezes also impact your plan.

You may do lots of recruiting, but no minorities apply. Or you may get applicants, but they don't meet your qualifications. You may offer them jobs, but they go elsewhere. All these are reasons why a goal might not be reached. If a goal turns out to be unrealistic, it can be changed.

2. Recruiting Applicants

The second requirement of Affirmative Action is to have an active recruiting program that targets underutilized groups.

Most companies send lists of job openings to various community groups. This is a bare minimum and rarely does any good. As the newsletter editor of a woman's professional group, I was inundated with job postings—all with application dates that expired long before our next edition was due. Recruiting requires networking with groups by attending their meetings and getting involved.

Many companies send recruiters to black colleges. But don't ignore the minority students at the universities where you already recruit. Contact the student professional associations for women, blacks, Hispanics, and Asians that exist at all major college campuses.

A friend who is an affirmative action manager told me about one recruiter's unique approach. The recruiter attended a National Association for the Advancement of Colored People (NAACP) convention. She called back excitedly. "I'm making a lot of good contacts. I met this one lady, she's 85 years old and really helpful."

My friend said, "Uh, what kind of job does she want?" The recruiter said, "It's not for her. It's for her kids and grandkids. They're all engineers!"

3. Hiring the Best

Affirmative Action allows you to hire the most qualified candidate. You decide what the qualifications are, based on legitimate business reasons.

True affirmative action employers consider it a plus when an employee is "different." They like having different perspectives on such issues as product design, marketing, and customer service. They see Affirmative Action as part of the trend toward globalization.

Those employers hire and promote women and minorities even when they are slightly less qualified in some areas, because the company considers them to be better qualified overall as a result of their different perspectives.

AFFIRMATIVE ACTION FOR PEOPLE WITH DISABILITIES

In 1973, Congress passed a law requiring Affirmative Action for people with disabilities.[43] Unlike Affirmative Action for women and minorities, there are no goals and timetables for hiring employees who are disabled. Instead, the law encourages you to hire as many qualified applicants as possible.

The company is required to have a written Affirmative Action plan for hiring and promoting people with disabilities. Although the law does not require any particular program, government regulations suggest that at least some of these steps should be followed:

1. Gain support for Affirmative Action from the top down.
2. Post job openings with disability community groups and government agencies.
3. Recruit from training programs and schools for people who are blind, deaf, or disabled.
4. Promote and train current employees who are or become disabled.
5. Picture workers who are disabled in ads, company newspapers, and annual reports.
6. Evaluate managers on their affirmative action efforts and results.

THE RIGHTS OF VIETNAM-ERA VETERANS

Congress passed another law[44] in 1974 to protect men and women who served in the American armed forces anywhere in the world during the years of the Vietnam war (August 1964 to May, 1976). Like the other Affirmative Action laws, it applies only to government contractors, subcontractors, and public employers.

The law prohibits discrimination and requires Affirmative Action.

The war in Vietnam greatly divided the American people. Some took out their frustrations on the returning veterans. Some vets were spat upon, called names, and harassed. They couldn't get jobs. That's why this law was passed.

The law requires that you

1. Treat veterans the same as all other employees in hiring, evaluating, training, transferring, paying, and terminating. You must have a legitimate business reason for treating a veteran inconsistently.

2. Don't single out veterans for conversation about Vietnam. Asking questions about war experiences, bringing up the latest Vietnam war movie, or talking about some psychopath recently in the news who also happens to be a veteran can be offensive. Like most people, veterans don't want to be singled out for being different. If veterans want to talk about Vietnam, they'll bring it up.

Affirmative Action also requires a written plan for recruiting, hiring and promoting Vietnam-era veterans. The plan should have the same steps as plans for employees who are disabled. You don't set goals and timetables for hiring Vietnam-era vets. Instead, hire and promote as many as possible.

HOW TO BE AN AFFIRMATIVE ACTION MANAGER

In the spirit of affirmative action, you have four major responsibilities as a manager.

1. *Evaluate applicants for employment, transfer, and promotion consistently:* Have legitimate business reasons for your decisions. If you don't discriminate, chances are you will meet affirmative action goals.

2. *Know the Affirmative Action goals for your area:* If your area is under-represented in females, minorities, people with disabilities and veterans, go out and find some! Don't wait for the personnel department to recruit people. There are literally hundreds of professional associations and organizations for people in Affirmative Action categories. Find out who they are and let them know about job openings. Join. Give money. Become a visible sponsor.

3. *Support Affirmative Action employees after you hire them:* Help them become part of the team. Some companies have found assigning a mentor or buddy to new employees is helpful. That person doesn't have to be another minority. The idea is to have someone initiate the new employee into your unique company culture in a way that you, the manager, cannot. (And, yes, you must assign a buddy to every new employee, whether or not minority.)

   Prepare women, minorities, people with disabilities and veterans in your area for transfers and promotions, including promotion into your job. After all, if you are irreplaceable, you can't get promoted. As a manager, you should be grooming one of your subordinates to replace you. That person should be picked based on legitimate business reasons. One of those reasons can be meeting Affirmative Action goals.

4. *Document your efforts:* Affirmative Action does require you to fill out additional paperwork to prove you made good faith efforts to recruit candidates. If the company doesn't reach its Affirmative Action goals, it must be able to prove with documentation that a good faith effort was made.

One of my corporate clients was audited by the OFCCP. The company was behind on its goals, so it entered into a conciliation agreement with the government. Under this agreement, the company agreed to step up its efforts.

A few years later, the agency came back to follow up. The auditor first asked to see the conciliation agreement. The company couldn't find it. Then the auditor asked to see documentation of the company's recruitment efforts. The company had done some recruiting, but there was no documentation.

Finally, the auditor asked to see the applicant flow data showing how many women and minorities had applied. The company did have a form attached to its application to get this information. But applicants weren't given the application to fill out. Employees were asked to fill out the application only after they were hired.

As a result, the company had no documentation of its good faith efforts. That's why they had to hire me.

It's a lot cheaper to document your efforts than to hire a lawyer after you get caught.

VALUING DIVERSITY

The equal employment opportunity law was the first step toward achieving equality. Affirmative Action was the second step. Both these laws successfully created opportunities for people who otherwise would have been left out of the system.

But both of these laws were flawed. They divided us. EEO made us pretend we're color blind. We're not. Then Affirmative Action required us to be color bound. It violated our sense of fairness.

Valuing diversity goes beyond the laws. It sees difference as value added. It celebrates our differences. It's the spirit of equality.

Chapter 3

THE RIGHT WAY TO FIRE EMPLOYEES

The Law of Wrongful Termination

*T*he chief executive officer (CEO) of a local manufacturing company called me one day. He wanted to fire his national accounts sales manager. The reason: the manager didn't come to work. When he showed up, he fell asleep. When he woke up, he criticized the product to customers.

Those are good reasons for firing. It's the sales manager's job to promote the company's product. The CEO had a right to be angry.

But he couldn't fire him. Why? For a number of reasons.

His sales were up. His last performance appraisal was good. There was no documentation of these recent problems. Also, I was afraid these problems might be caused by some illness. We didn't want to discriminate against him if he was disabled.

After a long conversation, the CEO agreed to take it slow.

First, he had a heart-to-heart talk with the sales manager. The CEO said he was concerned about his health. He offered to pay for medical specialists. He offered time off for disability.

The manager insisted he wasn't sick and refused to cooperate.

We followed up with a letter. "If you are disabled, we will reasonably accommodate your disability as required by law. If you continue to refuse medical treatment, we will have no choice but to begin disciplinary procedures for poor performance unless there is immediate improvement." We also said he would be fired immediately if he talked down the product again.

He stopped the bad-mouthing. But his attendance didn't improve. We gave him a written warning that he had 30 days or he would receive a final warning.

Thirty days later, we gave him the final notice. "If your attendance and performance do not improve in the next 30 days, your employment will be terminated."

As the last day got closer, I met with the CEO to discuss our termination strategy. Our bottom line: we were willing to pay the sales manager three months' severance pay. But in exchange, we wanted his agreement not to sue for wrongful termination. I drafted a release that said we would pay him one month's severance.

The day after he was fired, he hired a lawyer. Although she made a lot of noise, the lawyer didn't have a case. After all the arguments, the lawyer "won" her client two months' severance pay. For a small fee, of course.

We fired this employee the right way. It was "right" for two reasons:

1. We prevented a lawsuit.
2. We treated him fairly.

TERMINATING "AT WILL": WHAT IS FAIR?

What is fair? The best definition comes from Judge Conrad Rushing, who said managers must ensure that "like cases be treated alike."[1] In other words, be consistent and have a legitimate business reason for everything you do.

"Treat employees fairly" is the most important rule for preventing wrongful termination or discharge lawsuits.

It wasn't always this way. The idea that an employer must treat employees fairly wasn't adopted by the courts until the 1980s. Since then, courts in 46 states have adopted some form of wrongful termination. As of July 1992, only Florida has rejected wrongful termination outright. Louisiana, Mississippi, and Rhode Island have had no definitive decisions.[2] See the chart on wrongful termination law by state at the end of this chapter.

Despite the rise of wrongful termination cases in recent years, the basic law still is that most employees are terminable at will. The idea of at-will employment comes from old England. In those days, the terms "employer" and "employee" weren't used. Instead, it was "master" and "servant."

A master can be completely arbitrary. He can fire a servant on the slightest whim. Servants don't have employment rights.

The master-servant tradition was adopted by the U.S. colonies when they first codified their laws. It has continued until today. But instead of using the word "servant," most laws declare employees to be "at will."

An at-will employee can be terminated at any time, for any reason, or for no reason at all.

Exceptions to the At-Will Rule

Throughout history, there has always been one exception to the at-will rule. If the employee and employer agree employment will last for a specific period of time, it is not at will. The employee can be fired only at the end of the contract, unless the employer has "good cause" for termination.

For example, football coaches typically are hired for one, two, or more years. They can't be fired before their contracts are up, unless the team has good cause.

Having good cause to terminate an employee is the same as having a legitimate business reason. For example, poor job performance, chronic tardiness, and abuse of sick leave all are examples of misconduct that legally justify firing an employee. See the accompanying box for more examples.

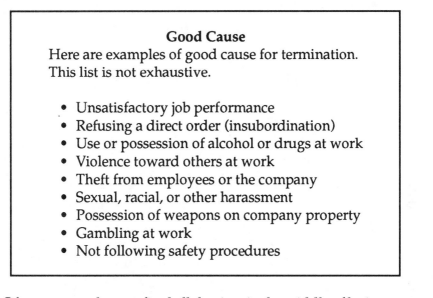

Good Cause
Here are examples of good cause for termination.
This list is not exhaustive.

- Unsatisfactory job performance
- Refusing a direct order (insubordination)
- Use or possession of alcohol or drugs at work
- Violence toward others at work
- Theft from employees or the company
- Sexual, racial, or other harassment
- Possession of weapons on company property
- Gambling at work
- Not following safety procedures

Of course, coaches are fired all the time in the middle of losing seasons. But losing usually is not legal good cause for termination, depending on how the contract is written. In those cases, the team still must pay out the contract, keeping the coach on salary until the time is up.

The same is true if your company hires a new CEO or other key player and promises a minimum term of employment. They can be fired without legal good cause ("differences in philosophy"), but you have to pay them off. This is the basis for so-called "golden parachute" or "golden handshake" agreements.

THREE RULES FOR PREVENTING WRONGFUL TERMINATION LAWSUITS

Most employees are not hired for a specific period of time. Usually you don't tell new employees they are being hired for one or two years. You hire them to work indefinitely.

Since most employees are hired for an indefinite period, they are considered at will under the *statutes* of most states. But in recent years, the *courts* have interpreted these at-will statutes narrowly. The courts have expanded employee rights so that today, there are three new exceptions to the at-will rule.

These exceptions can be stated as three basic rules for preventing wrongful termination lawsuits:

1. Keep your promises.

2. Treat employees fairly.

3. Don't fire whistleblowers.

These three rules should be followed whenever you terminate an employee. Even if you don't think you're subject to wrongful termination law, you don't want to be the landmark case in your state that says you are.

These three rules generally apply only when employees are terminated. As long as you don't fire, lay off, or force an employee to quit, technically you don't have to follow these rules.

That's because the courts abhor injecting themselves into the employer-employee relationship. Only when the employment relationship is over will a court review what happened—and then only in a limited number of cases.

After an employee is terminated, courts will review the entire employment relationship from beginning to end. So although this chapter is about preventing wrongful termination lawsuits, most of it has nothing to do with termination. Instead, we'll be looking at offer letters, employee handbooks, performance appraisals, and disciplinary warnings.

You never know when an employee might quit, get fired, or be laid off. As a practical matter, you should assume everyone will be terminated eventually—and follow these three rules.

Keep Your Promises: Written, Oral, and Implied Contracts

The very fact that employees work for you means they have contracts with the company. The contracts say they will show up and work. In exchange, the company pays them money. That is the basic employment contract.

But the courts have said that many companies, by their words and actions, have expanded their contracts with their employees. A contract is a promise. If you or your company make promises to your employees, you have to keep those promises.

There are three kinds of promises or contracts found by courts in wrongful termination cases: written, oral, and implied. It's very easy for courts to enforce written contracts that are entitled, "Employment Agreement." But since few employees have written contracts, the legal battles have been fought over other types of documents.

The Employee Handbook: A Critical Legal Document for Your Company

One of a company's most important legal documents is its employee handbook. Employee handbooks are contracts in at least 30 states.[3]

Courts have said employees have a reasonable expectation that if they work at a company with policies, the company is going to follow those policies.[4] So you want to make sure the policies you have are the ones you want to follow. Then, you have to follow them.

There are four critical areas in employee handbooks:

1. The welcome to the company, letter from the president, or other introductory comments

2. Any mention of reasons or cause for termination, including in probationary periods

3. Disciplinary procedures, up to and including termination

4. The employee acknowledgment section

Introductions

Your employee handbook could be legally correct throughout only to be torpedoed by the president's welcoming letter. Here are some remarks commonly found in handbook introductions.

"Welcome to the XYZ Company family." If I'm joining a family, I can't be fired, right? And I have to be treated more fairly by a family than a company.

"As President, I want you to feel free to use our Open Door policy if you have a concern." An open-door policy is great. Just make sure it's not empty rhetoric. Have a procedure in place. And don't actively or passively discourage employees from using it.

"We look forward to you having a long and successful career with the company." This could be interpreted as a promise that employees will be allowed to stay at the company until retirement. Maybe they will, but you don't want to be legally bound to it.

"Ever since we started as a small company, we have been committed to treating our employees fairly." Although you should treat employees fairly, it's best not to promise it in writing. The law requires every employer to meet minimal standards of fairness, as you'll see in the next section. But if you promise to be fair, a court might require you to exceed the legal minimum in every case.

Some companies choose to treat employees fairly. That's great! Those companies are probably the best places to work. Just make sure your decision is made after weighing the risks involved. As one company's director put it, "We still made the same decision, but we made it as a conscious choice, rather than out of ignorance."

Cause for Termination

Usually found lurking throughout a handbook is the phrase, "cause for termination." For example, "Violation of the sick leave policy is cause for termination." What's wrong with that? It implies the company must have cause whenever terminating employees.

If you promise employees in the handbook, either directly or indirectly, that you are required to have cause to fire them, you could be required by a court to prove you had legally sufficient good cause.

Most employees are terminated for cause. Of course you had reasons for firing them. However, proving it in court is another matter.

To eliminate this risk, wherever the phrase "cause for termination" occurs, replace it with "could lead to termination." The example would be changed to, "Violation of the sick leave policy could lead to termination."

Notice I did not say a violation "will lead to termination." The words "will" and "shall" are mandatory. They require you to terminate. But you don't want to limit your options. Perhaps an employee violated the sick leave policy, but there are mitigating circumstances. If you don't fire in that case, then other employees who later are fired for violating sick leave can claim unfairness, because you didn't apply the policy consistently.

Failing to follow a mandatory policy is worse than having a nonmandatory policy. The words "could" and "may" indicate nonbinding policies. You are just predicting one of many possible outcomes when you say a violation "could" lead to termination.

A related problem area is "probationary periods." Most handbooks read something like this:

> *The first 90 days of employment are a Probationary Period. The company reserves the right to terminate your employment at any time within this period.*

This section says employment is at will the first 90 days. That's how it should be. You want flexibility in terminating all employees, especially new hires.

But once you state employment status for one group of employees (new hires), you must state the status for all employees. Otherwise, a court could draw a negative inference. In other words, because you've gone to great lengths to say probationary employees are at will, nonprobationary employees must be the opposite—they only can be terminated with good cause.

To give yourself the most protection, the company should state it reserves the right to terminate *all* employees at will.

Another handbook might say

> *Your first three months of employment give you the opportunity to decide if the job is right for you, and for us to decide if you are right for the job. If during this period we determine you are not a good fit, we may terminate your employment.*

This section implies you need good cause to terminate employment during the probationary period. That's because termination is phrased in terms of the employee's ability to do the job. To be truly an at will employer, you must reserve your right to terminate arbitrarily—for no reason at all.

If probationary employees can be terminated only for good cause, a court might then take the next "logical" step. It doesn't make sense to give probationary employees more rights than regular employees. A court could reason that regular employees also should be entitled to termination only for good cause.

You see how simple words can be interpreted so many ways by a lawyer. Granted, this is all subjective. It's a judgment call. The phrases are ambiguous. That's why there could be a lawsuit.

Either example might be followed by the phrase, *After probation, you will become a permanent employee.* That compounds the problem. Courts have said if you imply long-term employment, including calling employees "permanent," they're permanent![5] You can't fire them except for legally sufficient good cause.

To avoid these problems, don't call it a probationary period. Call it "employment status" and describe it something like this:

> Your first three months of employment will be your Introductory Period. During this time, you will not receive certain employee benefits. After that, you may become a regular employee. We reserve the right to terminate your employment at any time, with or without notice, and with or without cause.

If you have decided to commit to providing a progressive discipline system (described in the next section) you could add a sentence like this:

> During your first 90 days, you will not have the benefits of our progressive discipline policy as described in this handbook.

Discipline and Termination

The third critical area is disciplinary procedures, including terminations.

Some disciplinary policies require that before being terminated, an employee first must receive three warnings, perhaps first an oral warning, next a written, and then a final written warning. This is called progressive discipline, because it requires the manager to progress through each disciplinary step.

If the handbook says before being terminated employees "will," "must," or "shall" be given three warnings, then legally, three warnings must be given. If, instead, it says warnings "may" or "could" be given, then you don't necessarily have to follow the policy step by step. This is preferable. You don't want to limit your options. Managers should have the flexibility to skip some of the steps, depending upon the circumstances.

Of course, with flexibility comes responsibility. You still must treat like cases alike.

Read your company's policies carefully. Follow all mandatory procedures.

Employee Acknowledgment

The last page of the handbook should be an employee acknowledgment form. There should be one in the handbook and a signed original in the employee's personnel file.

The acknowledgment must be written carefully. In some states, the words, "This handbook does not create a contract," have been held to create at-will employment. In other states, this language is considered to be denying the existence of the contract the courts already have held is contained in handbooks. If you deny the existence of a contract, you could be held to have acted unfairly. You could be sued for wrongful termination for treating employees unfairly because you used these words.

The acknowledgment that follows has been refined over the years in response to new cases. However, every court that has ruled on such acknowledgments has given each phrase its own twist. The language here is not guaranteed, and like all suggestions, should be reviewed by a local employment attorney.

> I have received, read, and understood this employee handbook. I understand my employment is terminable at will by the company, with or without cause, and with or without notice. [Dated and signed by employee.]

> *practical pointers:* Of course, before you can ask employees to sign, they have to be given an opportunity to read it. If possible, send new employees the handbook before they start work. This gives them the chance to back out if they don't like your rules. On the first day of work, go over it with them, have them sign the acknowledgments, and let them take the handbook home.

> As for all important employment documents, the handbook should be translated for non-English speakers. Arrangements should be made to read the handbook to people with reading disabilities or to make an audiotape available.

Some companies maintain the handbook is company property and insist employees return it upon termination. That's a dumb idea. If your handbook is legally correct, and written in such a way that it helps you, you want the employee to have it after termination. The handbook is one of the first documents an employee's lawyer wants to see. One written within these guidelines will discourage an attorney from taking the case.

Such an employee handbook will not protect you from discrimination claims, whistleblower suits, and complaints of unfairness. And it will not protect you from a contract-type wrongful termination case if there are other written documents or oral promises contradicting the handbook. The handbook is only one piece of the puzzle. But it's a very important piece.

You Can Change The Rules

Can the company change the handbook? Specifically, can the employment status of employees be changed?

Let's say your current handbook implies that cause is needed in order to terminate employees. Your current employees believe they cannot be fired arbitrarily.

Now you understand the legal implications of the handbook. You decide to change it. You are going to declare all your employees at will.

New employees will be hired under the new rules. But current employees were hired under the old rules. Can you change the rules in midstream, without the employees' consent?

It depends.

In some instances, a policy change simply can be announced. For example, Advanced Micro Devices (AMD) for years had a "no-layoff" policy. In Silicon Valley, where layoffs were a way of life, AMD advertised its no-layoff policy to attract and keep good people.

One day, AMD held a news conference and renounced its no-layoff policy. A layoff was not planned at that time, but the company wanted everyone to know layoffs were now an option.

Inevitably, AMD's first layoffs were announced a few months later. But employees couldn't sue based on the no-layoff policy, because it had been renounced. The employees had plenty of time to look for work elsewhere if the new policy was not acceptable to them. By continuing to remain employed, the employees accepted the new terms. If they didn't like it, they could quit and (theoretically) get a job at another company with a no-layoff policy.

Before changing a policy concerning termination or at will status, you should check with a lawyer. In some cases, a one-time payment ("independent consideration") must be made.

> *practical pointers:* If you institute a new employee handbook, and current employees refuse to sign it, do not terminate their employment. Instead, send them a memo: "Your signature is not necessary for the terms of the handbook to be effective. You are expected to abide by all the rules and regulations."

Be sure to highlight any changes in your handbook so employees can't later clam they didn't know about the new rules.

What to Include—and Omit—in Offer Letters

Offer letters also have been held to be written contracts.

The same kinds of statements made in the introductory paragraphs of employee handbooks also sometimes are found in offer letters, with the same effect.

Most experts say that stating the salary to be paid as an annual figure ("the job pays $30,000 per year") implies the employee will be employed for a minimum of one year. However, only one or two cases actually have held that.[6] Most cases hold that annual salary does not create an implied contract. But just to be on the safe side, most experts suggest quoting the salary on a biweekly basis. If new employees can't figure out the annual amount, you don't want them anyway.

The offer letter should include a description of benefits. If you are an at will employer, that should be stated. Offer letters should be signed by employees and kept in their personnel files.

Oral Promises: Don't Make If You Can't Keep

Oral promises made to employees also are enforceable. You may know the saying, reminiscent of Yogi Berra, "Oral contracts aren't worth the paper they're written on." Not in the employment area. Oral contracts are worth a lot.

As a manager, whenever you talk to an applicant or employee, you are a representative of the company. If you make promises, the company is making promises. The company can be sued for not keeping those promises, even if you're no longer employed there.

Don't make promises like these if you can't keep them:

"Don't worry, you won't be laid off."

"Next time there's an opening, you will get the promotion."

"After a year, you will get a raise."

These comments imply employees will have job security, raises, and promotions. Maybe they will. But you don't want to be legally bound to it.

Long-Term Employees and Implied Promises

You don't have an employee handbook. You haven't made any promises. A court still could imply that you must have good cause to fire an employee if the employee has worked at the company for many years.

The courts have said if employees work for a company a long time, they have a reasonable expectation they will continue to work there as long as they are performing well. These courts have found implied contracts as a result of the longevity of the employees.

In the early cases, the employees who were found to have implied contracts had been employed for more than 25 years.[7] But in 1988, the California Supreme Court found there was an implied contract where the employee had been employed for just over 6 years.[8]

The court said it's not how many years an employee works at the company. It's what the company does during those years. If the company fires people only for good cause, other employees can expect that they, too, will be fired only for legitimate business reasons.

As a practical matter, it's pretty tough to argue in court that you are an "at-will" employer. The attorney for the employee will get you, the manager, on the stand. The cross-examination will go something like this:

Lawyer: Have you fired employees before?

Manager: Yes.

Lawyer: Did you have a good reason when you fired them?

Manager: Of course.

There goes your at will defense! If you can't prove you are an at-will employer, you must be able to prove you had good cause for firing the employee. That's the first rule for preventing wrongful termination.

FOUR TARGET AREAS FOR TREATING EMPLOYEES FAIRLY

The second rule for preventing wrongful termination lawsuits is *treat employees fairly.*

The first rule, *keep your promises,* was based on contract law. The second rule is based in part on contracts, and in part on tort (personal injury) law.

Just as the courts have implied contracts between employees and companies, they also have implied sections of those contracts.

The courts have said that every contract, including the basic employment contract, contains an implied covenant. A covenant is simply one section of a contract. This section requires the employer to treat the employee fairly. It is called the covenant of good faith and fair dealing.[9]

Once you accept the idea that every employee has a contract, it makes sense to require employers to treat employees fairly. In other contexts, the courts have said that if the parties to a contract are in an unequal bargaining position, the weaker party should be protected from the stronger one.[10]

In the employment area, employees generally are the weaker parties. They have very little say about the amount of pay they receive, the kinds of work they do, and their working conditions.

In the past, it was thought that if employees didn't like the working conditions, they could leave to work elsewhere. But in recent years, the courts have recognized that requiring employees to leave creates a hardship for them, particularly as they get older. So gradually the courts have come to the conclusion that employers should treat employees fairly.

Ideal managers help employees achieve success. They treat the employment relationship as an ongoing process of constant communication, accurate feedback, and gentle correction. They give positive reinforcement. They take the time to be good coaches.

Fortunately for those of us humans who become managers, the law does not require us to be ideal. Although there is a lot of language in their opinions about fairness, the courts actually have required fairness only in a few limited situations.

There are four areas where courts have required managers to treat employees fairly:

1. Evaluating performance
2. Investigating complaints
3. Disciplining for misconduct
4. Terminating employment

Performance Evaluations: How They Can Make or Break Your Case

Performance appraisals are critical documents in every employment lawsuit. They can make or break your case.

Appraisals should tell the story of the employee's life with the company. They should be given regularly to create a complete picture of the employee's job history.

> *practical pointer:* At a minimum, give appraisals after three months, six months, and then yearly on the anniversary of the hire date.

Whether representing employers or employees, lawyers look at the appraisals and ask questions. Do the appraisals show the employee was a good performer for years? Then why the sudden termination? It looks suspect. But if the appraisals show two years of declining performance, the termination looks legitimate.

Sometimes appraisals show years of substandard performance. If the employee continued to receive pay increases, it appears that you condoned it. It will be difficult for you to justify termination for poor performance if you've put up with it for long. If the employee was so bad, why didn't you terminate before?

Appraisals should answer these questions, or better still, never raise them.

Preparing for Appraisals

Before you do this year's appraisal, look at last year's. If the employee has shown improvement over the year, note that. If performance has deteriorated, say so. If the performance appraisal this year is significantly different from last year's, say why.

If another manager wrote the last performance appraisal, your ratings may be very different. Employees who have worked under the same manager for years learn to do their jobs in a certain manner. When new managers come in, or when current managers take training courses, they often want to change old ways of doing things.

Just note that on the form itself. "Your last manager rated you excellent even though you were 85% of quota. I rate employees excellent only if they reach 125% of quota." As long as you are consistent and have a legitimate business reason, you can change performance standards.

You also can change employees job responsibilities. You should have a legitimate business reason. You must inform them clearly of the new job requirements, either in the performance appraisal or other written memo. You must give them time to achieve the new goals. As long as the assignments are achievable by a reasonable person, you can implement your changes—even if your particular employees can't achieve them.

Appraisal Do's and Don'ts

Appraise performance accurately! This seems like common sense, but it's not.

Remember the national accounts sales manager at the beginning of this chapter? While we had him on final written notice for poor attendance, his performance appraisal came due.

The CEO called. "Should I give him his appraisal?"

I said, "Yes. We don't want to be accused of unfairness because he didn't get it. And it will be one more nail in the coffin."

"I figured you'd say that, so I got it ready. I'll go give it to him."

"Wait, Pat. Fax me a copy first."

Later, I called back.

"You rated this guy average on attendance! Why did you do that?"

Pat said, "I just looked at last year's appraisal and rated him two steps down in everything. I guess I didn't look that closely at the categories."

That could have been a costly mistake. If we had given him that appraisal, it would have nullified the final warning. We couldn't fire him for attendance if it was average. By definition, you can't fire an average employee.

practical pointers: When you write appraisals, give specific, legitimate reasons for every criticism.

Appraisals sometimes are conclusory, rating on attributes like attitude, leadership, and initiative. These are admirable characteristics and can be rated. But you must give the facts to back up your conclusions in these categories.

Find the good, and praise it.

Avoid the halo effect. This is where you rate highly employees who you like and fail to see their weaknesses. The opposite of that—the devil effect—means you rate employees lower than deserved in all areas because of poor performance in one, or because you don't like them.

Don't emphasize areas that aren't legitimate job requirements. For example, leadership skills should be recognized no matter who has them. But nonmanagers shouldn't be penalized for not having leadership ability.

Employees should never be rated "must improve" in the same category year after year. If they're that bad, get rid of them. Of course, if there are major problems, you shouldn't wait until performance appraisal time. You should give warnings and then terminate.

Appraisal Forms Should Be Fair

For appraisals to be accurate, the form itself must be fair. In my opinion, the longer the form, the worse it is. There are companies with six-page forms, manuals of definitions, and lists of codes. To complete the form is a major expenditure of time. Managers dread doing it, so when they do, they make mistakes, like Pat.

A good performance appraisal documents your management efforts for the employee over the year. It summarizes the results of the past year, and plans for the next.

Here is a simple performance appraisal form you can use.

Performance Appraisal Form

Date:
Supervisor's Name:

Employee's Name:

1. List present job requirements:

2. Describe how the employee has performed the job requirements:

3. State the objectives from last year's appraisal:

4. Describe how the employee has achieved the objectives:

5. Comment on the employee's strengths and weaknesses:

6. What career opportunities should the employee consider:

7. List the specific objectives to be accomplished the next review period:

8. Employee's comments:

9. Employee's signature:

Compare it to the form in use at your company. In addition to sheer length, look at what categories are rated.

The sample form doesn't have a numerical rating scale. Numerical ratings are perfectly legal. It's just a matter of preference.

If you have numerical rating, you should rate most employees in the middle of the scale. The middle is average. That's where most people should be by definition. It's more accurate. If the numerical rating scale is expressed in words, look closely at the words used. They can skew results.

If an overall rating is given, you should not just average the scores of the different categories. You should weight the relative importance of the various categories to different jobs. For example, "initiative" is very important for a manager, whereas good "work habits" are almost assumed. The relative importance of these categories might be the opposite for a production worker.

Employee Self-appraisal

Some managers like to have employees fill out the appraisal themselves, to see their self-evaluation. Considering the employee's point of view is a good way to show you treat employees fairly. It also is useful in deciding how to rate the employee.

One of my secretaries had been given two written warnings in two months. Then her performance appraisal was due. I asked for her self-evaluation.

She wrote she was an excellent performer in every area and didn't even mention the pending warnings. The fact that she hadn't acknowledged her weaknesses made me realize I was going to have to be more critical in the appraisal than I planned.

Another secretary made one mistake six months before her appraisal. She apologized for it in her self-appraisal and reminded me of new procedures she had implemented to prevent future problems. In her case, I praised her for learning from the experience.

If you do accept employee self-appraisals, keep them with yours in the personnel file. This does not mean you have to accept the employee's version of the facts. If the employee is accurate, acknowledge that. But don't back down from a poor review if one is warranted.

In an article written for Women Organized for Employment, the author advised employees:

> Remember that your boss may be reluctant to fill out your review because he may not be the type to criticize another. Firms do not generally train their managers in how to evaluate an employee. You can turn this to your advantage by taking the initiative and covering yourself in advance. Pull out of your boss any praise for the work you have done.

Don't allow this to happen to you.

Guidelines for Investigating Complaints Against Employees

After performance appraisals, the second area where courts have required fairness is in investigating complaints against employees. These may be complaints brought by one employee against another or your own complaints about the employee's behavior or performance.

Whenever you first learn of a problem with an employee, you hear only one piece of the story. You need more information before you can take action. Even if you think you saw everything, something could have happened before you got there that would put the situation in an entirely different light.

As an opposing lawyer once said, "No matter how thin the pancake, there are always two sides."

You need to do an investigation to learn all the facts. Most important, you need to hear the accused employee's side of the story.

Although not all employees legally have due process rights, as a matter of fairness they should be told of the charges against them and be allowed to respond to those charges.

However, they should not be allowed to confront their accusers. In fact, it's usually best to keep the name of the person who complained confidential, if possible.

How do you keep the complainant's name confidential if you are required to tell the accused of the charges? Approach the investigation interview with the accused like a conversation. Don't begin with an accusation like, "Chris complained that you . . .". Not only does this reveal the name of the person who complained, it also will put the accused on the defensive and is not likely to result in you obtaining much useful information.

Instead, start off with a general statement like, "I heard there was a problem yesterday. What happened?" You could have heard about it from a witness. Even if no one witnessed the incident, you could have heard about it from someone who heard about it from the complaining person.

If the accused demands to know how you heard about it, you can say, "I can't reveal that information." If the accused asks, "What did you hear," you can respond, "I'd rather hear it from you."

If a general statement doesn't work, you can get slightly more specific, "I heard you and Chris had words. Tell me what happened." If the accused still denies, then get very specific, "I heard you called Chris a . . . . Is that true?"

In conducting an investigation, you must be scrupulously fair. Anything you say or do that appears to be biased or prejudiced can be used against you later. An example of a biased investigation occurred in one of my cases. Joy was the secretary for Bob, a middle manager at a *Fortune* 100 company.

During Joy's first year of employment, she became increasingly concerned about Bob. He routinely took off Mondays and Fridays, arrived late, left early, took long lunches, and always smelled of alcohol. He had erratic mood swings and verbally abused her and others.

Finally, Joy went to her personnel representative. She told him what she had seen. She said she was concerned that Bob might be an alcoholic. She said, "I don't want to get him into trouble. I hope you will help him into the employee assistance program."

The rep said, "I'll look into it."

The entire conversation lasted 15 minutes. The rep then sat down at the computer and generated two single-spaced pages about his impressions. The notes began, "Joy came in today accusing Bob of being an alcoholic. Why is she out to get him? Why is she concocting this story? Investigate Joy."

Once the rep began his investigation, he asked people in Joy's department if they had any problems with *her*. His notes state he didn't want to bring up Bob's name "to maintain confidentiality."

The rep also wrote this: "In the past there has been hall talk about Bob being an alcoholic, but he's not." There were no facts proving Bob wasn't an alcoholic, just the bald assertion.

All these are examples of a biased investigation. And was it ever biased. The end result—Joy was fired!

I represented Joy in her suit against the company. When we obtained the notes of the rep, the case quickly settled. The investigation wasn't fair; neither was the termination.

Generally, an investigation should include not only talking to the accused, but also talking to witnesses, reviewing documents, and going back to the complaining employee for more information. You should use the following investigation checklist to make sure you cover the important steps.

Although this checklist is extensive, in practice it can be implemented fairly quickly. It also represents the ideal. An investigation probably will be considered fair even if you do less than this, as long as you act fairly.

Checklist for Investigating Complaints

- All conversations must be in private.
- Listen.
- Take good notes.
- Ask for names of people who saw or heard this or similar incidents.
- Ask if there are any notes or a diary of the events, and if so, ask to see them.
- Tell the person who complained that you intend to talk to the accused and other witnesses.
- Make a date for a follow-up meeting within one week.
- Decide whether you can impartially investigate; if not, call in someone who can.
- Make an appointment with the accused.
- Tell the accused in general the nature of the complaint and ask for response.
- If accused denies knowledge, tell specific instances and ask for response.
- If accused denies everything, ask if there is any reason or motive why anyone would lie and make up charges; if so, obtain all facts and witness names.
- Make a follow-up appointment with the accused.
- Talk to witnesses.
- For all witnesses, determine if they have any bias against either person involved, and interpret their version of the facts in that light.
- Review any relevant documents, including the personnel file of the accused and, if appropriate, the person who complained, and other witnesses.
- Meet separately with the accused and the person who complained at the agreed times, whether or not you have reached a conclusion.
- Inform them generally of your actions.
- Ask them to explain any contrary information you've received from others.
- Make follow-up meeting appointments to inform them of result.
- Decide if you have enough information to reach a conclusion.
- If you can't determine what happened, bring in someone else to conduct another investigation.
- Decide the appropriate action to take—ranging from disciplining the accused to disciplining the complainant if you can prove the complaint was a lie.
- Prepare all necessary paperwork such as disciplinary forms and final paycheck.
- Meet with the person who complained and inform generally of action taken; maintain the privacy of the accused by not revealing the specifics.
- Meet with the accused to take appropriate action: discipline, counsel, or clear the record.
- If the accused and the person who complained remain employed, counsel them not to retaliate against each other. Monitor their relationship.

Investigations Can Be Wrong

The benefit of conducting an investigation is that it may protect you from a wrongful termination lawsuit even if the results of your investigation are wrong. An influential opinion by the Oregon Supreme Court held that an investigation could protect the company.

In that case, two women were accused of making violent threats against a coworker. An investigation was conducted. Witnesses were questioned. Then, the accused employees were told of the charges against them. The women gave their side of the story. They denied making threats. After listening to them, the company decided to believe the other employees and fired them.

The women sued for wrongful termination. They said they didn't make threats, and they could prove it. But the court said their proof was irrelevant.

The court ruled that even assuming the investigation turned up the wrong result, the company still could not be sued for wrongful termination. As long as the company conducted an investigation, it acted fairly. It's irrelevant that the company came to the wrong conclusion.[11]

In most states, your investigation doesn't have to be right, just fair.

Of course, it's better to be right. One of my pet peeves frequently occurs in the investigation of harassment complaints. The manager says, "Well, she complained, but he denied it, and there aren't any witnesses. So since there's no evidence, I can't do anything." *Wrong.* The complaint is evidence. Yes, it may just be one person's word against another's. But it's evidence.

You must do an investigation, and if you can't decide, kick it up to someone who can. Making no decision is in effect deciding the person who complained is lying. And that's not fair.

Counseling and Discipline: Give Employees a Chance to Improve

The third area where fairness is required is in counseling and disciplining before firing.

Employees should never be surprised about being fired. They should know they're going to be fired, and they should know why, long in advance.

The law assumes if you warn employees, they will improve. So you are required to counsel them before firing them. You have to give them the opportunity to improve.

Avoiding lawsuits is only one reason you don't want to fire employees. You don't want to fire an employee unless it is absolutely necessary. It's expensive to hire a new employee. Do you want to go through the process of writing up the job description, buying an ad, receiving a bunch of resumes, screening them, interviewing people, and training a new person? Or would you rather have one counseling session with your problem employee? If the employee improves, you don't have a problem.

One day, I was having lunch with some of the managers who were in my seminar. A department head told me about an engineer he wanted to fire for incompetence.

He said, "Personnel wouldn't let me fire the guy until I counseled him. I said, 'Look, I don't have time for that. I'm working 60 hours a week as it is. He's not going to get better anyway.' But they said, 'Just do it.'"

The manager said, "I sat down with him once. Went over things slowly. And . . . he got better. Nobody could believe it! He's gotten better and better, and now he's one of the best people in the department!"

Although everyone agrees employees should be counseled and disciplined, they disagree about how to do it. The continuum runs from the gentle approach to kick-em-in-the-pants.

Al Neuharth, founder of *USA Today,* says in his *Confessions of an SOB,*

> Too often CEOs act more like politicians than like bosses. Employees do not want to be wooed. They don't want soft soap. They like plain talk. And as Gannett CEO I delivered plenty of it—in writing. I called my memos on peach-colored paper Love Letters whether they were tender or tough. . . . Sure, I sometimes used tough language and I got pretty personal. . . . I wasn't trying to win a popularity contest. What I wanted was results.[12]

Mary Kay Ash, founder of Mary Kay Cosmetics, has a different approach. In *Mary Kay on People Management*, she says,

> Never giving criticism without praise is a strict rule for me. No matter what you are criticizing, you must find something good to say—both before and after. This is what's known as the "sandwich technique." Criticize the act, not the person. And try to praise in the beginning and then again after discussing the problem. Also strive to end on a friendly note. By handling the problem this way, you don't subject people to harsh criticism or provoke anger.[13]

Legally, both these approaches are fine. Most managers will probably use something between these two extremes, and that's fine, too. As Andy Grove, Intel CEO, says in his book, be straightforward and direct.[14]

According to personnel expert George Tansill, one of the biggest mistakes a manager can make is waiting to warn. We silently let little things slide by until we're so mad, we want to fire the employee.

Don't wait. A quick verbal counseling, with a note in your documentation, may solve the problem. If not, you have prepared the record for firing the employee.

If you have a problem employee, don't try to avoid a one-on-one counseling session by making a general announcement at a meeting. Its ineffective. You don't get the employee's feedback. And if everyone knows you are really talking to that one person, the employee could claim public humiliation because you singled him or her out for discipline in front of everyone else.

Almost more important than what you say, is how you treat employees in their counseling sessions. Listen to them. Ask questions. Find out their reactions. When people feel listened to, they feel they've been treated fairly.

Listening was mentioned in the section on investigation, and it will come up again later. Listening is one of the most important skills a manager can have.

There isn't room to talk about listening skills here. The effective listening checklist that follows is a brief overview of essential listening skills.

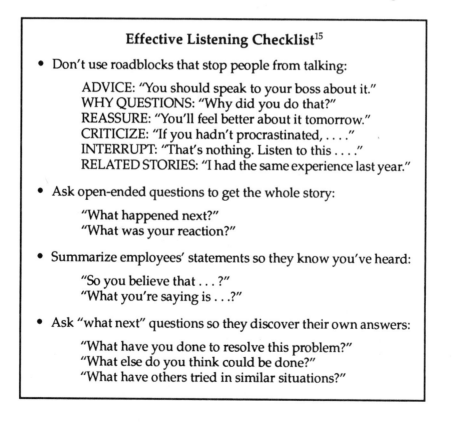

Effective Listening Checklist[15]

- Don't use roadblocks that stop people from talking:

    ADVICE: "You should speak to your boss about it."
    WHY QUESTIONS: "Why did you do that?"
    REASSURE: "You'll feel better about it tomorrow."
    CRITICIZE: "If you hadn't procrastinated, ..."
    INTERRUPT: "That's nothing. Listen to this . . . ."
    RELATED STORIES: "I had the same experience last year."

- Ask open-ended questions to get the whole story:

    "What happened next?"
    "What was your reaction?"

- Summarize employees' statements so they know you've heard:

    "So you believe that . . . ?"
    "What you're saying is . . . ?"

- Ask "what next" questions so they discover their own answers:

    "What have you done to resolve this problem?"
    "What else do you think could be done?"
    "What have others tried in similar situations?"

How to Write a Disciplinary Memo

Once you've verbally warned an employee, you must prepare written documentation. If this is the first mention to the employee ("heads up!"), your documentation might consist of a few words jotted down in your calendar.

An "oral warning" is more formal. You should at least write a memo to file. Some companies require "documented oral warnings" or "written orals." Calling them "oral" is just a throwback to the old days, before documentation was necessary.

Written warnings typically are given as the second and third steps before termination.

To document that you have been fair and have given warnings, I recommend the use of a form similar to the model warning form that follows.

Model Warning Form

Date:

Employee's Name:

Manager's Name:

level: first ___ second ___ other (specify)_____

Policy Violated:

Problem Behavior:

Desired Outcome:

Intended Improvement—Employee Comments:

Timetable:

Consequences:

"I have received and read this warning."

Employee Signature:

Whether or not you use the model warning form, you should cover the following areas:

Date: All your documentation should be dated, particularly warning forms. And don't forget the year!

Policy: State what policy has been violated. Even if there is no written policy, you can write, "It is a violation of company policy to . . . ."

Problem Behavior: This is where you list the objective, verifiable facts that created the problem. This should be specific and narrowly written to put the employee on notice of the exact problem.

For example, in my educational programs I show a video of a sexual harassment situation and ask the managers to write a disciplinary memo to the harasser. Some managers will write in this section, "You sexually harassed a female employee." That sweeping statement doesn't tell the employee anything. Exactly what did he do wrong?

Other managers write, "You showed her a pornographic picture." That's better, but what's pornographic? Not even the U.S. Supreme Court has been able to define pornography. The best examples are those that say, "You showed her a *Playboy* centerfold." Now that's specific, objective, and states exactly what occurred.

Desired Outcome: Whereas the *Problem Behavior* section is written narrowly, *Desired Outcome* should be written expansively. It should include not only the behavior that led to the warning, but any other behavior that's related.

For example, in the exercise just described, some managers write, "Don't show her any more centerfolds." That's a license to the employee to harass her sexually some other way or to show other women nude pictures. A better way to put it is, "Do not violate the company's sexual harassment policy again. Treat all women co-workers in a professional manner." This is broad enough so that if there are similar, but not identical, problems in the future, this warning will count and you can go right to the next warning.

Intended Improvement—Employee Comments: This is where employees state what they'll do to improve. This might include taking classes, obtaining counseling, or simply promising to change. This section is recommended to get the employee to buy into the need for change.

Timetable: The model form, like warning forms in use at many organizations, has a "timetable" section: the period of time the employee is given to show improvement. You should use a timetable only in cases of poor performance, not misconduct. "Misconduct" refers to breaking company rules, while "poor performance" is job related.

When employees don't perform, they must be given an opportunity to improve. The amount of time they should get is a reasonable time. What is reasonable depends on how long the employee has worked at the company, how long poor performance has been tolerated, the kinds of mistakes being made, and how quickly a new employee could be expected to get up to speed.

Hewlett-Packard, which is known as a pro-employee company has given one month to improve for every year of employment. I've seen them take two years to terminate a 24-year employee. And it worked; I didn't sue them.

In contrast, in the case of misconduct, you want "immediate and sustained improvement." Don't do what one company did.

My client was sitting at her desk one day when a coworker walked up, pulled out the top of her sweater, looked down, and made a comment about her breasts. The company gave him a warning which read, "If you sexually harass anyone in the next year, you will be fired."

One year and two days later, he sexually harassed her again. The company said, "We can't fire him, because he made it past a year." They were right. They couldn't fire him. They had painted themselves into a corner by the warning.

In my opinion, they could have fired him on the spot the first time, because this action was gross misconduct. Or they could choose to give him a lesser discipline, which is what they did. But the warning should not have included a timetable.

It also is important not to have a timetable in poor attendance and tardiness cases. It is amazing how some employees are able to achieve perfect attendance during whatever period of time they're given, and the day after they are off the timetable, they call in sick.

Consequences: No one should be surprised about being terminated. If an employee is surprised, you haven't done a good job of warning. To prevent surprise, you should tell the employee about the consequences of not improving. The consequences are the next level of discipline: written warning, final warning, disciplinary probation, suspension, or immediate termination.

It's only fair to warn of the consequences, but at the same time, you don't want to limit your options. Describe consequences this way: If there is no improvement I will take further disciplinary action, up to and including immediate termination.

> *Employee Signature:* Many managers find it is more difficult to get the employee to sign the form than anything else in the process. I think if the employee refuses to sign, that's relevant to your evaluation of how serious the employee is about improving.

You want employees to sign it so you can prove they saw it. If they refuse to sign, you can ask them to write "I disagree" or "I refuse to sign." About half the time, they'll be glad to write and sign that.

If they still refuse to sign, bring in a personnel representative or another manager to witness. They should say to the employee, "Have you read this warning?" When the employee says, "Yes," the manager should write on the warning form, "Employee has read but refuses to sign," and sign off on it.

What if you don't have a company policy requiring warnings? A court still may imply that it is only fair for you to give warnings before terminating. Not warning employees could be seen as trying to set them up to be fired, particularly if they're fired for violating an unwritten rule.

When Terminating Employees: Be Consistent

The final area where courts have required fairness is in actually terminating employees.

You must be consistent when it comes to disciplining and firing employees. You must give the same level of discipline for the same type of misconduct. You can't fire one employee for poor attendance if other employees with worse attendance aren't dismissed.

Another example of unfairness is where the supervisor encourages employees to break a rule. The supervisor can't turn around and fire them for that.

One of my colleagues represented three young people who were sales associates at a furniture store. They were told by their boss to push the store's waterproofing service, which she described as "pure profit." One day a nationwide waterproofing sales contest was announced. The boss said she would do anything to win. She said if a customer refused the service, the salesperson should discount the furniture and record the difference as a waterproofing sale. She also told the employees to sell small discontinued items like lamps and pillows and ring them up as waterproofing.

The employees were glad to follow these orders. If their store won the contest, they would all get big bonuses.

Sure enough, they won. A few days after they received their bonus checks, management realized the store had sold more waterproofing service than furniture. The company sent an investigator to talk to the store manager.

She denied any knowledge, accused the employees of pulling the scam on their own, and fired them.

That's a wrongful termination.

Terminating employees fairly means terminating them only for legitimate business reasons. You should not fire employees for what they do or say away from work, unless it affects their performance or that of their coworkers.

For example, a salesman was owed commissions by his employer. He stayed on the job and performed well. But he filed a lawsuit against the company. As a result, he was terminated. He sued for wrongful termination and won. The court said any time an employee is terminated for a reason not directly related to the job, that is a factor extraneous to (or outside) the employment contract.[16] Firing for a reason outside the contract is not fair, and it's a wrongful termination.

Tell the Truth About Termination

If you have written accurate performance appraisals, counseled to improve, investigated fairly, and given progressive discipline, on the fateful day it should be obvious to the employee that termination is inevitable, and why. You will say, "As you know, you were given 30 days to improve. You haven't improved, so you are being terminated today."

As easy and obvious as that approach is, some managers choke when it comes to looking employees in the eyes and firing them. Some managers want to let employees (and themselves) down easy. Or maybe the manager legitimately is concerned about the employee's welfare. The manager knows if the employee is fired, he or she may not be eligible for unemployment benefits from the state.[17]

In those situations, it's tempting for managers to give employees false reasons rather than the real reasons for their terminations. For example, the manager says, We've decided to reorganize the department, and your job was eliminated. In fact, the employee is being dismissed for poor performance.

This can backfire. If you tell employees they are being laid off, and they later discover they were replaced, they begin to wonder what other lies you told them. They are more likely to go to attorneys if they believe you lied to them.

Courts have held it isn't fair to the employee to give an untrue reason for termination. It is particularly unfair if, as a result, the employee loses out on the protections of the employee handbook. If your company has a mandatory progressive discipline program, you must follow it to dismiss a poor performer. If instead of following the policy you concoct a layoff, you have violated the employee's contract. Worse, you have acted as if there was no contract.

If you are sued for lying about the reason for termination, you will have a tough time defending yourself in court. The attorney representing the employee will cross-examine you something like this:

"You told my client that you reorganized the department, right?"

"Yes."

"But in fact, you didn't reorganize, did you?"

"Well, no."

"So you lied to my client, didn't you?"

"I wouldn't call it a lie, exactly."

"What do you call it when you don't tell the truth? You lied didn't you?"

"Yes, yes, I lied."

On redirect examination, your attorney will have the opportunity to "rehabilitate" you.

"You testified that you told the employee there was a reorganization. Why did you tell him that?"

"I wanted to let him down easy, and I knew if he told the State we had a reorganization, then he would get unemployment benefits."

"And why did you want him to get unemployment benefits?"

"Because I cared about him as a person. I cared about his family."

When the employee's attorney made you out to be a liar, you got your "foot in the mud." When the company's attorney helped you recover, you got your foot out of the mud. But you still have a muddy foot. And you will be dragging it behind you for the rest of the trial, leaving a path of slime.

For example, when the employee's attorney questions other witnesses, the attorney might say, "We heard earlier testimony from the manager who lied about the termination that . . . ." The attorney will keep reminding the jury you have a muddy foot.

At final argument the attorney will say, "Ladies and gentlemen of the jury, you heard the manager admits he lied to my client. The manager is an admitted liar. What else did she lie about? Everything! The manager testified she had a legitimate business reason for firing my client; that's a lie. The manager testified that she warned my client; that's a lie. . . ."

How to Terminate

Harvey Mackey, author of *Swim with the Sharks Without Being Eaten Alive*, says, "It's not the people you fire who make your life miserable, it's the people you don't fire." I agree.

In an interview, Mackey admitted that firing "sometimes is the toughest thing I have to do. I know it's right and that I should do it, but I still have a problem." [18]

I agree. The first time I terminated an employee, he had been with me only two weeks. I cried all morning before I fired him. The next one was a little easier.

Like any other management skill, it takes practice to perfect the art of terminating employees. If you have followed progressive discipline, it will be relatively easy to tell the employee, "I've decided to let you go." But there are a number of other items you should consider. Although these may not be required by a court of law in all instances, following these steps help you look more fair.

First, decide if the employee can remain for a transition period. Letting employees stay on for a few weeks, and allowing them to look for other jobs while training their replacements, is a very humane approach. It's usually the least disruptive. But sometimes you can't afford.

I once received a frantic phone call from one of my corporate clients, a foreign-owned company. The manager said, "I fired our computer systems operator, but he refuses to leave. What should we do?" I said, "Call the cops." The manager said, "That's not how we do it in our country. Employees just leave when they're fired." I said, "They usually leave in this country, too, but when they don't, you have to call the cops."

The company was very concerned about its image, so they didn't call the police. They allowed the employee to stay the rest of the day.

The next day, the employee came back. This time, the manager called and said he had to meet with me right away. An hour later, he came in with the employee's supervisor, the controller of the company, and the president. I said, "Where is the employee now?" They said, "At work." I said, "Who's watching him?" They said, "No one." I said, "Get back there and keep him away from the computer!" But it was too late. By the time they returned, the employee had corrupted the entire database. It put them back three months.

We ended up filing a temporary restraining order against the employee, hiring a private security guard to prevent him from coming into the plant the next day, changing the locks and security passes, and generally disrupting the entire work force. In this case, it would have been better to escort the employee off the premises immediately.

Always alert your security department before firing. An officer usually needn't be in the room, or even in the building. But someone on call nearby (even a fellow manager) can prevent disaster.

Once you decide to tell employees they're fired, do it quickly. It shouldn't take more than 10 minutes. Do it privately, in their office or in a conference room, not your office. This allows you to cut off the meeting even if they don't want to.

If you do give the employee some advance notice, you may want to give an exit interview on the actual last day of work. Although the personnel department gives a separate exit interview, you may learn some useful information from departing employees.

Even if you don't learn anything useful, it gives employees the chance to vent their feelings of hostility against you. After they've let off some steam, they may feel better and be less likely to seek other ways of getting back at you.

When should you tell employees they're fired? Most managers do it on Friday afternoons, having put off the unpleasant task all week. This is the worst day for employees to be fired. It gives them an entire weekend to nurture revenge fantasies, with no opportunity to do something constructive until Monday.

Instead, do it first thing the morning their final warning period expires. The employee can immediately go out, get a newspaper, prepare a resume, and start a new job search.

You should never fire an employee on the spot, in a fit of anger. At most, you should immediately suspend them, and order them to leave the premises. Think about it overnight. Do an investigation. Hear the employee's side. If after all that, you decide to fire, you can turn the suspension into a termination.

If you can, help employees get new jobs. This keeps down their potential damages. Attorneys generally won't take cases if the actual amount of pay lost by employees is minimal. Even if you terminate employees wrongfully, if they get jobs the next day, they don't have any actual or out-of-pocket losses. The case will be less attractive to an employee's attorney.

Consider taking these steps:

1. Allow employees to use the office, phone and secretarial assistance for a few weeks so they appear to be currently employed.
2. Refuse to discuss them on the phone with potential employers, so you don't accidentally reveal negative information.
3. Pay the final paycheck, accrued vacation, and commission checks when due.
4. Provide salary continuation or severance pay while they are unemployed.
5. Don't contest their applications for unemployment benefits (but see Chapter 8).
6. Offer outplacement services.

Yes, some of these are expensive. But they're cheaper than hiring a lawyer.

Alternatives to Termination

A wrongful termination lawsuit can be avoided almost completely if you don't fire the employee at all. Consider these alternatives to terminating employees to avoid lawsuits:

- Restructure employees' jobs.
- Change their reporting relationships.
- Move their workstations.
- Transfer within the company.
- Call an executive recruiter to find a position for them outside the company.
- Give them time off to look for work.
- Give them counseling or therapy from an outside professional.
- Offer them leaves of absence.
- Place them on disability leave.
- Agree with them that they will leave at a later date.
- Offer early retirement (but see Chapter 2).

My most successful termination occurred with a secretary who had been with me for over two years. She was competent when we first hired her, but over time the office had doubled in size and complexity. She simply couldn't keep up with it.

Not only that, she was making mistakes and then denying them. I had given her two written warnings and a poor performance appraisal, but she hadn't improved.

Finally, one day I sat down with her and said, "You know, we've really expanded in the last two years, and we're going to expand more. Since this is the first law firm you've worked for, you don't have the experience we need to get to the next level. This could be a good opportunity for you to move to a bigger law firm and get that experience."

She admitted she was thinking of looking for work elsewhere, but didn't want to hurt us by leaving. We agreed she could start looking for a job during working hours, and the firm would look for her replacement.

Within one month, she was happily ensconced in another firm, making more money, with more benefits. We had avoided a messy termination. We had prevented a lawsuit. And probably we even got some good PR. Most important, we maintained the good relationships that had developed at work. By treating her fairly, we all benefited.

WHISTLEBLOWERS: DON'T FIRE THEM!

The third type of wrongful termination lawsuit protects employees who complain about unlawful actions by their employers. Employees who blow the whistle are protected because they are attempting to uphold a public policy of the state.

For example, you can't fire an employee who reports to the state water quality board that your company is dumping toxic wastes in the river. The purpose of a clean water board is to protect the public. Reporting a violation is a public duty. It would be ridiculous for the state to encourage employees to report violations but then allow them to get fired as a result.

Here is another example: employees who believe they should be paid overtime when you think they're exempt from the overtime laws. If they complain to the Labor Department, you can't fire them in retaliation.

Even if the employee complains only to you and not to a government agency, the employee still may be protected from being fired. In one case, a respiratory therapist refused to work with another who, she said, was a danger to the patients. She was fired. She sued and won. The court said the law requires medical workers to give good patient care. She was allowed to do anything to convince the employer that she was serious about preventing the dangerous coworker from working.[19]

A new trend is lawsuits against government contractors for fraud. When employees discover their employers are defrauding the government, they can file "qui tam" actions. *Qui tam* is Latin for "he who." These are the first two words of a phrase that basically means, "He who digs up the dirt gets the treasure."

Employees who file qui tam actions are protected from retaliation, discrimination, and wrongful termination. They also are entitled to a finder's fee because they dug up the fraud. This fee can range from 10% to 30% of the defrauded amount. Since some of the fraud involves billions of dollars, the employees in these cases stand to make hundreds of millions.

See the accompanying box for more examples of protected whistleblowing.

Protected Whistleblowers

Employees in many states can't be fired for:

Reporting government fraud and waste

Questioning the safety of consumer goods

Expressing their political beliefs

Serving on a jury or as a witness

Complaining about unsafe working conditions

Reporting tax code violations of the company

Refusing to commit perjury for the company

Refusing to take a lie detector test

Receiving one wage attachment or garnishment

Refusing to serve unsafe food

Refusing to support political candidates or issues of the company

Taking time off for military duty

Entering an alcohol or drug treatment program

Complaining of harassment or discrimination

Demanding overtime pay if not exempt from overtime laws

Determining What a Public Policy Is

There is a split among the courts about whether employees are protected only when they complain about violations of specific statutes.

Some courts will protect any public policy that can be implied from existing laws or found in court opinions.[20] Other courts have said there must be a specific statute prohibiting the conduct. Even if there is a specific statute, a court still may not find a case.

The California Supreme Court, for example, ruled that the employee must be blowing the whistle to protect the public, not to protect a private interest. This ruling was made in 1988 in the case of Daniel Foley, a branch manager of Interactive Data Corporation, a computer information service.

Foley learned that his new boss was under investigation by the FBI for embezzling money from his former employer. Foley immediately informed top management. He was told to forget what he heard.

A few weeks later, the new boss fired Foley, supposedly for performance reasons. Foley had worked there for over six years and had an excellent performance record.

Six months later, the new boss pled guilty to embezzling from his former company.

On the surface, it would seem that Foley's termination was a violation of public policy. After all, he blew the whistle on his new boss. He did so to protect the interest of the company.

But the court said the company's interest is a private one; in other words, only a few people will benefit if the company doesn't hire an embezzler. The public at large will not benefit. Thus Foley was not acting in the public interest. Therefore, he couldn't claim whistleblower protection. (He won on contract grounds.)

The result in the Foley case would have been different if he had worked in a bank. Then, embezzling would have endangered people's money. His whistleblowing would have been protected in the public interest.

How Circumstantial Evidence Can Prove Retaliation

You may have no intention of retaliating against whistleblowers. But if they are not performing, you may want to terminate them. Unfortunately, if it appears you did not begin disciplinary proceedings until after the employee filed a complaint, the circumstantial evidence tends to prove you retaliated.

Circumstantial evidence does not prove a fact, but facts can be inferred from the circumstances. For example, if you have been in a windowless room all day, you don't know what the weather is like outside. If I come into the room wearing a raincoat, dripping wet, and shaking my umbrella, the circumstances would lead you to believe that it's raining outside.

Similarly, if an employee who has received outstanding performance appraisals complains about a problem, and the next day is fired without warning, the circumstances would lead one to believe the reason for termination was the complaint.

You can rebut circumstantial evidence with direct evidence that shows the employee's poor performance. You can terminate any employee who does not perform, even a whistleblower, if you are consistent, have a legitimate business reason for the termination and document it.

How to Handle Layoffs

So far, we've covered involuntary terminations due to firing. There is another type of involuntary termination: the layoff due to reorganization, plant closing, or reduction in force (RIF).

In some states and at some companies, the term "layoff" means the company is required to reinstate employees if their positions come open later. A "reduction in force" refers to a permanent loss of employment with no opportunity for reinstatement. With that one exception, the terms will be used interchangeably here.

If your company has a layoff policy requiring reinstatement, like all policies it must be followed. Courts rarely second-guess a company's decision to have a layoff, RIF, or other reorganization. Even if as a result of the reorganization, the company loses money, the courts don't question it. After all, a company has the right to run itself into the ground. As a result, wrongful termination cases rarely arise out of layoffs.

The three areas that can lead to cases are:

1. Whether the layoff in fact was legitimate
2. The criteria used to select employees for layoff
3. The impact on groups protected under discrimination laws

How to Tell If the Layoff Is Legitimate

I once represented a salesman who was laid off due to a reorganization. Under the reorganization plan, all the salesmen were to be promoted to area managers. Their former sales manager was to be demoted to area manager. Since there were only as many areas as there were salesmen, this meant there was one "extra" sales rep. My client was picked for layoff.

This plan was never put in writing. There were no minutes or notes from the many meetings before the reorganization. My client was one of the oldest and had been with the company for over 16 years.

Despite these failings, on the surface the layoff looked legitimate. It involved just a handful of people at a small company, so formal documentation wasn't expected. And despite his long years of service, my client had the *least* amount of seniority of all the employees.

A few days after the sales manager was told of his demotion, he opted to take early retirement. This meant a position was now open, and my client's layoff could be countermanded. In fact, he was still on the payroll because he had been given two weeks' advance notice.

The company didn't tell him the position was open. Instead, they contacted an executive recruiter. Within a week, they hired an outsider. The day after my client officially was off the payroll, the new employee began working.

That was not a legitimate RIF. My client's position was refilled.

My rule of thumb: If a laid-off employee is replaced within six months, the RIF looks suspicious. Companies sometimes try to make the layoff look legitimate by waiting longer to hire a replacement or by giving the new employee a different job title.

These subterfuges rarely work. One advantage laid-off employees usually have is friends back at the company who tell them exactly what is going on.

What if you have a legitimate RIF and then later your budget is restored? Even if it's been six months since the layoff, the former employee may still be unemployed. Most people would be delighted to go back to work. And you as a manager in most cases will benefit from rehiring an experienced employee.

You may have decided to restructure the job. Perhaps you want to strengthen an area the laid-off employee was weak in. You can change job requirements, for legitimate business reasons. But you still should interview laid-off employees.

Even if you're sure they can't fulfill your new requirements, as a matter of fairness, it's best to interview them. Maybe they have talents you are unaware of. If not, at least you treated them fairly.

What if you don't want the former employee back? Maybe you used the layoff to get rid of a nonperforming employee. You can use a legitimate layoff to get rid of a nonperformer.[21] But it's best if you have documentation to back you up.

How to Select Employees for a Reduction in Force

Some companies have written policies that establish criteria for selecting employees for layoff. Typical criteria include:

Seniority: Employees are laid-off in order of reverse seniority ("last hired, first fired").

Job Titles: Certain job classifications or departments are eliminated.

Skill Sets: Employees with the least number of skills and abilities are let go

Merit: Poor performers are laid-off.

All these are legal as long as they are applied consistently.

Some companies leave RIFs up to the managers. They allow managers to use their discretion. Managers establish their own criteria.

This is dangerous. One court found a RIF to be discriminatory where the company did not have written criteria for evaluation, layoff and recall to guide the managers.[22]

Criteria must be based on legitimate business reasons and should be in writing. If your company leaves the decision up to you, write down your own criteria.

The Adverse Impact of Layoffs

One obvious criterion for layoff is salary. If you want to cut costs, it makes economic sense to RIF the highest-paid people in each job group. But if you do, the RIF might include a lot of older workers. That's because salaries tend to increase with age. If you terminate highly paid people, chances are they will be older than the average employee.

If a RIF has an adverse impact like this, it may be age discrimination. You can pick the highest-paid people for layoff only if older workers are not disproportionately impacted.[23]

In other words, if the department work force is 50% over the age of 40, then no more than 50% of the people laid-off should be over the age of 40. This type of analysis should be done at the department level, not companywide.

Seniority is a criterion that could have an impact on women and minorities. By laying off in order of reverse seniority, the last hired are the first fired. If women and minorities have been hired recently, they will be adversely impacted by a layoff.

But this adverse impact is *not* illegal. Federal and state statutes specifically exempt seniority systems from the discrimination laws. The one exception is for organizations under court-mandated affirmative action requirements.[24]

Whatever criteria you use, once the layoff list is assembled, review it for adverse impact on any of the protected groups discussed in Chapter 2.

> *practical pointer:* Although not required by law, it's a good idea to act compassionately. If people feel good about the way the layoff is handled, they are less likely to go to an attorney.

One of my clients was called into his boss's office, informed he was laid-off, handed a box, and told he had 15 minutes to clear his desk. He was not allowed to say goodbye to the people he had worked with for years. At age 68, the one thing he said over and over was, "I just wish I could have had a retirement party."

Although legally we couldn't do anything about that, it was his feeling of humiliation and embarrassment that caused him to seek an attorney. We successfully sued on other grounds.

In the best layoffs I've seen, employees were allowed ample time to say goodbye. The company hired a fleet of taxi cabs to drive them home. The company provided a career center with job opportunities, resume writing service, and telephones. It made the layoff a little easier.

There is one technical requirement: Under the Worker Adjustment and Retraining Notification (WARN) Act, the company must give 60 days' advance notice of a mass layoff or plant closing. The law applies only to companies with 100 or more employees and only to certain types of layoffs.[25]

If you don't give advance notice, you must pay employees one day's pay for every day less than 60 days of notice.

TIME LIMITS FOR FILING A WRONGFUL TERMINATION LAWSUIT

Unlike a discrimination claim, a wrongful termination case cannot be brought to any government agency. It's begun by filing a lawsuit in court.

Since wrongful termination cases are based on contract, tort, and public policy, the time for suing or statute of limitations vary from state to state and also according to the circumstances. In California, for example, the time to file an action based on an oral contract is two years and four years if based on a written contract.

A tort (or personal injury) claim based on fairness must be filed within one year. Whistleblower cases in California can be filed within three years, unless the case is based on a statute that contains a different limitations period.

Check with a local employment lawyer to find out the time deadlines in your state.

THE FAIRNESS FACTOR

Wrongful termination law covers the entire employment relationship from beginning to end.

It comes down to one word: fairness. Have you been fair? If you have, you probably won't get sued. If you're sued, you probably will win.

And no matter what happens, you'll feel good about yourself for treating people fairly.

Wrongful Termination Law by State[26]

Y = This form of wrongful termination is recognized by state
N = This form not recognized
NC = no cases or clear expression
NR = no definitive state ruling

State	Contract	Fairness	Public Policy
AL	Y	Y	Y
AK	Y	Y	Y
AZ	Y	Y	Y
AR	Y	N	Y
CA	Y	Y	Y
CO	Y	Y	Y
CT	Y	Y	Y
DL	N	Y	N
DC	Y	NC	Y
FL	N	NC	N
GA	Y	N	N
HI	Y	NC	Y
ID	Y	Y	Y
IL	Y	N	Y
IN	N	N	Y

State	Contract	Fairness	Public Policy
IA	NR	Y	Y
KS	Y	N	Y
KY	NC	NC	Y
LA	NC	NC	N
ME	Y	N	NC
MD	Y	N	Y
MA	NC	Y	Y
MI	Y	NC	Y
MN	Y	N	Y
MS	NC	NC	NR
MO	N	NC	Y
MT	Y	Y	Y
NE	NC	NC	Y
NV	NC	Y	Y
NH	Y	Y	Y
NJ	Y	N	Y
NM	Y	NC	Y
NY	Y	N	N
NC	N	NC	Y
ND	NC	N	Y
OH	Y	NC	Y
OK	Y	N	Y
OR	Y	NC	Y
PA	NR	N	Y
RI	NC	NC	NC
SC	Y	NC	Y
SD	Y	N	Y
TN	N	NC	Y
TX	Y	NC	Y
UT	Y	NC	Y
VT	Y	NC	Y
VA	NR	NR	Y
WA	Y	N	Y
WV	Y	NC	Y
WI	Y	N	Y
WY	Y	N	Y

Chapter 4

NONE OF YOUR BUSINESS?

The Law of Privacy and Drug Testing

O ne of my clients was a book publisher with 15 employees. The company was too small to have a personnel department. Instead, the president's secretary was responsible for personnel.

One day she called. One of the supervisors had come in that morning with a problem. A few weeks before, he had asked to borrow an employee's car. The employee said yes and gave the boss his keys. The boss got into the car and drove off on his errand.

When he arrived at his destination, he pulled the key out of the ignition. That was when he noticed something unusual. On the key ring was a small, glass vial filled with white powder.

He didn't know what to do. Here he was in possession of some kind of illegal drug. He figured as soon as he got back, the employee would want his keys. He didn't want to confront the employee until he knew what the stuff was, but he knew he couldn't keep the vial without confronting him.

He decided to take out a little bit of the powder so he could have it tested by a laboratory. Then he went back to work and returned the keys as if nothing happened. That night, he took the sample to a testing lab. He waited 10 days until he got the test report which showed the powder was cocaine.

This morning, he had presented the report to the president's secretary and demanded she prepare the paperwork to terminate the employee. She called me to okay the termination. Certainly it is legal to terminate an employee for bringing drugs to work. But in getting the evidence, they had conducted a search of the employee's personal belongings. Opening that vial was a search. Taking the powder was theft. Having the powder analyzed was a type of drug test. Was all this legal?

If just one of these wasn't legal, terminating him wouldn't be legal either. Even if he wasn't terminated, he still could sue for invasion of privacy if it was an illegal search.

You will see later what happened. But the way this search was conducted raised so many issues, it seriously narrowed our options. The lesson to be learned from this experience is you should analyze the employee's privacy rights *before* you conduct a search.

WHAT IS PRIVACY?

Plaintiffs' lawyers, the attorneys who represent employees, predict that privacy will surpass wrongful termination as the hot issue of the 1990s. Yet the concept of privacy is so broad, it's difficult to even define.

Originally, privacy was defined as the "right to be left alone." This meant you could not intrude upon my seclusion[1] or publicize private facts about me.[2] Today, the definition has expanded. Privacy includes ideas like human dignity or self-respect and autonomy or self-governance. Privacy also has been called secrecy, anonymity, solitude, psychological integrity, and personality. Privacy means you can't make me do what I don't want to do. What I do in private is none of your business. I have the right to control my own life.

Texas is one of the leading privacy states. One court there said, "The heart of this privacy interest is the individual's exclusive perogative to determine when, under what conditions, and to what extent he will consent to divulge his private affairs to others."[3]

The idea that one person could sue another for invasion of privacy is only 100 years old. Originally, only the government could be sued for invasion of privacy, under the Bill of Rights of the U.S. Constitution.

The First Amendment to the Constitution allows freedom of speech, religion, and of assembly. Freedom of assembly also is referred to as freedom of association, and it means that people are allowed to gather and join with others as they wish.

The Fourth Amendment prohibits unreasonable searches and seizures of "persons, houses, papers and effects." It protects our most personal spaces.

The Fifth Amendment provides that no one can be compelled in a criminal case to be a witness against himself. Also known as the privilege against self-incrimination, this amendment protects our minds from intrusion.

These amendments, by their terms, limit only the power of the government. For the most part, they have been applied to put limits on the police. But they also have been interpreted to protect employees who work for the government.

For example, a woman worked for a county sheriff in Texas in 1981. When she heard that President Reagan had been shot but not killed, she said, "If they go for him again, I hope they get him." She was fired on the spot.

The U.S. Supreme Court held she could not be fired.[4] She worked for a governmental agency. She was exercising her freedom of speech. She could not be deprived by the government employer of her freedom to speak out on a matter of public interest.

What of the rights of employees who work for nongovernment employers? Historically, they didn't have any privacy. Seventy years ago, Ford Motor Company checked the cleanliness of employees' homes, the neatness of their gardens, their attendance at church, and the kinds of cars they drove. Employees who didn't meet the company's standards legally could be fired.[5] Ford employees couldn't sue for invasion of privacy because the Bill of Rights didn't apply to them.

It didn't seem fair that government employees had freedom of speech and other privacy protections when nongovernment employees didn't.[6] But if the Bill of Rights didn't apply to them, what law did?

In 1890, the idea was proposed that everyone has a common law right to privacy. In 1905, the Georgia Supreme Court was the first to say that people have the right to be free of intrusion upon seclusion.[7]

Today, the right of privacy is recognized to some extent in every state. This right protects us from invasion of privacy by the public, the press, and employers.

In this chapter, you will see examples from many different states. Most of these cases would be decided the same in any state. These cases illustrate generally accepted privacy principles.

PRIVACY LAWS BY STATE

This chart shows which states protect privacy in the listed areas. Many of these statutes are not comprehensive; for example, a state may protect the personnel files only of police officers. For more information, contact a local employment lawyer.

State	General Privacy Statute	Drug Testing	Personnel Records	Electronic Surveillance	Polygraphs	Free Speech
AL	Y					Y
AK			Y		Y	Y
AZ		Y				Y
AR			Y			Y
CA	Y		Y	Y	Y	
CO					Y	Y
CT	Y	Y	Y	Y	Y	Y
DE			Y		Y	
DC					Y	
FL		Y	Y			Y
GA		Y	Y	Y	Y	Y
HI		Y			Y	
ID			Y		Y	Y
IL	Y	Y	Y	Y		Y
IN	Y					
IA		Y	Y		Y	Y
KS		Y				Y
KY			Y			Y
LA		Y	Y	Y		Y
ME		Y	Y		Y	Y
MD		Y	Y	Y	Y	Y
MA			Y		Y	Y
MI			Y		Y	Y
MN		Y	Y		Y	Y
MS		Y				Y
MO			Y			Y
MT		Y			Y	Y
NE		Y			Y	Y
NV			Y			Y
NH			Y			Y
NJ				Y	Y	Y
NM						Y
NY			Y		Y	Y

State	General Privacy Statute	Drug Testing	Personnel Records	Electronic Surveillance	Polygraphs	Free Speech
NC		Y	Y			Y
ND						Y
OH			Y			Y
OK			Y			Y
OR		Y	Y		Y	
PA			Y	Y	Y	Y
RI		Y	Y		Y	Y
SC	Y		Y			
SD						Y
TN		Y	Y		Y	Y
TX						Y
UT		Y	Y		Y	
VT		Y			Y	Y
VA			Y	Y	Y	
WA			Y	Y	Y	Y
WV				Y	Y	
WI			Y	Y	Y	Y
WY			Y			Y

Craig Cornish, an employee's attorney from Colorado who is recognized as a national expert on workplace privacy, says there are six types of privacy cases.[8] The six types, and the issues they raise, can be seen in the box.

Type Of Privacy Issue	Situations Where It Occurs
Collecting information	Drug tests
Method and means of collection	Polygraphs, searches, mail, telephone and computer monitoring, video surveillance, investigating
Retaliating against employees who refuse to give information	Questioning employees, wrongful termination
Using private information against the employee	Free speech, sexual orientation protection, arrest records, defamation, false light, appropriation

Type Of Privacy Issue	Situations Where It Occurs
Disclosing private information to others	Revealing medical information, personnel files, home address, and phone
Infringing the dignity of the employee	Asking personal questions, relationship restrictions, life-style discrimination, appearance standards

All these situations will be discussed in this chapter.

FOUR WAYS TO TELL IF AN ACTION IS AN ILLEGAL INVASION OF PRIVACY

To analyze whether an action is an illegal invasion of privacy, courts use different legal standards. A simplified version of the analysis courts use in privacy cases is this four-step process:

1. What is the zone of privacy being invaded?
2. What is the person's reasonable expectation of privacy?
3. Is there a sufficient reason to justify intrusion?
4. Are the means used rationally related to the end sought?

1. Zone of Privacy

The zones of privacy can be seen in the illustration on the following page. The areas in the center are the most personal: our bodies, our minds, and our homes. Next most personal is our personal belongings. Less personal are the desk and files we have at work. Less still is the office we use, then the general workplace, and last the parking lot.

2. Reasonable Expectation of Privacy

Once you know what zone of privacy is affected, you can determine the reasonable expectation of privacy. The zones closest to the center have the highest expectation. For example, we have a very high expectation of privacy in the contents of our pockets. We don't expect other people to go through our pockets without our permission. The more personal the zone of privacy, the higher the expectation of privacy.

An employer can change employees' reasonable expectation of privacy in some cases by notifying them in advance that the company reserves the

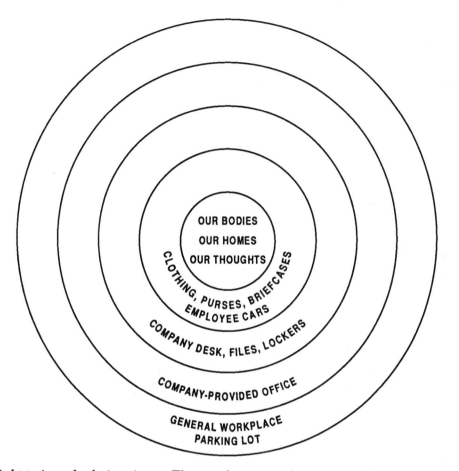

OUR BODIES
OUR HOMES
OUR THOUGHTS

CLOTHING, PURSES, BRIEFCASES

EMPLOYEE CARS

COMPANY DESK, FILES, LOCKERS

COMPANY-PROVIDED OFFICE

GENERAL WORKPLACE
PARKING LOT

right to invade their privacy. The employer's right to do this, and limitations on this right, will be discussed if applicable in each section of this chapter.

3. Reason to Invade Privacy

Even if we have a reasonable expectation of privacy, the law still may allow our privacy to be invaded if there is sufficient reason to justify it. A "compelling interest" is required to invade areas that have a high expectation of privacy. A "rational basis" is required to invade areas with lower expectations of privacy. Both of these are higher standards than the "business necessity" standard discussed in Chapter 2, on discrimination law.

Just as police officers must have reasonable suspicion before they can search people, employers must have compelling or rational reasons to invade privacy:

Reasonable suspicion of theft at work

Reasonable suspicion of intoxication at work

Maintaining plant security

Measuring work performance

Protecting trade secrets

Ensuring workplace safety

Preventing bribery of employees

Preventing conflicts of interest

4. *Means Reasonably Related to Ends*

Assuming the employer has a compelling or rational reason to invade privacy, then the means chosen must be rationally related to the end sought. This is determined through a balancing test. The need of the employer to obtain information is weighed against the extent to which the employee's seclusion is invaded.[9]

For example, if a company wanted to protect trade secrets, it might decide to prohibit employees from dating employees who work for competitors. But if such a policy applied to all employees, whether or not they had access to trade secrets, it would not be rationally related to the ends sought. We would say the policy is overbroad. It would be interfering in the private lives of many employees, when only a few employees are at risk. Therefore, such a broad policy is an invasion of privacy.[10]

When there are alternative means that don't invade employees' privacy but achieve the same result, the balance is likely to tilt in favor of the employee. For example, if a company's no-dating policy applied only to people with access to trade secrets, it still invades their privacy, but the policy is reasonably related to the ends sought and is more likely to be upheld.

The problem of overbroad policies can best be seen in the controversy surrounding drug testing.

WHEN COMPANIES REQUIRE DRUG TESTING

There are six types of drug tests: preemployment to screen out applicants, "for cause" testing of employees upon reasonable suspicion of intoxication, postaccident, regularly scheduled tests (usually part of a general physical), unannounced random tests, and follow-up tests to confirm an employee is maintaining sobriety after testing positive.

The Department of Defense (DOD) requires noncommercial defense contractors to drug test some employees.[11] Covered companies also are required to have drug awareness education, employee assistance and rehabilitation programs, and procedures for identifying illegal workplace drug use.

Under DOD rules, employees must be drug tested if they have access to classified information or are in positions that, for reasons of national security or health and safety, require a high degree of trust and confidence. It is up to the employer to decide what type of testing to perform. However, if state or local laws or union contracts prohibit drug testing, DOD contractors are not required to test.

The U.S. Department of Transportation requires drug testing for drivers in interstate commerce,[12] airline personnel,[13] and railroad employees.[14] These regulations require preemployment, for cause, postaccident, and random tests for sensitive positions.

According to a 1992 study, 69% of private sector companies conduct drug tests.[15] An estimated 10 million employees were tested in the United States in 1991. According to one sample, 8.8% of employees and applicants tested positive for drugs, a 50% decrease since 1987.[16]

But just because all this testing is going on, doesn't mean it is legal. Many drug tests have been challenged, and in many cases the employees won, because the tests illegally invaded their privacy.

How Courts Decide Drug Testing Cases

Let's go back to the four-step process for analyzing privacy claims to see how the courts have decided the drug testing cases.

1. What is the zone of privacy?

Drug tests invade the most personal zone—our bodies, our minds, and, by extension, our homes. From analyzing urine, much more can be known about our private lives than illegal drug use. To have accurate test results, employees must disclose the prescription and over-the-counter medications they take. Thus an employer will know about medication taken for diabetes, epilepsy, high blood pressure, depression, birth control, and many other sensitive medical conditions.

2. What is the reasonable expectation of privacy?

Drug tests normally are based on urine samples. As the Supreme Court notes, passing urine is one of the most private things we do in our society. It is done behind closed doors. It's illegal if done in public. And in drug tests, not only must we pass it on demand, but often someone watches as we do it.

As a New Jersey court put it,

> We would be appalled at the spectre of the police spying on employees during their free time and then reporting their activities to their employers. Drug testing is a form of surveillance, albeit a technological one. Nonetheless, it reports on a person's off-duty activities just as surely as someone had been present and watching. It is George Orwell's "Big Brother" Society come to life.[17]

3. Is there sufficient reason to invade privacy?

The U.S. Supreme Court has held that employers must have a compelling reason to drug test and has found drug testing justified in two instances.

The Court has said railroads have a compelling reason to test employees for drugs immediately after train accidents.[18] The Court reasoned that the fear of having a drug test would discourage employees from taking drugs. A decrease in drug use presumably would decrease accidents and increase passengers' safety. Society's interest in protecting the safety of passengers outweighs the railroad crew's right of privacy.

In another case, the Supreme Court said there was a compelling reason to give drug tests to candidates for promotion in the U.S. Customs Service.[19] Customs officers' jobs require them to search for illegal drugs. Drugs often are in their possession and control. If the government hired drug abusers in those jobs, they could be susceptible to bribery and might have a conflict of interest between their addictions and their jobs.

4. Are the means rationally related to the end sought?

This is where the problem of an overbroad test comes in. In the first year of postaccident testing, 3.8% of all railway accidents involved employees who tested positive for drugs.[20] In 1991, only 2.6% tested positive.[21] So 97% of the good, honest employees who were involved in accidents suffered the added insult to injury of being treated under suspicion, guilty until proven innocent.

Similarly, the Customs officer case relies on faulty assumptions. In his dissenting opinion, conservative Supreme Court Justice Scalia pointed out that employees who use drugs are no more likely to accept bribes from drug dealers than officers who wear diamonds are likely to be bribed by a diamond smuggler.

> Nor is it apparent to me that Customs officers who use drugs will
> be appreciably less sympathetic to their drug-interdiction mission,
> any more than police officers who exceed the speed limit in their
> private cars are appreciably less sympathetic to their mission of
> enforcing the traffic laws.[22]

Another reason drug tests are overbroad is they do not measure current impairment. Unlike blood alcohol tests, which detect the amount of alcohol currently in one's system, drug tests generally measure only inert metabolites that are the end products of drugs. These metabolites have no psychoactive effect themselves, and they are excreted from the body more slowly than drugs. Drug tests show past drug use; they do not show current impairment.[23]

The U.S. Supreme Court has recognized the problem of overbreadth and generally has required proof of impairment at work. In a 1987 case, the Court allowed a papermill worker, Mr. Cooper, to be reinstated to his job. He was fired after he was found in the company parking lot in his car, which was filled with marijuana smoke. Gleanings of marijuana later were found in the upholstery. The Supreme Court said, "The assumed connection between the marijuana gleanings found in Cooper's car and Cooper's actual use of drugs in the workplace is tenuous at best."[24]

Drug tests are overbroad for another reason: many studies have found alarming rates of false positives. The most optimistic study found that 1% to 2% of the samples tested positive for drugs when in fact no drugs were present. Although proportionately small, given that 10 million employees are tested each year, hundreds of thousands are being falsely accused of drug use on the basis of faulty tests. Some experts believe the rate of false positives is as high as 62%.[25]

Finally, there are less intrusive alternatives to drug testing. Performance Factors, a California company, has developed tests that measure people's reaction time, visual acuity, and other job-related abilities.[26] Much like a video game, the test is used by employers in such areas as railroads, steel mills, and transportation to test employees at the beginning of each workday.

This test does not invade privacy. Unlike drug tests, it catches people when they're impaired, before they get into accidents. And it catches them when they can't perform for reasons other than drugs, such as lack of sleep, depression, or hangovers.

Despite the problem of overbreadth, the Supreme Court upheld drug testing of railroad employees after accidents and of Customs officers. Other federal courts have upheld testing for other jobs.

When Random Drug Tests Are Allowed

In the following cases, the courts have allowed random and all other drug tests for employees in sensitive positions:[27]

> Employees with national security clearances
> Airline personnel
> Corrections officers with prisoner contact
> Transportation employees
> Employees at chemical weapons plants
> Army civilian employees
> Employees with top secret clearances
> Police officers
> Nuclear power plant workers

Some federal testing requirements have not been upheld. The U.S. Department of Agriculture was sued for requiring all food and nutrition service employees to be tested if the supervisor had reasonable suspicion of off-duty drug use.

The agency argued it had a legitimate interest in stopping off-duty use: users' work performance might be affected, they might buy drugs at work or steal to support their habits, and their drug use might erode public confidence in the agency.

The court of appeals said this was mere speculation and could not justify invasion of privacy. The court held that testing for off-duty use might be upheld for workers in safety- or security-sensitive jobs. But other workers could not be tested unless there was reasonable suspicion of on-duty drug use or drug-impaired work performance.[28]

State Drug Testing Laws

These federal court decisions are only the beginning. There is much more to the law of drug testing. Every state has some privacy protections, and 15 states have statutes specifically regulating drug tests.

A state's privacy statute may be interpreted by that state's courts more broadly than the Supreme Court interprets the U.S. Constitution. If the state's law gives more protection to privacy, generally it must be followed instead.

For example, a New Jersey court held in 1992 that preemployment drug testing is an invasion of privacy.[29] In California, preemployment testing has been upheld,[30] but not random tests for employees in nonsensitive positions.[31]

Most state courts that have ruled on tests allowed preemployment and postaccident tests. Reasonable suspicion of on-duty drug use also has justified tests, as long as the manager was able to document why he or she had reason to believe the employee was on drugs.[32]

State drug test statutes also vary widely. Some states, such as Utah, almost encourage employers to drug test. Other states limit employers' use of tests. For example, Maine's law[33] requires employers with 20 or more full-time employees to have an employee assistance program (EAP) before beginning any drug testing. Employers' drug prevention and testing policies must be approved by the state before being implemented.

The Maine statute also regulates how test samples are collected. Employers are allowed to drug test all applicants, and employees may be tested if they are suspected of using drugs at work. Random tests are allowed only in safety-sensitive positions or for employees who are undergoing rehabilitation. In Maine, you can't terminate employees for drug abuse unless you first give them the opportunity to participate in a rehabilitation program for at least six months. If employees refuse rehabilitation, they can be terminated immediately.

Whether or not your state has a drug law, drug tests may not be given in a discriminatory manner. If applicants are to be tested, all must be—from janitor to CEO.

If drug tests uncover employees addicted to drugs, you may be required to offer them rehabilitation under your state's law. The Americans with Disabilities Act (ADA) also may require you to send employees to rehabilitation.

> *practical pointer:* Because this is a volatile area, it is highly recommended that you conduct a full investigation of the law and practice in your community and industry before you begin a program. Consult with attorneys and other experts to implement drug testing. See the following box for a checklist of items to consider before starting drug testing.

Drug Testing Checklist

1. Identify a reputable testing lab.

2. Prepare legal notices for employees/applicants to read and sign.

3. Establish the mechanics of obtaining samples, including whether people will be monitored while giving samples.

4. Establish chain of custody controls so samples are not confused or tampered with.

5. Budget to include a second (different) test in case of positive results, to minimize possibility of false positives.

6. Designate an individual in your company to receive test results.

7. Establish confidentiality controls for test results.

8. Decide how employees/applicants will be informed of results.

9. Provide process for appealing the results.

10. Establish procedure for referring them to rehabilitation.

What to Do If You Think an Employee Is Abusing Drugs

If you don't have a testing program, what should you do about drugs in your workplace? If you suspect employees are abusing drugs or alcohol, document the objective, verifiable facts that prove their work is affected. You want to show they are arriving late, falling asleep, or slurring their words. Document their emotional mood swings and irrational outbursts. Start a program of counseling and disciplining them just as you would anyone else who isn't performing.

Even if you have a drug testing program, you still must document poor work performance to justify your reasonable suspicion for ordering an employee to take a test.

Don't do what one manager did. He fired an employee for documented poor performance. But when he fired him, the manager said, "Off the record, I think you're a drug addict." There's no such thing as off the record. Such an accusation could lead to a claim of defamation, intentional infliction of emotional distress, or invasion of privacy.

You may have a duty under the ADA to give the person the opportunity to self-identify. In other words, you can't accuse them of an addiction, but you can ask, "Is there any reason you are having these performance problems?" If they reveal problems with drugs or alcohol, you should then refer them to rehabilitation.

Federal Drug-Free Workplace Act

One other statute applies to drugs. The U.S. Drug-Free Workplace Act[34] requires all federal government agencies and contractors, including vendors with purchase orders totaling $25,000 or more, to adopt a policy statement and distribute it to employees. See the sample policy.

It also requires companies to develop drug awareness programs. The program must include information on the dangers of workplace drug abuse, the company's antidrug policy, and the penalties for violating the policy. You also must inform employees of any available rehabilitation and counseling programs. Some states have adopted similar programs for state government contractors.

Sample Drug-Free Workplace Policy

If you use drugs at work, you are a hazard to your safety and the safety of your coworkers. For that reason, it is company policy and a requirement of the Drug-Free Workplace Act to prohibit the unlawful manufacture, distribution, dispensation, possession, or use of a controlled substance at the workplace.

This means that if you are found in the possession of, or under the influence of, any drug at work, or while on Company business away from the workplace, you are subject to disciplinary action, up to and including immediate termination.

Some of the controlled substances that are prohibited are marijuana, cocaine, methamphetamine, PCP, LSD, and barbituates. These drugs, as well as alcohol and prescription medications, are dangerous at work because they interfere with your concentration, coordination, memory, judgment, perception, and mood.

We recognize that drug dependency is an illness and major health problem. This company has a drug rehabilitation and counseling program. If you use drugs, you are eligible for and encouraged to participate in this program. If you voluntarily admit your addiction and request to enter the program, you will not suffer any job loss as long as you conform to the program requirements and perform your job satisfactorily after returning to work.

continued

> If you are convicted by a court of a criminal drug violation in the workplace, you must notify the company within five days of your conviction.
>
> The company is committed to keeping a drug-free workplace to ensure the safety and health of employees, as well as a productive environment for our customers.

HOW COMPANIES COLLECT INFORMATION ABOUT EMPLOYEES

The right to privacy involves much more than drug tests. In the following sections, we'll cover the other protected areas.

Polygraph (Lie Detector) Tests

I once was asked by a woman to represent her against her employer. She had been caught stealing—on videotape. She denied the charges, but was fired. She said she wanted to take a lie detector test to prove her innocence. I frankly told her a polygraph wasn't very good evidence against a video, but she insisted. I referred her to a polygraph examiner.

The next day, the examiner called and said she had failed the test. That night, I told my husband about the result. He said, "What will you say to your client?" I said, "Well, I'll tell her polygraphs aren't very reliable . . ." He said, "Yeah, tell her, 'Polygraphs aren't reliable—and neither are you!'"

It's because lie detector tests aren't considered reliable that they are illegal in almost every situation under U.S. law. The Employee Polygraph Protection Act of 1988 prohibits employers from requiring, requesting, or suggesting that employees or applicants take lie detector tests.[35] Employees can't be fired, disciplined, or discriminated against for refusing to take them. If you violate this law, you can be fined up to $10,000 by the Department of Labor and sued by the employee.

There are a few exceptions. This law, like many other federal laws, does not apply to federal, state, or local governments. Contractors of the Department of Defense, National Security Agency, and the FBI may be required to take polygraphs under certain circumstances.

Some private security companies can give polygraphs if their employees are hired to protect facilities that have a significant impact on the health and safety of citizens, such as nuclear power plants, toxic waste dumps, and banks.

Any employer can ask an employee to take a lie detector test *voluntarily* if

- It is part of an ongoing investigation into theft, embezzlement or industrial espionage, *and*
- You have a reasonable suspicion that the particular employee was involved, *and*
- You inform the employee of the right to refuse to take the test.

If employees refuse to take polygraphs, you cannot use their refusal to "prove" their guilt.

If a test is given, there are numerous requirements about what employees must be told, what questions can't be asked, and how the information obtained can be used. A competent polygraph examiner will be aware of the legal requirements. These exceptions don't apply if your state's law is more favorable to employees. For example, in California all polygraph tests are forbidden except for employees of state and local governments.

> *practical pointer:* How do you discover the truth if you can't give polygraph tests? Follow the investigation checklist in Chapter 3. Or hire an outside investigator. Many private investigators are expert at judging when people are lying. They also can bring more objectivity to your investigation.

Searching Employees' Personal Belongings

Remember the coke on the key ring? Was it legal for the supervisor to open the vial, take out the powder, and have it tested?

Because keys are personal belongings, they are considered to be in a highly personal zone of privacy. But in this case, we decided the employee didn't have a reasonable expectation of privacy because he voluntarily gave his keys to the boss.

If the employee wanted to fight it, he could argue he didn't voluntarily give his keys to the boss. He could claim he was coerced. Even if the supervisor didn't intend to intimidate him, perhaps the employee was afraid to say no. If that could be proved, then the search would have been illegal.

If the police conduct an illegal search, the "fruits" of the search can't be used later in court. By analogy, it would be illegal to fire an employee as a result of the fruits of an illegal search.

Searches of employees' purses, briefcases, pockets, and cars[36] without their consent can be justified only if you have a compelling reason, such as reasonable suspicion a particular employee is hiding stolen property or is in possession of drugs

Mundane business reasons also may justify searches. For example, in one case the employer, a lawyer, was allowed to search another lawyer's briefcase in order to retrieve some documents due in court.[37]

> *practical pointer:* Inform employees of your intent to search and do so in their presence. If this is not possible, the search should be witnessed and documented so you can't later be accused of indiscriminately rummaging through their personal things.

In the case of the coke on the key ring, I wish the supervisor had come to personnel as soon as he found it. We could have brought the employee in and confronted him with the vial. Then we could give him a choice: rehabilitation, investigation, or resignation. He could enter a rehabilitation program. He could raise a defense (such as coercion), which we then would investigate. Or he could resign. This would have avoided claims of invasion of privacy, theft, and wrongful termination.

Searching Company-Provided Items

Companies assign employees lockers, cars, desks, and filing cabinets so they can do their jobs. Searches of company-provided items are generally less of a threat to privacy. But the courts will treat company property like employees' personal property if that's how you treat it.

Company lockers are relatively private, because they usually are reserved for personal belongings. But where employees sign agreements or there is written company policy that lockers may be searched at any time, there is no violation of the right to privacy when the lockers are searched.[38] Where there is no written policy, how much privacy lockers are given depends upon who has keys.

If the company provides the locks and employees are issued keys or combinations, they don't have any real expectation of privacy. They know the company could go in and look at any time.

If the employee provides the lock, and doesn't give a key to the company, the employee has a higher expectation of privacy. In one Texas case, the court held it was an invasion of privacy for K-Mart to break open employees' locks to search every locker for items missing from the store.[39]

A company-provided desk may be protected from invasion of privacy. According to the U.S. Supreme Court, whether employees have a reasonable expectation of privacy in their desks is decided on a case-by-case basis. Where there is a high expectation of privacy, searches must be reasonably related to a legitimate purpose, either work-related or an investigation of misconduct.[40]

In some companies, it's not uncommon for coworkers or supervisors routinely to look in employees' desks for office supplies, missing files, or other work-related items. If anybody could go in the office and open the drawers, there is a low expectation of privacy. If the company routinely searches offices for security reasons, the employee can't reasonably expect privacy.[41]

But if the desk has a lock and the employee has the only key, the employee has a higher expectation of privacy. In an Illinois case, the fact that a manager had given his secretary the key to his credenza meant he lost his expectation of privacy.[42]

A company car assigned to one person may be very personal, depending upon who else has a set of keys. A car used by many others is less personal. But the glove compartment and the trunk might have more privacy if they are locked.

File drawers would seem to be the least personal, unless they are locked and the employee has the only key. Files themselves are considered company property unless marked "personal."

Even where you have the right to search, it is not unlimited. Clothes hanging in a company locker, purses inside desks, and briefcases inside company cars have higher expectations of privacy. They should not be opened without a compelling reason.

> *practical pointer:* Most companies want to protect themselves from employees walking in with weapons or walking out with inventory. You can have policies that reserve your right to search company property and personal belongings. You can keep duplicate keys for desks and lockers. That way you don't create an unreasonable expectation of privacy among employees.
>
> At the same time, your policy can affirm your respect of employees' privacy where it is unrelated to work performance. See the sample policy in the box.

Sample Privacy Policy

The company respects the privacy of all its employees. At the same time, the company must take reasonable measures to maintain security.

We reserve the right to inspect and search any person entering or leaving company property, including any briefcase, purse, lunchbox, toolbox, locker, vehicle, package, backpack, or other personal belongings brought onto or carried from company property.

Any stolen items, drugs, weapons, or other contraband found in such a search may lead to discipline, up to and including immediate termination.

The company is concerned with employee off-duty behavior only when it affects the employee's ability to perform the job or affects the reputation of the company in a major way. Only when the company's legitimate interests are substantially injured by an employee's off-duty behavior will that behavior result in disciplinary action.

Mail at Work

The privacy of mail received at work depends on the appearance of the mail and the company's practice or policy.

Generally, there is a low expectation of privacy in mail received at work that appears to relate to work. When employees are away from work, usually it is expected others will read and perhaps respond to their business mail and save personal notes for their return. Even when the employee is at the office, if a clerk routinely opens and sorts business mail, there is no expectation of privacy.

But mail marked "personal" or "confidential" has a high expectation of privacy. It cannot be opened without a compelling reason.[43] Not only is the privacy interest of your employee to be protected, but also the privacy of the sender.

What is the expectation of privacy in interoffice mail? It depends on how it is sent: face up, in an unsealed envelope, in a sealed envelope, or sealed and marked "personal."

practical pointer: You can have a policy prohibiting employees from receiving private mail at the office. The policy may be enforced by returning mail to the sender unopened. Such a policy does not justify opening the mail.

Computer Files and Electronic Mail

At the high-tech companies where I consult, people disagree about how files and mail on computers should be treated. Company policies state they reserve the right to search computer files. Yet all employees have their own private passwords (keys), and many programmers encrypt their files to prevent reading by others.

Electronic mail (E-mail) is correspondence among employees, just like interoffice mail. E-mail also can be sent between employees and outsiders, like U.S. mail. To a programmer, most E-mail is open for the world (and the employer) to see. But many nonprogrammers mistakenly believe passwords keep their E-mail confidential.

These companies also have policies prohibiting employees from reading each other's computer files and mail. Whether courts will say these policies create an expectation of privacy remains to be seen.

Absent a policy, should the company have the right to read E-mail or computer files? Several cases are in litigation as of January 1993 to determine this question. Company telephone answering machines and voice mailboxes probably also would be treated like mail.

Even if mail is private, you can read it if you have a compelling interest. For example, a company received a sexual harassment complaint from a woman who was sent pornographic E-mail by a man at work. Disgusted, she erased it. After several weeks, she decided to report him. The company had the right to search his computer files for that day to see if he had saved a copy of the offending message.

practical pointer: While searching files, whether on paper or computer, do not look in files clearly unrelated to the purpose of your search. Once you open a file, if it is not what you are looking for, immediately close it. Save items marked "personal" for last. Don't reveal personal information you learn to anyone else.

Monitoring Telephone Calls

Title III of the Omnibus Crime Control and Safe Streets Act of 1968 restricts when employers can listen to telephone calls, whether on an extension or through more sophisticated means.[44] The law applies to anyone who uses the phone.

Phone monitoring is allowed in the ordinary course of business.[45] For example, companies may monitor their customer service representatives, telemarketers, and order takers.

When monitoring calls for business reasons, you can't continue to listen once you realize a call is personal. Personal calls may be monitored only to determine if a call is personal or not. As one court put it, "a personal call may be intercepted in the ordinary course of business to determine its *nature* but never its *contents.*"[46]

Personal telephone calls can be listened to only if the employee is notified and consents to it.[47] This consent can't be implied just because the employee has been notified the company has the capability or practice of monitoring. Consent is implied only if the employee knows the line is being monitored at a particular time.

For example, in an Oklahoma case, the employee knew the line was always monitored. He had been warned repeatedly not to make personal phone calls on this line and other phones were provided for personal use. In that case, it was implied that he agreed to be monitored.[48]

In some states, not only do you have to notify the employee, you also must notify the person on the other end. Both sides must give their consent.[49]

Computer-Based Monitoring of Work Activities

Computer-based monitoring is the computerized collection, analysis and reporting of information about employees' work activities. Computer-generated statistics are used to evaluate part or all of the work performed by about 4 to 6 million office workers in the United States. Employees such as data entry clerks, reservation agents, and directory assistance operators have their keystrokes counted by their machines. Many more millions of employees have computer statistics collected on them every time they use their terminals, but these records currently are not used to evaluate their performance.

Computer monitoring may soon be restricted if any one of several bills proposed in Congress passes. One proposal restricts collecting information about employees by computer, telephone call accounting, or other forms of surveillance.

Also proposed is legislation that prohibits employers from collecting information that is not relevant to the employee's work performance. It requires companies to give employees notice of the monitoring and allow them access to the information collected.

Whether or not this particular legislation is passed, this type of monitoring is controversial and may be the subject of state laws. Computer monitoring also has led to claims for stress disability under worker's compensation (see Chapter 7).

Watching Employees with Undercover Investigators

Watching employees work is a time-honored method of supervision. There is no invasion of privacy in that, because the employee knows the supervisor is there.

Claims for invasion of privacy have been made where spotters, checkers, or undercover investigators were brought in by the employer to watch employees. For example, employees who work for retail stores and bus companies routinely have their performance checked by auditors posing as shoppers or bus riders.

As an alternative to drug testing, companies have hired undercover investigators to identify employees who are using, buying, or selling drugs on company property. To date, the use of undercover investigators has not been found to be an invasion of privacy.

Another form of undercover surveillance is the use of video cameras. If video cameras also capture sound and are used to monitor telephone calls, they are subject to the same rules as telephones under Title III.

Using video cameras with or without sound also would be restricted by the proposed legislation that covers computer monitoring.

Even if there are no special statutes, common law privacy would allow you to video employees only for work-related reasons and only if they are informed of it. Videos cannot be used in places where there is a reasonable expectation of privacy, such as in the bathroom.[50]

Following Employees Home

Since one of the most protected zones of privacy is our homes, you might think employers could not follow employees to their homes or watch them once there. But for the most part, shadowing employees has not been held to be invasion of privacy.

In one case, the employer, a private security company in Louisiana, watched who went to and from the employee's home, took down the license plate numbers, and ran license checks on each guest. This was held not to be an invasion of privacy because comings and goings are open for anyone in the public to see.[51]

How far an employer may be able to go is illustrated in a Michigan case. An employer hired two private investigating firms after an employee filed a claim for worker's compensation. The private investigators entered the employee's home under false pretenses to look around, watched him inside his home through the windows, and followed him to his doctor's office. They even flagged down the garbage truck and asked the driver about the employee's health.

This was held not to be invasion of privacy because, according to the court, the intrusions would not be objectionable to a reasonable person since the employer had a legitimate right to investigate the employee's claim that he was disabled.[52]

But even where the employer has the right to investigate, watch, trail, shadow, or keep employees under surveillance, it can't be done in an offensive or improper manner. For example, in one case it was held improper for investigators to enter a man's home under false pretenses and then use a concealed camera to photograph him.[53]

RETALIATING AGAINST EMPLOYEES WHO REFUSE TO GIVE INFORMATION

How to Question Employees Without Coercing

The U.S. Supreme Court has said it is a violation of the First Amendment right of freedom of speech to force employees to admit wrongdoing by threatening to fire them. A forced confession "is the antithesis of free choice to speak out or to remain silent."[54]

In addition to forcing confessions, courts in many states have held these situations are outrageous conduct and invasion of privacy:

> In Arkansas, an employee was interrogated for six hours by company officials who berated her, accused her of sexual improprieties, and would not allow her to eat, smoke, or defend herself against the accusations.[55]

> In Colorado, an exemplary employee was questioned in a small room for over two hours by a manager who yelled at her, made

her cry, and repeatedly accused her of theft despite her repeated denials.[56]

In Vermont, an employee was fired after he was coerced into signing a confession by being kept in a meeting for three hours without a break.[57]

practical pointers: When questioning an employee, never make threats, such as "If you don't confess, you'll be fired." At the same time, don't make promises of leniency or other favors if the employee cooperates.

The purpose of an interrogation is to get information. The disciplinary action resulting from an interrogation is a separate matter. It's best if the person questioning employees is not in a position to make the decision to terminate or discipline them.

There should never be a show of force. A normal speaking tone should be used.

Have a witness, and if the employee agrees, tape the meeting. This will avoid later questions of who is telling the truth about what happened during the interrogation.

A confession or other statement should be written by the employee, in his or her handwriting. Preparing a statement for the employee to sign smacks of coercion.

The room in which the interrogation is conducted should not be small, hot, or cold. It should have normal lighting. Tell the employee he or she can leave at any time and offer frequent breaks.

Wrongful Termination and Invasion of Privacy

When it is an illegal invasion of privacy to collect information, an employee who is fired for refusing to go along with it may be able to sue for wrongful termination in addition to invasion of privacy.

A California employer required all employees to take a pupillary reaction eye test for drugs. The test involved shining a light in the employee's eyes and watching the reaction. If the pupils dilate, then the employee is considered possibly under the influence of drugs and is sent for urinalysis.

In California, random drug tests of current employees in nonsensitive positions are illegal. In this case, the employee refused to allow the employer to shine the light in his eyes. He was terminated. The court held this was an invasion of privacy and wrongful termination.[58]

It is also a wrongful termination where the employee is fired for refusing to violate another person's privacy. For example, a Maryland apartment manager was asked by his boss to enter tenants' apartments without their permission and to search their papers for phone numbers, salary records, and other private information. He refused and was fired. He was allowed to sue for wrongful termination.[59]

Using Private Information Against an Employee

Free Speech in the Workplace

Forty-three state constitutions have provisions guaranteeing free speech.[60] This is the principle that employees can't be discriminated against for what they say, nor can they be forced to support something against their will. To date, the courts have held these Constitutional provisions apply only to government employees.

Some states have statutes that directly protect employees' freedom of speech. Connecticut has a statute that guarantees free speech in the workplace. It applies to any employer, government or not, who disciplines or discharges an employee for exercising free speech.[61]

The U.S. Supreme Court has held that the Republican Party cannot force its own employees to belong to the party in order to be hired, promoted, or transferred. That would have a chilling effect on employees' freedom of speech and association.[62]

In a Pennsylvania case, an insurance company employee was terminated because he refused to lobby for a no-fault law favored by his employer. This was held to be an invasion of his privacy and freedom of speech.[63]

In another case, an employee of the U.S. Postal Service reported mail violations to her congressman. When the congressman asked the post office about her charges, the post office told him she also had filed a sex discrimination claim with the Equal Employment Opportunity Commission (EEOC). This was held a violation of her privacy rights.[64]

What are the limits of free speech? In the case of government employees, the courts have distinguished between speaking on matters of public interest versus speaking on matters of private concern. Comment on public issues is protected. But if I speak up about my paycheck, my disputes with the boss, or other personal issues, my speech is not protected.

Employers may restrict employees' speech or public issues if it substantially interferes with their job performance or their working relationships. But this must be proven, not assumed. That's why the Texas woman who worked for the sheriff couldn't be fired for her remark about shooting President Reagan. It was a matter of public interest, and there was no evidence her comment caused disruption.

Sexual Orientation Protection

Discrimination against gay men, lesbians, bisexuals, heterosexuals, and other sexual orientations is illegal only in a few places. Under federal regulations, a U.S. government employee can't be dismissed solely because of sexual orientation.[65] However, the regulations say that homosexuality combined with other factors will justify discharge.

What other factors justify discharge? According to the courts, people are unsuitable for federal employment if their homosexual conduct affects their job performance. But the employer can't assume, without any evidence, that gays bring the agency into public contempt or embarrassment.

How would homosexual conduct indicate someone's unfitness for duty? One court noted some of the ways. If employees are in security-sensitive positions, they might be susceptible to blackmail. According to the court, homosexuality might be evidence of an unstable personality, thus making people who are gay unsuited for certain types of work. If employees make offensive overtures while on the job, if their off-duty conduct is notorious, or if other employees and the public react negatively, their abilities to perform their official functions may be affected.[66]

For nongovernment employees, there are even fewer protections. Sex discrimination laws do not protect people who are gay. Only six states and the District of Columbia prohibit discrimination on the basis of sexual orientation: California, Connecticut, Hawaii, Massachusetts, New Jersey, and Wisconsin.[67] New York bans discrimination against gays in state employment.[68] Five of the seven states made discrimination illegal between 1989 and 1992.

Cities and counties have passed local ordinances when state legislatures are not. Those that have some prohibition of sexual orientation discrimination are listed in the box.[69]

Municipal Gay Rights Ordinances

Arizona: Tuscon
California: Berkeley, Cupertino, Davis, Laguna Beach, Mountain
    View, Oakland, Palo Alto, Sacramento, San Francisco, San
    Jose, Santa Barbara, Santa Cruz, West Hollywood
Connecticut: Hartford
Georgia: Atlanta
Illinois: Champaign, Chicago, Evanston, Urbana
Indiana: Bloomington
Iowa: Iowa City
Michigan: Ann Arbor, Detroit, East Lansing, Ingham County,
    Lansing, Saginaw
Minnesota: Hennepin County, Mankato, Marshall, Minneapolis
New York: Alfred, Buffalo, Ithaca, New York, Rochester, Troy
North Carolina: Chapel Hill, Durham, Raleigh
Ohio: Columbus, Cuyahoga, Yellow Springs
Oregon: Portland
Pennsylvania: Harrisburg, Philadelphia
Texas: Austin
Washington: Callam County, King County, Olympia, Pullman,
    Seattle

Where such laws don't exist, gay employees have argued that discrimination against them should be prohibited because it is an invasion of their privacy or otherwise unconstitutional.

So far, these arguments rarely have been successful. The California Supreme Court has held that an employer can't discriminate against employees who the company knows are gay because of their political activities.[70] In New York, marching as a gay pride contingent in a municipal parade has been held protected political speech.[71] In other cases, wearing a political button or holding a gay party have been held to be political speech and therefore protected.

A California court of appeals has held that asking questions about a person's sexual orientation is a violation of the state Constitution's privacy clause, even if the employee doesn't answer the questions.[72]

As of January 1993 Congress is debating whether to lift the ban against gays in the military. The courts have upheld the current regulations which allow people who are gay to be excluded from jobs requiring U.S. government security clearances. Discharging gays and lesbians from the military has been upheld in almost every case. Where the discharge has not been upheld, it has been because of a technical or procedural issue.

In one case, the Army was informed that a soldier was gay, but allowed him to reenlist a number of times. Finally, they discharged him. The court of appeals held the Army was prevented from discharging him because by allowing him to reenlist, he was led to believe they would not enforce their antigay policy.[73] The Air Force also has been ordered to justify its discharge of a gay airman with an outstanding military service record.[74]

Teachers for the most part have not been protected from sexual orientation discrimination. Whenever the teacher's homosexuality becomes notorious, as a result of an arrest, public advocacy of the gay life-style, or applying for a marriage license, the discharge has been upheld.

Where the homosexuality is purely private, a few courts have allowed teachers who were fired to be reinstated.[75] A court in Kansas held in 1991 that a school board cannot consider the sexual orientation of a teacher in making a hiring decision.[76]

In the 1990s, the trend is toward recognizing the rights of people who are gay.

Arrest Record: Is It Relevant to the Job?

Some states have statutes that prohibit employers from considering the fact that an employee has an arrest record. Other statutes allow considering convictions, although convictions of minor offenses may not be used.

The fact that an employee is arrested or even convicted of a crime while employed may not be relevant to the job. If not, using that private fact about them to take an adverse employment action may be invasion of privacy.

Arlene Golden was a high school guidance counselor in West Virginia. She was shopping at a local mall when she learned her daughter had wrecked her car. Mrs. Golden hurriedly left the store, unconsciously putting some items in her purse as she did. She was stopped and arrested for shoplifting. She pleaded no contest and was fined $100 for petty theft. She was then terminated by the school board for "a serious act of immorality."

The court held that a misdemeanor conviction by itself was not immoral.[77] The court said the employer must show there is a relationship between the arrest and the job duties. In this case, she couldn't be fired unless her conduct indicated she was unfit to be a counselor. Or her behavior must have impaired or threatened the welfare of the school community because it had become the subject of notoriety.

Even where there is publicity about an arrest and conviction, there still may not be sufficient notoriety to justify termination. In a West Virginia case, a substitute teacher was found guilty of illegal possession of marijuana in his home. This was held not sufficiently job related to justify his termination even though the charges were publicized.[78]

In contrast, if the arrest is specifically related to the job, the employer may be justified in terminating on that basis. For example, United Parcel Service (UPS) terminated a driver who was charged with theft while making a delivery to a UPS customer. He was arrested but freed pending trial.

The driver was questioned by his superiors about the incident. Based on his responses, he was terminated. Later, he was acquitted of the criminal charges and applied for reinstatement. UPS refused to rehire him. A Pennsylvania court upheld the company. Given the sensitive nature of UPS delivery jobs, the company had a legitimate interest in maintaining even the appearance of honesty among its employees.[79]

Injuring Another's Reputation: Defamation and False Light

Defamation is the general term for any untrue statement which injures the reputation of a person. Written lies are called libel; spoken untruths are slander.

If you tell your boss about an employee's poor work performance so you can get advice on how to handle the problem, anything you say is probably privileged. That means you can't be sued, even for lying, if you limit your comments to people who need to know and discuss only the employee's work performance.

Comments made about an employee's work performance to people who don't need to know (coworkers, for example) may lead to a defamation claim. Comments about an employee's personal life—made to anyone—are likely to result in a lawsuit.

False light invasion of privacy is like defamation, but the two are not identical. Whereas defamation is an untrue statement, false light usually consists of actions that are interpreted to injure the reputation of the victim.[80]

For example, when Merrill Lynch terminated a trader on the Chicago Board of Trade, they put him in a false light. Management made a surprise visit to his office, refused to allow him to speak to his staff, prevented him from taking all his personal belongings, and escorted him out of the building. They interrogated employees and others about entries in his travel and entertainment expense account. All these actions implied that he was terminated for gross misconduct, when in fact he was not. An Illinois court held he was put in a false light.[81]

Using Someone's Name or Picture Without Permission

Appropriation is using someone else's name or picture without their permission.[82] For example, a Vermont employer put an employee's name and picture in a newspaper ad with the words, "it has been exciting and reassuring to know that Continental continues to expand its equipment and services to meet its obligation to serve you." Because she had never said this, it was held invasion of privacy by appropriation.[83]

Another example of appropriation is seen in this Far Side cartoon.

THE FAR SIDE   By GARY LARSON

© 1986 Universal Press Syndicate

"Coincidence, ladies and gentlemen? Coincidence that my client just *happened* to live across from the A-1 Mask Co., just *happened* to walk by their office windows each day, and they, in turn, just *happened* to stumble across this new design?"

Disclosing Private Information to Others

Medical Information: When to Keep Quiet and When to Tell

Medical information and employee medical records are "classically a private interest."[84] They are protected under the common law in almost every state. Some states, such as California, also have statutes protecting the confidentiality of medical information.[85]

Courts in some states, such as Oklahoma,[86] follow the old rule that an employee cannot sue for invasion of privacy unless the confidential information is publicized to a large number of people. But the trend is to protect employees' medical information from being disclosed to even one person.

Medical information comes to the attention of managers in a number of ways. Employees often volunteer it in the course of calling in sick, requesting a leave of absence, or asking for light-duty work. But just because they tell you, doesn't mean you can tell anyone else, unless that other person has a legitimate need to know.

If you promise to keep medical information confidential, you have a duty to do so. For example, an Illinois employee told the company nurse that she had undergone a mastectomy. The nurse promised she would keep the information confidential, but later revealed it to one other employee. The court held the company could be liable for invasion of privacy.[87]

Even when the information is very sensitive, it may be revealed to protect the safety of others. In one case, an employee was diagnosed as suicidal, homicidal, and potentially dangerous to other employees. His supervisor told his union representative. The West Virginia court held that communicating the information was in the interest of the employer and employees and was therefore not an invasion of privacy.[88]

Even if employees' safety is not directly threatened, the employer may have a legitimate reason for revealing medical information. A Massachusetts supervisor sent a memo to Personnel, revealing an employee had been diagnosed by the company doctor as paranoid. This was held not to be an invasion of privacy because management needed the information to evaluate the employee's ability to continue working.[89]

In another case, a woman who worked in a Mississippi nuclear power plant fainted while doing decontamination work. Her coworkers were concerned she had radiation sickness and were afraid they might become ill too. The supervisor told them the coworker had not fainted because of radiation but because of a recent hysterectomy. This was held not to be an invasion of privacy because the coworkers had a legitimate interest in the information.[90]

If employees don't guard their own medical information, it is no longer confidential and can be revealed to others. In a recent Kansas case, a woman told seven friends she was entering a drug and alcohol treatment center. She did not ask them to keep the information confidential. She also told her supervisor he could "tell anyone who asked." The company then sent a memo to 110 employees informing them of her treatment. This was held not to be an invasion of privacy because it was no longer a private fact.[91]

Employers often have a legitimate reason to inquire about an employee's medical condition. Before you ask a doctor to tell you about an employee's medical condition, you may need a release. This is an agreement signed by the employee authorizing you to talk to the doctor.

There is a split among courts about whether a release is needed for an employer to talk about an employee with the *company* doctor or nurse. In a Massachusetts case, a release was not required.[92] In Ohio, a release has been held necessary.[93]

You must get releases from employees before you can contact their own doctors. Once you have a release, you must scrupulously follow its terms.

An Oregon case demonstrates how narrowly courts construe medical releases. An employee allowed her psychiatrist to write a letter to her employer stating she needed a two-week medical leave due to severe anxiety neurosis. The company's Employee Assistance Plan (EAP) representative then met with the psychiatrist to follow up, asking if the employee would be able to continue her employment. The court held this was invasion of privacy, because the employee had not authorized the follow-up visit.[94]

Information given by an employee to a counselor or doctor who is part of the company's EAP is confidential and can't be revealed to the employer.

Preemployment Medical Exams

Preemployment medical exams are allowed under the law to ensure applicants are fit for duty. Under the ADA a medical examination cannot be required before an offer of employment is made. Instead, you make an employment offer contingent on the applicant passing the medical exam.

The doctor who conducts the examination should have an accurate job description. Better still, the doctor actually should see the work performed in jobs that are physically demanding.

The doctor will be able to ask detailed questions about the applicant's medical history that would be illegal if asked by the company. But the doctor's report should not reveal this information to the company. Instead, it should state the applicant is able to work, unable to work, or able to work with restrictions.

The restrictions should be spelled out but not, in most cases, the reasons for the restrictions. For example, if an applicant can't lift more than 30 pounds due to a bad back, the report should merely state, "no lifting over 30 pounds."

In the case of applicants who are disabled, the doctor can reveal information to the employer which would be necessary to know in case of an emergency.

Psychological exams also are allowed in order to determine fitness for duty. These are allowed both before hiring or after employment begins, if there is a reasonable belief that an employee poses a hazard to a safe and healthy work environment.[95] As with physicals, the psychotherapist's report should state only that the individual is able to work, unable to work, or able to work with restrictions.

Personnel Files and Information

A federal law known as the Privacy Act limits the type of information federal agencies, the military, and government corporations may maintain on their employees.[96]

Thirty-five states have laws about personnel files. Most require employers to give employees access to their own files within a reasonable time after they request it—usually within seven days. These statutes generally apply both to employees and former employees.

Michigan and Pennsylvania allow employees to correct inaccurate information contained in their files. New Hampshire allows employees to copy their entire file; California employees are entitled only to copies of documents they sign.

Several states protect the privacy of other people who are mentioned in employees' personnel files. For example, Delaware allows companies not to give employees copies of letters of reference and reports of criminal investigations.

Wisconsin allows employers to keep confidential business information contained in personnel files if it relates to staff management planning (e.g., comparative rankings of employees, staffing projections).

As a manager, you may look into an employee's personnel file if you have a legitimate business reason. You may need to look at the last performance appraisal to measure progress over the year. You may have to check attendance records, vacation time accrued, or past warnings.

While looking for legitimate information, you might inadvertently see private information. An employee's claim for worker's compensation includes medical information. A request for insurance benefits for an employee, spouse, or dependent may contain confidential information. You should not read this confidential information, and you should not reveal it to others.

An employer must be cautious about revealing to other employees the reason employees have been terminated. They have a right to privacy. But employers often want to publicize why employees have been terminated so other employees will know that the company's rules are enforced.

A Wisconsin employer printed in the company newsletter the names of employees leaving employment and the reasons for their terminations. Included were such damaging reasons as "falsification of application." The court allowed it, saying the employer had a legitimate interest in letting employees know why a coworker was no longer employed.[97]

But the company can't announce it to people who have no reason to know. A California employer posted the reasons for an employee's termination in a public place that could be seen not only by coworkers but also members of the general public. This was held to be invasion of privacy.[98]

> *practical pointers:* An employee's personnel file should be kept locked up. Personnel files should be restricted to employees who have a need to see them. Medical information, including worker's compensation claims, insurance forms, and the like, should be kept in a separate file, or at least segregated within the file.

> You should not send copies of the entire personnel file to outsiders. For example, your worker's compensation carrier might ask for the personnel file to investigate an employee's past claims history. You should only give them information relevant to their investigation. There is a lot of information in files that isn't relevant, such as performance appraisals, disciplinary warnings and requests for (unrelated) sick days.

> Some supervisors keep a working file on employees with brief documentation of events that haven't resulted in any action. You cant hide documentation that you've used to make a decision. Your backup documentation for a warning should be in the official personnel file. But ongoing documentation that hasn't resulted in a poor performance appraisal, warning, demotion, or other ad-

verse employment decision generally can be kept separately and need not be shown to the employee.

Releasing an Employee's Home Address and Phone

A person's home address would seem to be very private. However, courts routinely have allowed employers to disclose the names and addresses of their employees to labor unions who are attempting to organize their workers. This is not usually an invasion of privacy because address is not considered a private matter—anyone could follow you home and see it.[99]

However, it also may depend on who requests the address. We would expect the employer not to give information to others without inquiring into whether they have a legitimate need for the information.

The Oregon Supreme Court held it was an invasion of privacy to give out a home address where the individual specifically had requested it not be, because she was being harassed. The court said this was personal information, which it defined as information which "normally would not be shared with strangers."[100]

An employee's home phone number has been held private by a court in Illinois.[101]

INFRINGING ON AN EMPLOYEE'S DIGNITY

Asking Personal Questions

Asking personal questions has been held to be invasion of privacy. For example, the Alabama Supreme Court found invasion of privacy in a case where a woman janitor was sexually harassed by the owner of the company. Within a few weeks of starting her job, he called her into his office and asked how she was getting along with her husband. A few days later, he again called her into his office, locked the door, and asked her how often and in what positions she and her husband had sex.

He continued this intrusive interrogation for weeks and finally demanded she have oral sex with him. She sued for sexual harassment. She also sued for invasion of privacy. The court held it was invasion of privacy merely to be asked the questions. The fact that she didn't answer them did not make them any less intrusive.[102]

Many courts have held that law enforcement and other government employees can't be forced to reveal personal information. Questions to police officers about personal and family history[103] and sexual history[104] have been held to invade privacy.

Relationship Restrictions

The courts have protected the right of government employees to enjoy freedom in their relationships.

The U.S. Supreme Court has held it was an invasion of privacy to dismiss a teacher who was getting a divorce.[105] Other courts have said police officers and presumably other government employees cannot be dismissed for these reasons:

Dating the daughter of a known mobster[106]

Having a past affair with another police officer[107]

Living with an unmarried woman[108]

Living with an 18-year-old girl.[109]

In a few cases, courts have upheld dismissals that were rationally related to legitimate government interests. For example, a rule prohibiting police officers from living with each other was held reasonable to maintain the discipline necessary in a quasi-military unit.[110]

A Pennsylvania court allowed termination of a bail commissioner because his wife became a political party ward. This was justified by the compelling state interest for the bail commissioner to avoid even the appearance of partisanship.[111]

Historically, nongovernment employees have received much less protection. Companies have been allowed to dismiss employees for these reasons:

Having extra marital affairs[112]

Attending a business convention with someone not a spouse[113]

Becoming engaged to be married[114]

Dating coworkers.[115]

But despite these cases, the recent trend is to expand employees' relationship rights.

The leading case in the country is California's *Rulon-Miller* v. *IBM*.[116] In this case, a saleswoman in the typewriter division was fired for dating a man who worked for a competitor of IBM computers. She did not have access to IBM trade secrets, and there was no evidence she was giving him any confidential information. In fact, he played on the IBM softball team, so he knew many IBM employees.

IBM had a written policy expressly guaranteeing employees the right to privacy. The policy provided in part,

> We have concern with an employee's off-the-job behavior only when it reduces his ability to perform regular job assignments, interferes with the job performance of other employees, or if his outside behavior affects the reputation of the company in a major way. . . . Action should be taken only when a legitimate interest of the company is injured or jeopardized. Furthermore, the damage must be clear beyond a reasonable doubt. . . .

The court held that Rulon-Miller had a privacy right to date whoever she wished as long as it was not to the detriment of IBM.

Similarly, a New Jersey court held that an employee could not be fired as a result of extramarital sexual activities if the company would have to intrude upon his privacy to enforce its rule prohibiting affairs.[117]

Courts also have found invasion of privacy where employees have been harassed for interracial relationships. An Indiana court held this because of the strong public policy against race discrimination.[118]

Life-style Discrimination

Employers concerned about rising health care costs in recent years have adopted life-style restrictions. Companies have refused to hire applicants and have fired employees who are overweight, smoke cigarettes, have high cholesterol, or engage in high-risk activities such as sky-diving. Most of these restrictions have not been ruled on by the courts.

Requiring employees not to exceed maximum weight standards have been upheld for the most part. The courts have not been persuaded by statistics that show women are disproportionately excluded by various weight standards. The courts have held that weight is not immutable, but a characteristic that can be changed.[119] Therefore, they have held it is not deserving of protection, unless it is specifically protected by law, as in Wisconsin, or it is caused by or related to a disability (Chapter 2).

Seven states have laws prohibiting life-style discrimination unless it is job related: Colorado, Kentucky, Oregon, Rhode Island, South Carolina, Tennessee, and Virginia. Other states prohibit discrimination against smokers; see Chapter 7.

Establishing Dress Codes

Establishing appearance standards or dress codes has long been held to be the right of the employer. Today, in some localities, this historic right is being challenged.

The general rule still is that employers have the right to set appearance standards. Dress codes have been upheld that require employees to "achieve the Brooks Brothers look" as long as it was applied to men and women equally.[120]

Dress codes have been struck down by courts where they are discriminatory. In one case, a retail store allowed male salesclerks to wear street clothes, but required female salesclerks to wear uniform smocks over their clothes. The court held this was illegal sex discrimination.[121]

But simply having different requirements for men and women is not necessarily sex discrimination. Courts recognize that in the professional world, women wear earrings and men don't. Men wear pants and women wear skirts. Men wear neckties and women don't. These distinctions have not been held to be discriminatory, because they do not put an undue burden on either sex.

In 1990, an Oregon court allowed a company to fire a male employee for refusing to take off an earring, even though women were allowed to wear them.[122]

A schoolteacher who was fired for wearing short skirts lost her case. The court held the school had administrative reasons that made the dress code necessary.[123] A woman who wore tank tops to work could be fired for wearing provocative clothes.[124]

A woman attorney couldn't complain of sex discrimination when her boss said her dress was "too flashy" and she should tone down her style, because male attorneys probably were given similar advice.[125]

In line with these cases, the U.S. Supreme Court came to a similar result when it ruled on appearance standards in a 1990 case.[126] Ann Hopkins was an associate accountant at Price Waterhouse. Of the 88 people in her class at PW, she was ranked number one in terms of performance. Despite that, she was one of the few who was not offered a partnership.

Among the reasons given were that she didn't dress femininely. In finding that Ms. Hopkins had been discriminated against, the Supreme Court noted it was unlikely that any man had been denied partnership on this basis. However, if the employer had said she didn't look "professional," perhaps the result would have been different.

Hair and beard regulations also have had mixed success. Short hair for men has been upheld for the military, including reservists.[127] An airline was allowed to prohibit employees from wearing cornrows.[128] But teachers in Mississippi successfully challenged hair and beard regulations, on the theory that they were not reasonably related to the job.[129]

Washington, D.C., and Howard County, Maryland, have ordinances that prohibit discrimination on the basis of physical appearance. These ordinances allow employers to have dress codes for legitimate business reasons but prohibit them from applying their dress codes inconsistently.

Privacy Issues of the Future

Some experts say that the next big areas of threat to our rights to privacy are genetic testing and the employer's use of subliminal messages.

What about going to the bathroom? The Japanese currently have on the market a smart toilet that analyzes our seat print and what we eliminate. It can create a complete report showing our current health, everything from blood sugar level to heart rate.[130] What an invasion of privacy if an employer decided to install these!

Other privacy issues include handwriting analysis and psychological tests. These are covered in Chapter 5, on hiring. The rights of smokers and people with AIDS are covered in Chapter 7, on safety.

Money Damages: How Much Is at Stake?

If an employee's privacy is invaded, what are the available damages? Although the law does not protect the "neurotically thin-skinned,"[131] there does not have to be any economic loss, or even any discovery of private information, for employees to win damages.

They don't have to show they were embarrassed or suffered emotional injury. It is enough that their privacy was invaded. As a New Hampshire court put it, an invasion of privacy "impairs the mental peace and comfort of the individual and may produce suffering more acute than that produced by a mere bodily injury."[132]

According to one study, during the period from 1985 to 1988, 72% of the privacy cases were won by employees. The average jury award was $375,307.[133]

Six Principles that Will Help Prevent Invasion of Privacy

There are six general principles that you can adopt to prevent invasion of privacy:

1. Establish reasonable work standards and objectively measure employees against them.
2. Advise employees in advance about what information is collected, why and how.
3. Guarantee information will not be disseminated to outsiders without the employee's consent.
4. Give employees access to records and opportunity to correct inaccuracies.
5. Collect information only that is relevant to the job.
6. Gather information in the least intrusive way possible.[134]

Joseph R. Grodin is a former California Supreme Court justice who is a leading thinker in the field of privacy. He believes that privacy is a fundamental principle of U.S. law. He says the U.S. Constitution is based on the idea that the individual surrenders to government only what is reasonably necessary to be governed. Similarly, employees should be required to give up only what is necessary for the employer to do business.[135]

Privacy is precious. We should do all we can to protect the privacy of others. It is by protecting the privacy of others that we protect ourselves.

Chapter 5

HOW TO HIRE THE BEST

and Prevent Suits from the Rest

I once interviewed a woman for a job as a trial lawyer. My first impression was that she was overweight, slovenly, and ugly. As soon as I saw her, I knew she could never represent my firm in front of a jury. I couldn't wait to get that interview over with.

Fortunately, my associate also was in the room. He asked her some questions about her experience. She started talking about her past victories in court. Her face lit up as she described in vivid detail the trials she had won.

After listening to her for about 15 minutes, I no longer remembered what she looked like. She was a masterful storyteller. She held us spellbound. She was a perfect trial lawyer.

After she left, I turned to my associate, "She doesn't exactly have the image I was looking for." He said, "At first I noticed that, but as she talked I saw all her clients. I saw animals come alive as she described a 'witness as prickly as a raccoon.' She was wonderful! We should hire her."

Unfortunately, I didn't listen to him. Instead, I spent days checking and rechecking her references, only to find out she walked on water. One of her former employers was willing to pay for her to commute back to Atlanta every week!

Still, I agonized. I put off making the decision for weeks. Finally, I decided to offer her the job. But when I called, she said she hadn't been able to wait. She took another job! I lost a terrific employee because of my first impression. If instead I had judged her strictly by the results of the interview and references, I would have made the correct decision in time.

The same hiring techniques that make good legal sense also make good business sense.

In the previous chapters you learned about the laws of discrimination, wrongful termination, and privacy. All these laws impact how you conduct interviews for hiring and promoting employees. In this chapter, you will learn the legal requirements for hiring and some practical ideas for finding the best qualified candidates.

Hiring Checklist

- Write a job description.
- Advertise the opening.
- Post the job internally.
- Contact recruiting agencies.
- Ensure application forms are legal.
- Accept resumes.
- Screen applicants.
- Write out interview questions.
- Conduct interviews.
- Give necessary tests.
- Perform background checks.
- Call references.
- Write the offer letter.
- Contact rejected applicants.
- Begin employment of the new employee.

HOW TO WRITE AN ACCURATE AND COMPREHENSIVE JOB DESCRIPTION

Before you hire someone, decide what knowledge, skills, and abilities you need. Yes, it's obvious. It's common sense. But it's rarely done, and when it is, it's done wrong.

First, get a job description. Not one of those things that some committee wrote years ago, but a real description of the job as it currently is performed.

The best person to write it is the one doing the job now. Have the employee keep a time log for a few weeks to get an accurate picture of the true job functions.

Once you have the incumbent's description, you may want to change it. Perhaps the current employee has been spending more time in one area than you'd like. Perhaps he or she has weaknesses you want to eliminate with the next employee.

You can restructure the job however you like as long as you have a business necessity. Justify in writing your legitimate business reasons for making changes.

Job descriptions not only should be accurate, they also should be comprehensive. The Americans with Disabilities Act (ADA) requires you to justify hiring decisions based on the essential functions of the job. If those essential functions are written in a job description, they are presumed valid. Job descriptions should list the physical and mental requirements of the job, including attendance, hours of work, travel, and paperwork.

Hiring Standards: Are They Permitted?

Can your job description include the sex, height, or age of the ideal candidate? Yes, in some cases.

After two years of law school, my best friend dropped out and moved from San Francisco to Santa Barbara. At first, she was picky about what kind of job she would accept. After a few weeks, she would take any job that would use her brains. She couldn't find one. One day she ripped this ad out of the paper to show me how desperately hard it was for her, at age 30, to find a job:

WANTED

3 Santa Barbara Girls

between the ages of 18 and 25, for promotional handout and display at local theaters in conjunction with the showing of "Asian Paradise" sponsored by Surfer Magazine. Must be young and athletic with outgoing personalities. Arrive in front of the Yacht Club. Please wear beach attire.

As depressed as she was about this ad, I had to tell my friend it was completely legal. Yes, it discriminates on the basis of sex and age and probably race, too. But discrimination is allowed if there is a bona fide occupational qualification (BFOQ).

A BFOQ says the purpose of the job is to fulfill a stereotype. Most

BFOQs are in the entertainment industry. Actors and models are picked *because of* the way they look. An international restaurant can hire only ethnic employees in keeping with its theme. The costumed characters at an amusement park must be certain heights and weights so they can fit into their outfits.

Another example of a BFOQ is in the making of the radar dish for the AWACS airplane. To build it required people who were short. Height then was a business necessity.

Similarly, firefighters must be in top physical condition because we want them to be able to carry adults out of burning buildings when the need arises. Peace officers on the front line must be able to run, climb, and crawl, even if they rarely actually do it. For those jobs, hiring physically fit applicants is a business necessity. (But if those employees become disabled after they get line experience, the employer may be required to reasonably accommodate them in other jobs.)

An employer can't use hiring standards that exclude disabled people unless the standards are job related. Job-related standards must be validated by an industrial psychologist or by your observation. Here are some examples of job requirements that exclude disabled people, and when they may be allowed:

> *Typing:* A person who is hired to type can be required to type. On the other hand, a person being hired for a professional job that requires the use of a computer may not require the same level of typing skills; in fact, although most people in that position type, perhaps there is no reason why a person could not perform those functions in another way. Voice recognition computers are here now. Soon typing will be unnecessary.

> *Lifting Requirements:* ("must be able to lift 30 pounds"): If the job requires lifting 30 pounds once a year, it hardly seems fair to make it a requirement. But it is legal to have a requirement if in fact lifting is required regularly, say, once a week or more. Even then, is it absolutely essential that the person you are hiring do it? Or is there some other way the job could be done? Could another employee do the lifting? Is there a forklift? Consider all the alternatives. If you still need someone who can lift, then you have a legitimate business reason.

The bottom line on hiring standards is this: make sure you have a business necessity.

Hiring to Accommodate Customer Preference

Can you limit who you hire because of what your customers prefer? The airlines argued in many early cases that their customers preferred young, slim, unmarried women flight attendants. The courts refused to accept these as BFOQs. The purpose of an airline is to deliver passengers safely, not to sexually titillate them.[1]

The customer preference argument today is used by companies hiring in the United States for employees to work overseas. Many of my clients argue they can't hire women to work in Japan, because they won't be accepted by the Japanese. This argument ignores the facts. Women, both native Japanese and U.S.-born, have won acceptance in Japan and do hold positions of responsibility. As one savvy manager told me, "A woman from the U.S. is accepted the same as any other *gaijin* (foreigner) in Japan."

You can have neutral requirements if they are necessary for you to do business. For example, if you are hiring people to work in Japan, you can require them to be fluent speakers of Japanese and have extensive work experience in that country.

The only time international customers' preferences have been accepted is where that preference has the force of law. For example, Saudi Arabian law forbids non-Moslems to enter Mecca on penalty of death. A company that hired helicopter pilots to fly to Mecca required them to be adherents of or convert to the Moslem religion. This was upheld.[2]

Contrast that to a case where a hospital sent doctors to Saudi Arabia. Because of the history of anti-Zionist statements made by officials of the Saudi Arabian government, the hospital refused to send two Jewish doctors there. The court held this was not allowed. There was no evidence that the Saudi government would refuse to give American Jewish doctors work permits. In fact, other hospitals working in Saudi Arabia had negotiated nondiscrimination clauses in their agreements with the government.[3]

Can foreign companies doing business in the United States reserve top positions for foreign nationals? Yes, in some cases. Although the anti-discrimination laws apply to all companies doing business in the United States, they are overridden by Friendship, Commerce and Navigation Treaties entered by various countries with the United States.

For example the treaties between the U. S. and both Japan and Korea provide, "Nationals and companies of either [country] shall be permitted to engage, within the territories of the other [country] . . . executive personnel . . . and other specialists of their choice." These treaties have been held to allow foreign companies to save their top positions for people from their own countries.[4]

TIPS ON ADVERTISING THE OPENING

Once the job description is completed, you will advertise the position. There are legal requirements for ads, as well as some practical considerations.

Ads should never state a preference for age, sex, race, or other protected classification, unless it is a BFOQ. If you aren't in the entertainment business, the BFOQ probably doesn't apply.

Avoid descriptions of the job or your company that could lead to charges of discrimination, such as

Don't Use	Use
young (person, company)	high energy
recent grad	up-to-date knowledge
student	part-timer
coat and tie	professional appearance
Girl Friday	administrative assistant
couple	two-person job
married	stable
Hispanic	Spanish-speaking
salesman	sales representative
draftsman	draftsperson

As discussed in the discrimination section, it is illegal to require a college (or high school) degree without also considering experience. All ads should read "degree or equivalent experience." You decide what is "equivalent." Just be reasonable.

Define the amount of experience you want without putting an upper limit on it. For example, "3 to 5 years of experience" almost guarantees your applicants will be younger. Instead, say "3-plus years." This way you will not exclude older people who have more experience but who have chosen to take less challenging jobs.

So far, we've covered ads from the perspective of preventing discrimination lawsuits. Your job ads also can be used against you in a future wrongful termination case. They should be written carefully to avoid any appearance of offering long-term employment.

I once saw two ads for accountants in *The New York Times*. One offered "partnership potential." The other said, "career position." The first one offers only the hope of long-term employment; the second one virtually promises longevity. It takes a lifetime to have a career. And I can't be fired from a career, can I?

As a practical matter, it's a good idea to put any major negatives about the job in the ad. There is no reason for you to be inundated with resumes if many people wouldn't want the job on your terms.

One manager told me all the salaried employees in his area were required to work 60 hours a week. He said, "I don't tell applicants that, because then they wouldn't want to work here!" Yet he expressed surprise about the number of people who quit shortly after he hired them.

POSTING REQUIREMENTS

Postings are essentially internal advertisements. You are recruiting people from within the company rather than from the outside. Postings are subject to the same rules as advertisements.

Some companies don't post internal openings at all, others post some, and a few post all of them. When are you required to post openings?

Under Affirmative Action, all government contractors and subcontractors must post all openings internally.[5] If your company has a written policy which states jobs are required to be posted, they must be posted. If they aren't, it's a breach of contract.

Management experts say it's a good idea to post openings so people can move up within the organization. This contributes to better employee morale, continuity within the corporation, and growing your own management.

I agree. My only caution is that internal candidates must be fairly considered. If the posting is a sham, you will be worse off than if you had no posting at all.

HOW TO USE RECRUITING AGENCIES

Some managers use outside recruiters rather than advertising to find qualified applicants. Recruiters can make the hiring process easier for you. But because they are your agents, you are held responsible for their illegal acts.

I believe most agencies are law abiding. But in the early 1990s, a number of them were caught engaging in outright discrimination on the basis of sex, age, and race. Temporaries, Inc.,[6] Interplace, and Recruit all were named in

Equal Employment Opportunity Commission (EEOC) investigations and court cases alleging discrimination.[7]

In one case, recruiters used codes on job order forms to indicate the preference of the hiring manager. For example, "Talk to Adam" was written on the job orders if a male candidate was preferred; "Talk to Eve" if only a female would be considered.[8] In each of these cases, the agencies were sued by their own employees, who refused to go along with the scheme. But the managers who originally placed the discriminatory orders also would be liable to anyone who was screened out as a result.

On the other extreme, there are executive search and recruiting firms that specialize in finding minority and female candidates. It is not illegal to use these firms as long as you let them know you will consider a person of any group, and you use alternative sources to find nonminority candidates. Your hiring decision must be based on all qualifications, including Affirmative Action.

ACCEPTING APPLICATIONS: QUESTIONS TO AVOID AND WHY

After you advertise, people arrive to fill out applications. Now you have to sort through them without making any decisions based on illegal factors.

One way to make sure you don't is to use an application form that doesn't have any illegal questions on it. Application forms sold by mail order or in stationery stores may not comply with all applicable laws.

At a minimum, an application should not ask for any of the following:

Date of birth

Height, weight

Marital status

Color of eyes, hair

Place of birth

Dependents

Some other questions to avoid and why are the following:

Name of relative to contact in case of emergency? This could indicate marital status. You can ask for the name of a person to contact, but don't ask about the relationship.

Date graduated from high school? This indicates age. But you are allowed to ask date graduated from college, since not everyone goes right to college.

Are you a U.S. citizen? Remember, it's illegal to discriminate against noncitizens who are otherwise eligible to work in the United States. You are required to ask every applicant: "Are you legally entitled to work in this country? If yes, give visa or residency status."

Do you have a disability? This question is illegal under the ADA. Instead, the applicant should be given the job description and asked, "Are you able to perform all the essential functions of the job? If not, is there a reasonable accommodation that can be made?"

Have you been arrested? Blacks and Hispanics are arrested at a greater rate than whites, but are convicted at the same rate. Some states, including Hawaii, directly prohibit asking about arrests.[9] You can ask, "Have you been *convicted* of a felony?" Some states may require you to include the statement, "A felony conviction will not necessarily disqualify you."

Do you have military experience? Since many more men than women have military experience, putting undue weight on this factor can be discriminatory. If you ask about military experience, you also should ask about volunteer activities that may have developed job skills.

Do you belong to clubs and organizations? This may be relevant to the job, but you should include a statement that organization names which indicate the sex, race, religion, or other classification of the group may be omitted, and if included, will not be used to discriminate.

Some of the questions that are illegal to ask before hiring, are completely legal to ask afterward. Insurance forms ask for date of birth, sex, marital status, dependents, and so on. Affirmative Action data are collected. This information may be collected after hiring, but can't be used to discriminate or invade the privacy of employees.

Application forms can hurt you if they have illegal questions. When designed correctly, they can help you prevent not only discrimination claims, but also other lawsuits.

In Chapter 3, on wrongful termination, you learned that most employees are considered "at will." That means they can be fired for any reason or no reason. Wrongful termination cases arise when the company does something that leads employees to believe the company is promising them long-term employment.

You can try to ensure employees don't get this erroneous belief by including at-will language on your employment application. This is sometimes referred to as a waiver or disclaimer. The employees are signing a waiver of their rights, if any, to long-term employment.

A simple form of waiver is, "I understand my employment is at will and can be terminated at any time, for any reason or for no reason. I understand that any change in my at-will status can be only in a writing signed by the president of the company."

Language like this has been held by some courts to prevent wrongful termination lawsuits. The same language has been held by other courts to have no effect at all. Check with a local attorney if you are concerned.

Another way your application form can protect you from lawsuits is by including a release signed by the applicant. This release authorizes you to do a background check on the applicant. This way, you can't be accused of invading privacy.

It also releases the former employers of the applicant to give you information, without fear of being sued for giving negative references. References are covered at the end of this chapter.

Such a release might read: "I hereby authorize you to investigate the accuracy of the information submitted on this application, my resume, or any other information I provide. I release you and all persons and organizations from all claims and liabilities of any nature arising from such investigation or information given."

This release may or may not be effective, depending upon the law of your state and what information is given. Even if applicants sign releases, they still might be able to sue over a negative reference. They could argue they had not released former employers to give out *untrue* information about them.

One other piece of the application form for Affirmative Action employers is the applicant flow data sheet. This is usually a tear-off section attached to the form. It asks for the applicant's sex, race, disability, and veteran status.

It is mandatory for federal government contractors and some other employers to request this information from the applicant,[10] but voluntary for the applicant to provide it. Applicants are allowed to self-identify. Even if you don't think they are minority, if they identify themselves as minority, they are for this purpose.

RESUMES: WHAT TO IGNORE AND WHAT TO CONSIDER

Resumes prepared by applicants frequently have information that is illegal for you to consider. Just ignore it.

I once worked for a discrimination lawyer who was hiring a new law clerk. We received a huge pile of resumes from the law school placement office. There was no way to distinguish among the resumes. Everyone had two years of law school, had taken the same classes, and had no experience.

One of the resumes listed the height and weight of the student. "Look at that," my boss exclaimed. "She's only four foot nine! She's too short to work here." He tossed the resume on the reject pile.

At the time, we all laughed. In those days before the ADA, it didn't occur to us this could be considered a disability. But today our decision would be illegal. Worse yet, my boss circled the offending information on the resume so we wouldn't forget why we rejected the applicant.

I've seen resumes list marital status, number of children, and church activities. Many list health condition. They always say, "Health: good." Can you imagine someone writing, "Health: bad"?

Ignore this irrelevant information, and don't highlight it or ask questions about it in the interview.

On the other hand, a resume often unintentionally reveals the caliber of the person who prepared it. In many cases, it's legitimate for you to reject a resume on the basis of overall appearance, misspellings, grammar, and punctuation. If applicants don't present perfect documents to you when looking for employment, what will be the quality of their work after they're hired?

Judging an applicant based on misspellings or similar errors would not be appropriate for jobs that don't require writing. But the overall neatness of the resume probably is relevant to any position that requires attention to detail and quality.

THE GRID SYSTEM FOR SCREENING APPLICANTS

The owner of a small business shared the great method he used to pick secretaries with one of my classes. He said, "I just ask them if they're divorced and if they have kids. If they do, I won't hire them. If you don't hire divorced women, you don't have any problems!"

When I told him that was illegal, he said in despair, "Now how am I going to pick them?"

Go back to the job description you constructed. List each job requirement. Weight the requirements to reflect how important each one is. Base the weight on legitimate business reasons. Then rate each candidate against those requirements. The grid here is one systematic method for screening applicants.

Essential Functions	% Weight	Legitimate Business Reasons	Candidate A	Candidate B	Candidate C

This kind of grid system will support your hiring or promotional decisions. Courts love graphs, grids, and charts. They want to see that you created a decision system before you interviewed the first candidate. Then you just slotted the applicants into your decision system.

If you use this type of system, in most cases a court will not "disturb your discretion." A court will not second-guess your business judgment.

With this kind of grid system, you can identify the top 5 or 10 candidates. In some cases, you may want to interview them a little by phone. Or you may want to bring them all in for face-to-face interviews. Either way, you must prepare written questions.

How to Ask Behavior-Based Interview Questions

Before the interview, write out your questions. Base your questions on the requirements of the job. The job requires technical skills. Technical skills are "what a person does." The job also must be performed in a certain way. Performance characteristics are "how a person does it." Performance characteristics include

Reactivity

Judgment

Problem solving

Versatility

Assertiveness

Alertness

Planning

Commitment

Interaction

Team building

Friendliness

Thoroughness

Initiative

Foresight

These are sometimes called intangibles, but they're not. In fact, directly or indirectly, you routinely rate your current employees on these skills.

How do you determine if applicants have them? By asking questions about their past behavior. The best predictor of applicants' future behavior is their past work performance. Applicants will give you accurate information about their past if you ask them for specifics.

Interviewing expert Rick Smith says you have to "peel the onion" to probe for specific examples of past behavior.[11] For example, I interviewed a woman for a supervising position that required working with difficult people. She assured me this was one of her strengths. I asked her, "Tell me about a time when you worked with a difficult person."

She described in gory detail a coworker she disliked at a past job. Peeling the onion, I asked, "What did you do about it?" She said, "I quit."

This is what is known as contrary evidence. She has just contradicted her earlier statement that she works well with difficult people. But peeling the onion also means probing for more examples. Perhaps this was an isolated circumstance.

So I asked her to tell me about another time. Again she went into the story with great gusto, relishing the details of how difficult the offending subordinate was. Finally, I asked, "What did you do about him?"

She said, "I fired him."

This woman cannot work with difficult people! I discovered that by using behavior-based interviewing. Behavior-based interviewing is

- Asking for specific examples ("Tell me about a time when you . . .")
- Accepting silence while the applicant thinks of examples
- Peeling the onion by asking for dates, places, and numbers
- Probing for contrary evidence

After writing out your job questions, write out a few rapport-building questions to begin the interview. These are designed to put the candidate at ease. You can't ask any personal questions. The weather and the traffic are two safe topics of conversation.

You can also write out questions to wrap up the interview in a comfortable and legal way:

Is there anything about your experience you want to tell me?

Do you have any questions about the job?

Do you need more information about the company?

How to Conduct a Superior Interview

Start with your rapport-building questions.

After the candidate relaxes, explain how you will conduct the interview. My dad was a recruiter for Lockheed Missiles and Space. When I was a young girl, he told me his secret: "A good interview is divided into thirds. The first third, you tell them about the job. The second third, you ask them questions. The last third, they ask you questions and 'tell' you if they want the job."

If the applicant will be interviewed by peers, either with you or separately, make sure they know and follow all the rules about interviewing. The law applies to coworkers as well as managers.

Stick to your preplanned questions throughout the interview. Legally, the best interviewer asks everyone the same questions. Make notes of the responses. You need to document the interview like any other major employment event.

You should not refer in your notes to the physical appearance of applicants. Don't document things like young, old, good-looking, blond, gray hair, athletic, grandma type, and so on. For public contact jobs, you can note if the person is dressed professionally. But the wearing of religious garb, such as a turban or yarmulke, can't be considered.

One of the most subtle forms of discrimination is the short interview. You have an interviewing routine that probably will last an hour. If you break that routine when interviewing certain candidates, you can be accused of discrimination.

Your first impressions of candidates based on their appearance can be very misleading. You owe it to yourself and your company to give every candidate a complete interview. You may find that hidden in an unlikely exterior is a superior employee.

How to Handle Five Common Interview Hotspots

There are some areas in interviews that are hotspots. The questions are job related, but must be asked correctly in order to stay legal. The best guideline is to use the *statement-problem question* approach. Make a *statement* about the job, and then ask the *question*, "Do you have a *problem* with that?" If applicants say they can't meet the job requirements, they've selected themselves out of the hiring process.

Here are some common interview hotspots.

Hazardous Workplaces

If hazardous materials are used in your work environment, you should inform every applicant. Most people with experience in your industry know if they are likely to be working with toxic chemicals or be confronted with other dangers. But as a matter of routine, you should say, "You are going to be working with these chemicals. [Hand them a list.] Do you have a problem working with these?"

Asking the Applicant's Plans

You may want to consider an applicant's future goals and plans. You can ask about these areas if you have a business necessity and if you ask everyone. But you have to be careful about implying long-term employment.

Asking older applicants "When do you plan to retire?" is illegal. But if you are concerned about how long they plan to stay, you can ask all applicants their plans for the future.

Keep in mind two problems. If there is any talk of a long-term future with the company, you could later be sued for wrongful termination. So you have to say something like, "I want anyone who I hire to promise they will stay at least a year. Do you have a problem with that?"

> *Applicant:* "No problem. I want to stay here for the rest of my career!"

> *You:* "Well, we're not guaranteeing you will be here for any length of time. Business conditions may change, you may not work out, and we're an at-will employer. So I'm not making any promises. Do you have a problem with that?"

> *Applicant:* "No, that's understood. But I'm willing to stay at least a year."

Of course, even assuming the applicant tells the truth, no one can predict the future. If you hire applicants based on their stated plans to stay with your company, and they leave before the time promised, you can't make them stay. That's slavery.[12]

Dependability Requirements

Most employers want their employees to be dependable. For some jobs, it's critical. But some employers still determine dependability by asking applicants the question, "Do you have children?"

Traditionally, men weren't asked that, so this question was originally considered to discriminate on the basis of sex. Today, it also is considered discriminatory against male and female single parents (marital status discrimination).

You can't ask questions about children. Of course, some employees are unreliable because they have children. But if those employees didn't have kids, they would be unreliable for some other reason.

You can use the statement-problem-question format to determine how reliable the applicant is, without referring to children. For example, if you are worried about parents getting personal phone calls from their kids, say, We do not allow personal phone calls. Do you have a problem with that? As long as you apply your no-personal-phone-call policy to everyone equally, you are not discriminating.

Time Off Needs

Your need for dependable employees sometimes conflicts with the rights of employees who are religious or disabled. You can use the statement-problem question approach to inform employees of your attendance requirements. But what if employees say they need time off for religious holidays or regular medical treatment?

As discussed in Chapter 2, you must reasonably accommodate the special needs of employees who are religious or disabled, unless it would cause an undue hardship on the company.

Negotiating Salary

Negotiating salary is another hotspot. The law says employees must be paid equally for doing the same job.[13] The only differences in salary should be based on experience and ability. Salaries should not be based on the salary negotiating skills of the person you are trying to hire.

You can pay market value to get a new hire. But the current employees who are equally or better qualified should have their salaries raised so they are paid equally.[14]

You cannot establish pay based on the salary requirements of the applicant. Allstate Insurance Company tried that and lost.[15] The company asked applicants for insurance agent trainee what their salary requirements were.

The women on average gave salary requirements 20% lower than the men. Therefore, the women were paid on average 20% lower than men, even though they were doing the same job and had the same experience. The court held that was illegal sex discrimination. If paying based on salary requirements resulted in lower pay for other groups, it could be illegal age, race, or national origin discrimination.

Another reason managers like to ask about salary requirements is to screen out people whose answer is too high. The assumption is that a person who gives a high number will not be happy with less.

Like other assumptions, this one is illegal if it impacts some groups more than others. Instead of assuming, ask the statement-problem-question. "This job pays from _____ to _____. Do you have a problem with that?"

How to Answer Applicants' Questions About Sensitive Subjects

In recent years, some women and minority applicants have asked interviewers tough questions about their company's record of hiring and promoting a diverse work force.

If you are asked how many women are in management, whether opportunities for minorities are good, or other sensitive questions, follow these steps.

1. Tell the truth.

2. Don't guess.

3. Answer specifically to the extent you can.

4. Admit what you don't know.

5. Express the company's policies on EEO and Affirmative Action.

6. Offer to put the applicant in touch with your personnel department to get more complete answers.

7. Then document the questions raised by the applicant, so you can't later be accused of illegally bringing up the subject.

Fraudulent Concealment

Applicants sometimes ask about the financial condition of the company. You can't lie or answer in half-truths designed to conceal the truth. That's called fraudulent concealment.

A Colorado case illustrates this rule. Roberta Berger was recruited to work as a sales manager for Recovery Plus, a disaster recovery computer service. At the time, she was living in New Orleans. The job was in Denver.

At the interview, Ms. Berger asked about the company's financial status. The division president told her the division had no detailed financial records but that it was a wholly owned subsidiary of Security Pacific Corporation. He gave her the annual report of Security Pacific, showing it to be a multimillion-dollar company. He also gave her a magazine article which said that Recovery Plus had so many customers it was turning away business.

In fact, the company had only two or three regular customers. In fact, the division president knew at the time of the interview that his job was at risk and, indeed, all of Recovery Plus might be shut down. Despite that, he told her his career "was just beginning" at the company.

Ms. Berger was hired in January and began work in February. In March, Recovery Plus was shut down. As a result of losing her job, Ms. Berger defaulted on her home loan, sold her home at a loss, and was unemployed for two years. She sued for fraudulent concealment and won.[16]

The moral of the story: don't lie about the company's financial condition. In fact, you may have to volunteer bad news.

In Florida, dismissed employees may sue for fraudulent concealment if the company deliberately misleads them by concealing material information about the job. In one case, the employee was not told in the interview that his project was expected to fail. Nor was he told he would be fired when it did. The court said the employer had a duty to disclose these facts.[17]

Diversity Considerations

When you interview people from other cultures, there may be differences in style. If misinterpreted, you might not hire someone well qualified for the job.

According to the report *Workforce 2000* the majority of applicants entering the United States job market by the year 2000 will be minority and female.[18] In Silicon Valley, California, where I work, this milestone already has been reached.

When we evaluate candidates from other cultures, we should be mindful of stereotypes and assumptions about them. An example of cultural bias appeared in an article that advocated choosing people for certain jobs based on their handshakes. The author outlined 10 different handshake styles. Characteristics such as drive, leadership, and the like supposedly were reflected in the way a person shook hands.

But what of people from cultures that don't shake hands as we do in the United States? What of men and women who were raised not to shake hands with members of the opposite sex? What of the person with arthritis who can't get a firm grip?

There are plenty of books on cross-cultural communication. Read them. Your purpose is not to replace one set of assumptions with another, but only to learn of the wide diversity of styles. As diversity expert Lenora Billings-Harris says, "The issue is not that we behave a certain way because of the boxes we come in, but that we behave in similar and different ways despite our boxes."[19] Don't judge applicants by differences in body language, eye contact, or other culturally biased communication habits.

A related issue is getting people from different backgrounds to tell you about their accomplishments. The interview is the place for applicants to sell you on themselves. But many people, especially women, minorities, and foreign born, are hesitant to make themselves the heroes. They were raised to give credit to the team or the group. If you ask them for examples of their victories, they may be tongue-tied.

Instead of assuming they are incompetent, ask about successes in their departments. Ask about the overall accomplishment; then zero-in on the applicant's role in that success.

Another way to get applicants to talk about their accomplishments was suggested by Jim Kennedy and Anna Everest.[20] They ask this question: "If I were able to speak with your managers, what do you suppose they might say about you that would explain how you were able to do that?"

Applicant Fit

A manager once justified not hiring my client, a well-qualified woman, on these grounds. He was staffing a new group from scratch and wanted it to be highly compatible. United Air Lines had just laid off a large number of mechanics. The manager decided to hire only UAL mechanics, on the assumption they would work well together. It just so happened that all of them were male.

Compatibility of team members is a business necessity. But applicant fit must be measured, not assumed. The fact that the UAL mechanics had worked together for a long time might mean they were compatible. It also might mean they had hated each other for years.

Compatibility also does not mean sameness. You can have a diverse work group that is compatible. At one company where I regularly give legal training to managers, they tell me they don't like to hire older people because it's a young company (average age 37). I then tell them about my law firm, where the average age was 35. We hired an older woman to be a secretary, even though we wondered if she would fit in with our wild sense of humor. She turned out to be the wildest one of all!

Assuming applicants are equally qualified, you can choose among them based on compatibility, as long as you don't exclude people because they don't fit in with an illegal culture. For example, if people in your company tell lots of racist jokes, you can't refuse to hire applicants because they don't go along.

You can't hire or promote based on your "gut feeling." That's a subjective conclusion. Your decision must be based on objective qualifications.

PRACTICAL GUIDELINES FOR GIVING TESTS TO APPLICANTS

Before and after interviews, many companies give applicants tests. This area is fraught with danger for the unwary employer. The tests we'll cover here are performance, aptitude, handwriting analysis, integrity and personality. Medical, drug, and lie detector tests were covered in Chapter 4.

All these tests have one danger in common. If the applicants who fail the tests are disproportionately members of one group, you must show a business necessity for using the test.[21] A business necessity is more than a legitimate business reason.

Because of the danger of discrimination, most tests are subject to the federal government Uniform Guidelines on Employee Selection Procedures.[22] These guidelines come into play if a test has a disproportionate impact on minorities, women, or other protected group.

How do you determine if a test has a disproportionate impact? The measure used in the Uniform Guidelines is called the "four-fifths rule." If the pass rate for a protected group is less than 80% (four-fifths) of the pass rate for the majority group, the test is deemed discriminatory.

When there is disproportionate impact, the guidelines require tests to be valid. Validation means the tests accurately measure what they purport to measure. For example, a paper-and-pencil test on decision making may say more about applicants' reading and test-taking skill than their ability to make decisions.

Any reputable company selling tests will provide you with validation studies, references to other companies, and a way to measure whether the test is valid as used at your company. Employers that give frequent tests, such as government civil service exams, keep industrial psychologists on staff to perform validation studies.

Performance Tests

Performance tests are the most job related of all tests. Their purpose is to judge whether the applicant can actually perform the job.

To ensure a performance test is valid, it should

- Duplicate actual working conditions
- Test only the primary job tasks
- Have the applicant actually perform the job tasks

A good example is giving a typing test to a secretary. If the secretary will be typing, you have a business necessity to give the test. Other examples are driving tests for drivers, editing tests for editors, and so on.

How much weight you should give to the test depends on the task's significance to the overall job. It doesn't make sense to exclude applicants from jobs that require minimal typing because they're slow typists. Yet that's what we're tempted sometimes to do because it's one of the few objective measures we have.

Aptitude Tests

Aptitude tests are usually multiple-choice exams that are supposed to measure intelligence or ability. Standardized multiple-choice tests are the least related to job performance. We may live in a multiple-choice world, but in reality we aren't given five options from which to choose.

The U.S. Supreme Court and the federal courts have found many of these tests to be discriminatory against blacks and Hispanics. The tests ruled discriminatory include the Wonderlic Personnel, Bennet Mechanical, General Clerical, Scientific Associates Non-Verbal, and Flanagan Aptitude tests, the Beta Examination, and the General Aptitude Test Battery.[23]

In one early case, a company historically had reserved jobs for whites only. After the Civil Rights Act of 1964 passed, the company began requiring an aptitude test to be hired or promoted into the previous "white" jobs. Few blacks passed the tests, while many whites did. The company's managers admitted they didn't notice any improvement in the work force after the aptitude test was required. And in a validation study, the incumbents who were top performers couldn't pass it.[24]

If you want to use an aptitude test, you first must determine if it has a disproportionate impact on minorities, women, or other protected group. If it doesn't, you can use it safely.

Even if the test does have a disproportionate impact, you are allowed to use it under the Civil Rights Act of 1991 if you have a business necessity *and* there is no less discriminatory alternative.

Integrity Tests

After the polygraph law was passed in 1988, employers looked to other ways to measure the honesty of applicants. Multiple-choice integrity tests became a popular method.

These paper-and-pencil tests ask applicants a series of questions designed to prove whether or not they lie, cheat or steal. They include questions such as, "Should a person be fired if caught stealing $5?" and "Compared to other people, how honest are you?"

How accurate are these tests? The validity of honesty tests has been measured. The American Psychological Association (APA) issued its report on them in 1991.[25]

The psychology professors who led the research task force requested information from dozens of companies that sell honesty tests. Only a few responded. Of those that did respond, fewer still could prove what they claimed.

The APA report found that some (unidentified) honesty tests were valid. In other words, they had predictive ability. For example, a test was given to convicted thieves and members of the general public. The test scores showed which ones were the convicted thieves.

Employers who use these tests want to do more than screen out convicted felons. You want to know who will cheat on their time cards. Who will use inside information? Who has embezzled without getting caught?

The best honesty tests are able to find those people with reasonable accuracy—on the order of 30% to 40%. Although it seems like a low correlation, it may be higher than the predictive ability of the alternatives—interviews, background checks, and references.

The APA report stresses that an honesty test should be only one of many factors considered in determining the honesty of applicants. The report also strongly urges employers not to use tests if the test company refuses to provide documentation of their claims.[26]

Even if the test meets the APA requirements, using it still can lead to lawsuits if it's used inconsistently. Do you have a legitimate business reason for requiring hourly employees to take honesty tests, but not executives?

Personality Tests

Worse than the integrity tests are the personality tests some employers give to applicants. These attempt to predict job performance by determining the personality type of the applicant. For example, if the position is for a supervisor, a person who scores low on leadership or ambition would not be hired.

As with all tests, these must be validated as having an actual correlation between job performance and score. Validation trials must be performed in the working environment, not in psychological clinical studies.

Even if these tests are a valid predictor of future job performance, they still are subject to legal challenge. That's because many of the questions asked invade the privacy of the applicants or intrude into illegal areas. If you are not allowed to ask a question in an interview, you should not be able to ask it in a test.

One of the worst abuses of personality testing was practiced by Target Stores, which used a test called the Psyscreen to weed out applicants.[27] The test included questions about one's religious beliefs and sexual fantasies. Among the more intrusive: "I go to church almost every week" . . . "I believe in the second coming of Christ" . . . "I believe my sins are unpardonable."

Other offensive questions: "I am very strongly attracted by members of my own sex" . . . "I have never indulged in any unusual sex practices" . . . "Many of my dreams are about sex matters."

In the Target Stores case, the court said that asking these questions violated the California constitution, because they invade applicants' privacy for no compelling reason. Other states' privacy statutes, and the U.S. Constitution, may be interpreted the same way.

In the high-tech world, personality tests have been reduced to software packages.[28] Whatever the package, the same two questions must be answered: Is it valid? Even if it is, does it invade privacy?

Handwriting Analysis

Graphology, graphoanalysis, or handwriting analysis has received increased interest in the United States in recent years.[29] The origin of handwriting analysis has been traced to Aristotle in ancient Greece and is found in Chinese history.[30] It is highly accepted in parts of Europe, particularly France[31] and Germany.[32]

Handwriting analysis is a way to determine personality traits such as aggression, decisiveness, and dependability. Like all tests, handwriting analysis must measure what it says it measures. Although some studies have questioned its validity, the majority have found handwriting analysis to be valid.[33]

Does handwriting analysis have a discriminatory impact on some groups compared to others? Alfred Binet, the originator of IQ tests, found that age and sex could not be determined through handwriting analysis.[34] Among practicing graphologists, it is accepted that handwriting does not reveal ethnicity, religion, or other protected classification, unless, of course, the content of the handwriting sample gives such information.

People who are disabled must be reasonably accommodated if they can't write due to blindness, quadriplegia, or other impairment. That might mean none of the applicants should have handwriting analysis if a disabled applicant can't participate. Interestingly, graphologists claim they can analyze writing made by mouth and foot as well as by hand.

Another legal issue is whether handwriting analysis is an invasion of privacy. The legality of an employer analyzing personality through handwriting has not been decided by any court.

If the court was asked to rule, its analysis would start with the question, "Do applicants have the reasonable expectation of privacy?" One way to ensure they don't is to inform them their handwriting will be analyzed. Then they can't claim invasion of privacy. The theory is that if they don't want their handwriting analyzed, they don't have to apply.

Many states have privacy laws that sometimes are interpreted more broadly than the U.S. Constitution. California's Constitution, for example, prohibits employers from collecting information that is not job related. If handwriting analysis reveals information about one's personal life, that's invasion of privacy. For example, handwriting has been analyzed for psychosexual dimensions of personality.[35] Asking a graphologist for this type of information would invade privacy unless it was job related.

> *practical pointers:* If you decide to use handwriting analysis, these suggestions may prevent legal violations. Obtain handwriting analysis for all job finalists, not just a few. Have a legitimate business reason for requiring handwriting analysis for some jobs but not others.
>
> Give the graphologist a job description and list of job-related characteristics necessary for success. The graphologist's report should be limited to these characteristics. Document your legitimate business reasons for picking these characteristics

When you hire a graphologist, get a good one. Like all consultants, graphologists should have formal training, years of experience, and good references. Conduct your own validity studies. Hire an industrial psychologist from the local college to confirm results. At a minimum, review the outcome to ensure that no groups are excluded or impacted by the process.

Never use the results of handwriting analysis as the only factor in your hiring decision. The safest way to use it is in choosing between two candidates whose skills and experience are about equal. The most dangerous: choosing a candidate with less experience over one with more, on the basis of handwriting analysis.

How to Verify Information During Background Checks

After the interview and the testing process, you have one more step before making an offer: the background check.

As a practical matter, you should confirm the educational background, work experience, and criminal record of potential new hires. According to *Business Week*, one convenience store chain reduced worker turnover from 300% a year to 97%, and theft was cut in half after background checks were instituted.

At a minimum, you are allowed to verify any information relevant to the job given to you by applicants.

Credit Checks

A check on the credit of new hires is essential in some instances, illegal in others.

If you are hiring employees to handle your own or other people's money or valuables, you can run a credit check. A good credit rating decreases the likelihood of theft. Credit checks also have been allowed for police officers, who frequently are exposed to the temptations of bribes.

The U.S. Fair Credit Reporting Act[36] requires employers who request credit reports to inform applicants of that fact. The notification must be given in writing within three days of requesting the credit information. If the applicant is not hired based on the credit report, the applicant must be informed of that fact and given the name of the agency that gave the unfavorable credit information.

Employers who are found guilty of willful violations of the act can be sued for actual damages, attorneys fees, and punitive damages. Employees who are not responsible for handling money may be able to claim a credit check is an invasion of their privacy.

Criminal and Driving Records

There are legal restrictions on investigating criminal and driving records. As mentioned earlier, you can't ask applicants about arrest records, because it's race discrimination. Some state laws also prohibit asking questions about arrests, except for certain professions such as doctors and peace officers.[37]

Generally, you can refuse to hire people convicted of felonies or misdemeanors, but there are some exceptions under state laws. In California, you can't even ask about misdemeanors for minor marijuana convictions.

Poor driving record can't be used to exclude people who won't be driving on the job. Driving record is relevant for any person whose job requires driving, including salespeople, executives, and professionals.

A history of drunk driving arrests that led to diversion rather than conviction may not be used to exclude recovered alcoholics. You need current evidence that they are not rehabilitated. That's because under the ADA, a rehabilitated alcoholic is protected.

Not only will background checks help you weed out the liars and the cheaters, they also will help you defend against claims for negligent hiring.

Negligent Hiring and Retention

Negligent hiring lawsuits are not brought by your employees.[38] Instead, they're filed by your customers, clients, or third parties who are injured by your employees. A typical negligent hiring case would be brought by parents of a child abused in a day care center. They would claim you did not properly check the background of your employee. If you had, you would have discovered the past record of the employee for abusing children.

The negligent hiring claim can be won if

- You had a duty to your clients or others to check employees' backgrounds.
- Employees had past records that you would have discovered.
- As a result, someone was injured by them.[39]

When do you have a duty to check the background of new hires? When they are being hired for jobs which put them in positions of power, trust, or confidence. Jobs with children are the most obvious. Police, corrections officers, and security guards have positions of power, which in the wrong hands could be abused.

Any person responsible for handling other people's money or valuables should have a background check. Bank tellers, hotel employees, apartment managers, delivery persons, real estate agents, night janitors, and the like are held to a high standard. Personal attendants who live or work in private homes should be screened.

Hospitals must report to the National Practitioner Data Bank on doctors, dentists, and other health care professionals who have had malpractice claims, adverse licensing actions, or clinical privileges suspended or revoked. A hospital also must check the data bank every two years for information about its staff.[40]

Some states allow negligent hiring suits if the employee has *any* contact with the public. In one New York case, the employee was hired to work in a bowling alley. One night, he punched several patrons. They sued for negligent hiring. The court held the bowling alley liable because it didn't do an investigation when the employee was hired. Also, the employee had made "irrational remarks" to his manager on several occasions before the assault. The court said these comments should have alerted the manager to the employee's dangerous propensities. By retaining the employee after these remarks were made, without closely supervising him, the employer also was liable for negligent retention.[41]

Even if you don't do a background check, if you would not have discovered the past record anyway, you can't be sued for negligent hiring. For example, if the employee quit while under investigation for theft, the former employer may not have enough evidence to justify giving you a negative reference. In that case, you would not have been told even if you asked.

HOW TO STAY OUT OF TROUBLE WHEN GIVING OR REQUESTING REFERENCES

Getting references is essential for preventing negligent hiring suits. It also makes good practical sense. But these days, it's almost impossible to get references. Why? Because giving references for former employees can get you into trouble. Before we can talk about getting references, let's see why you should be careful about giving references for your former employees.

The basic rule is that you can't tell lies about former employees. Of course, most employers don't lie. But companies also are sued for giving out truthful information. The problem arises when the employees version of the truth is different from yours. You say the employee was fired for stealing. The employee denies it and sues you for defamation.

Defamation is an untrue statement made about someone that hurts their work reputation. Nothing hurts a reputation more than giving out negative references.

So the employee sues you, claiming it's not true. Do you really want to hire lawyers to go to court to prove it? Do you have enough evidence? Do you have enough time and money? The answer is No.

What You Can Say

To avoid a lawsuit, lawyers recommend you say as little as possible about former employees. Many companies give out only dates of employment and job title; sometimes they will confirm final salary. That's it.

Some employers believe it is their moral, if not legal, duty to warn other employers about bad employees. You do have a duty to give references if another manager at your company requests them. Internal references are "privileged," which means they can't be the subject of a lawsuit even if what you say is untrue. That's because the law allows companies to protect themselves from passing around their bad apples.

Some companies hope if they give references to outside companies they also will be able to get references when they're hiring. Your company cannot prohibit you from giving references for former employees who worked for you at other companies. But you still could be sued personally for giving negative information.

practical pointers: If you give references, here are some steps you can take to decrease your risk of being sued.

Your former employee should sign a release allowing you to give out reference information. Sample release language was given in the application section of this chapter. A release can be signed by your employees when leaving your employment. Or they may apply at a company that uses an application form with a release. If a company calls you for a reference, ask them for a copy of their release before you talk.

If you are called for a reference, make a note of the name of the caller, the company name, and the date and time of the call. If you don't know the caller personally, ask to call back later. If the caller hedges about you returning the call, watch out! Attorneys and investigators posing as employers routinely call former employers to find out if bad references are being given. Typically, they won't want to leave phone numbers.

Once you start talking, explain to the person calling that you are giving out confidential information. The caller should promise that anything you say will not be revealed to your former employee. This promise may not be enforceable, but it keeps most people from telling the applicant about your bad reference. (Some states prohibit keeping such information confidential from employees. Check with an expert before you agree to keep a reference confidential.)

When giving references, stick to the facts:

- Attendance record (don't say good or bad, just missed 5 days in 6 months)
- Tardiness record (more than 30 minutes late on 5 of the last 20 days of work)
- Production record (met quota 65% of the time)
- Completion record (completed 8 out of 10 goals last review period)

The more negative the information about the employee, the more objectively verifiable and documented it should be.

The following areas are dangerous ones to talk about to prospective employers of your former employees:

- Employee's attitude
- Reason for leaving
- Whether the employee is eligible for rehire
- Whether employee was fired or quit
- Employee's weaknesses

In these danger zones your perception is probably different from the employee's.

How Good References Can Backfire

When good employees move or are laid off, you may want to give them good references. Don't accidentally give a bad one.

My paralegal wanted a job closer to home. I gladly agreed to be her reference. The first potential employer who called was a good lawyer. He got me talking about her strengths. Then he asked the fateful question, "What are her weaknesses?" By now, he had me relaxed. So I told him, "She's not too good with details." We continued talking a bit and hung up.

The next day, she came into the office blazing mad. "I thought you were going to give me a good reference!" I said, "I did!" She said, "You told him I wasn't good with details." Oops, gee . . . sorry.

After that, when asked about weaknesses, I said she was a perfectionist and worked too hard. But that's not the answer, because although true, it's not the whole truth.

Techniques for Getting References

If employers follow the advice of most lawyers, you won't be able to get references for your new hires. These techniques may help you get more information.

Ask the applicant to bring copies of performance appraisals, letters of recommendation, completed projects, and other proof of good performance. Make sure these materials don't reveal any trade secrets.

Ask the applicant for the names of former coworkers and subordinates. They probably have not been told about the dangers of giving references. They are more likely to give you information. Since they aren't acting as managers, their comments generally do not bind their companies. And in many ways, their assessments may be more accurate than the supervisor's.

AT&T's Harry B. Thayer said,

> It is easy to fool yourself. It is possible to fool the people you work for. It is more difficult to fool the people you work with. But it is almost impossible to fool the people who work under you.[42]

HOW TO PREPARE THE OFFER LETTER

After all this, you finally are ready to make an offer to the candidate. The offer should be in writing, and like all legal documents, it should be written carefully.

Yes, an offer letter is a legal document. It can help you or harm you in any later case brought for wrongful termination.

An offer letter should not promise or imply long-term employment, unless that is your intention. Such statements as "we look forward to you having a long and successful career with the company" can lead to a later lawsuit if the employee is terminated. Review the section on employee handbooks in the wrongful termination chapter for other wording to avoid.

After you make offers of employment, it's reasonable to expect your new hires to make changes in their lives. They are relying on their reasonable expectation of employment. They certainly will quit their old jobs. Perhaps they will move, make major purchases, or get engaged.

Once they've done all that, can you revoke your offers? Are you allowed to call them up and say, "Sorry!"? Yes, in two situations:

- If your company announces a layoff after you made the offer, you may decide to eliminate the position or redeploy current employees. You are not forced to get rid of an experienced employee to bring in a new person.

- Even though you did a thorough background check, you may later discover the employee gave you false information. Employers routinely fire employees when they learn about lies on the application, even months after hiring them.

If you would have good cause to terminate employees after they're hired, you also have good cause to revoke their employment offers. But make sure you haven't violated any other contracts you've made.

In one case, the manager called the applicant and told him he could start work the next week if he quit his job and moved his home by then. The employee quit and moved. Then the company decided not to hire him.

The court held that the offer could be revoked since he was an at-will employee. He was not entitled to a job; therefore, he was not entitled to front pay damages. However, the court said the telephone call created an oral contract that if the employee moved, he would be allowed to work at least one day. By quitting and moving, he relied on the offer to his detriment. So he could sue for his losses as a result of quitting his old job and moving to a new house.[43]

Obviously, revoking an offer is a very serious matter. It will be terrible public relations for your company. It should be done only as a last resort.

TECHNIQUES FOR REJECTING APPLICANTS

After you decide who to hire, you should document the reasons why you rejected the other applicants. "Not as qualified" is *not* a reason. Be specific. "Less relevant experience." "No background leading teams." "Fired from last three jobs."

Do you have to tell applicants you're rejecting them? Or can you ignore them and hope they'll go away?

At some point, you will stop looking for candidates. That point in time should be documented. A good way to do that is to send brief letters to applicants thanking them for applying and saying, "Your qualifications do not match our current needs." Then invite them to reapply in the future.

Do *not* say that the application will be held for future openings unless it is true.

I represented a woman who applied for a heavy manufacturing job. She had several years of relevant experience. She wasn't interviewed, because a man with more experience was hired. The company sent her its standard rejection letter. "We will keep your application on file for a year and consider you for future openings."

One week before the year was up, another job opened. Her application wasn't pulled. A man with no relevant experience was hired instead. She was awarded almost $75,000 in back pay.

In most states, you are not legally required to send a rejection letter, as long as you can prove when you stopped accepting applications and when the application in question was received.

But management experts recommend sending rejection letters if only for the good public relations. As a matter of common courtesy, at least call people you interviewed.

Do you have to give them the specific reason they weren't hired? No statutes require this. You can be vague. Just remember, what you say can be used against you. For example, in one case the company told the rejected applicant for promotion that the successful candidate "had the best overall qualifications to lead the group." After the case started, the company said the real reason was because the successful person had more computer experience.

The court said the computer explanation "would have been such a straightforward answer to [the rejected candidate's] inquiries that one might expect that [her managers] would have mentioned it if it really was the explanation. That they instead gave vague explanations about 'overall qualifications' might suggest that the computer explanation was a later fabrication."[44]

After Hiring: How Managing and Training Go Hand in Hand

You've hired the best qualified people. On the first day of work, have them fill out all legal documents, including W-2s and Form I-9. They should read and sign for the employee handbook.

Hiring the best is only the beginning. You have to manage and train them to be the best employees for your company. You, as an employee, have the right to be managed. That means you, as a manager, have the duty to manage your subordinates.

Managing and training go hand in hand. As a trainer, naturally I recommend training. But there is more to training than an occasional class. The Japanese are excellent role models in this area.

I once wrote an article touting training. I wanted to compare the amount of time spent in training by Japanese and U.S. managers.

I researched for hours to find out this one fact. I called experts. I had the reference librarian at the Brooklyn business library work on it. We could not find any Japanese statistics comparable to the reams of data on U.S. training.

What I did find in every book and article on Japanese management was the same message: training begins from the first day of employment until the last. It's a part of daily life. The amount of training in Japan is immeasurable.

A good manager in the United States takes the same approach. Here, it's called coaching.

How to Hire the Best

You have the right to hire the best people. To attract the best people to your company, treat applicants with respect and dignity.

As plaintiff's lawyer Cliff Palefsky said to a personnel group, "You give applicants a psychological test, an integrity test, and a drug test, make them sign an at-will statement, and then say, 'Welcome to our great company!' It doesn't work that way."[45]

Chapter 6

HOW MEN AND WOMEN CAN WORK TOGETHER

The Law of Sexual Harassment

*E*arly in my career, I was asked by a company to represent a man who was accused of harassment. I didn't want to—after all, it was against my principles—but they offered me a lot of money, so I agreed.

When I met him I asked what happened. He said, "Our department hired a new secretary. She was really good looking. I asked her out a couple of times. She never said yes, but she never said no, so I figured she liked me."

I said, "Is that the complaint?" He said, "Not exactly. One day she and I were alone together in the copy room. I looked over at her, and she looked so good, I reached over and gave her a big hug and a kiss. The next thing I knew she ran out of the room yelling sexual harassment."

I said, "Why did you do that?" He said, "I don't know what got into me. I just couldn't control myself."

I thought, "Give me a break! You are an adult, you are a professional, certainly you can control yourself." I dealt with the situation constructively. But after that I would use this man as an example of the kinds of men we women have to put up with in the work place.

A couple of years later I was speaking to an all women's group. I was ranting and raving about these men who can't control themselves. All of a sudden I realized that I had sexually harassed one of my employees. It was one of the worst forms of harassment. I was a 25-year-old lawyer. He was a student intern. He was young and innocent.

One day he came to work wearing a tight pair of pants. I was walking through the office when he turned and bent over.

I did the only natural thing: I reached over and grabbed his buns.

He jumped and screamed, and then he laughed, which was fortunate for me. But I have to admit: I don't know what got into me! I just couldn't control myself.

The point is, anyone can be guilty of sexual harassment. That's because one of the reasons harassment occurs is a result of lust. At least That's what it was in my case.

THE CAUSES OF SEXUAL HARASSMENT

Harassment also occurs because of power, where one person uses his or her power to harass. This is called *quid pro quo* harassment when managers use their power over subordinates to get sex. "If you don't sleep with me, you're fired." It's *hostile environment* harassment where coworkers use sex to get power over their peers.

Sexual harassment occurs because of lust, because of power, and for bizarre reasons we don't entirely understand. Sex is irrational, it's emotional. Sometimes we don't know why harassment happens.

This was proven by a very scientific and rigorous study that was reported in *Ms.* magazine several years ago.[1] A woman walked down the street, and every time a man whistled or catcalled she stopped, pulled out a questionnaire, and said, "Excuse me, you've been chosen to participate in a study." Then she asked, "Why did you do that?"

Most of the men whistled only at good-looking women. They said they did it just to have fun. But some said they only whistled when a woman was ugly, because they wanted to make her day!

We don't always understand why sexual harassment occurs. But we do know that it does occur. The federal government reported on over 8,000 employees who were studied from 1985 to 1987.[2] It found 42% of the women were sexually harassed during those years, and 14% of the men. Of the women, 95% were harassed by men. Of the men, 22% were harassed by other men, the rest by women.

Sexual harassment occurs across gender lines and across sexual orientation lines. All of it is illegal.

WHY HARASSMENT IS ILLEGAL

Harassment is a form of discrimination. It is illegal to harass any employee on the basis of the protected classifications: sex (including pregnancy), age over 40, race and color, national origin, religion, citizenship, and disability. In addition to sexual harassment, there is also gender (or "sex-based") harassment. This is making derogatory comments about men or women in general. "Women don't make good supervisors." "Men can't work in day care."[3]

One of my clients was 68 years old. When he made a mistake, his manager said, "You're getting senile." Every morning the manager came in and said, "When are you going to retire?" Finally, he brought in brochures from retirement villages, all of them conveniently located thousands of miles away and said, "Wouldn't you like to live here?" That's age harassment.

Telling ethnic jokes is racial or national origin harassment.[4] Making degrading comments about another's religion is religious harassment.[5] Refusing to work with someone with AIDS is disability harassment.

Sometimes employees claim that being criticized or disciplined at all is harassment. Unless the discipline is explicitly related to a protected classification, it is not illegal under these laws.[6] In some states, general harassment is illegal under the law of intentional infliction of emotional distress or outrage.[7] And, if employees become stressed by discipline, they may be able to get worker's compensation benefits.[8]

In addition to the harassment laws, other laws prohibit some of the same conduct. Claims can be filed for battery, wrongful termination, defamation, and false imprisonment.

Since the basic concepts are the same for all types of illegal harassment, and since sexual harassment complaints are the most frequent, we will focus on sexual harassment in this chapter.

FOUR WAYS TO PROVE SEXUAL HARASSMENT

Four factors are necessary to prove sexual harassment. All four must be present for a victim to win.

Four Factors Prove Sexual Harassment

1. It's explicitly sexual.
2. It's repeated or gross.
3. It's unwelcome by the victim.
4. The employer knew or should have known it was occurring, but did nothing to stop it.

---

1. *Sexual Harassment Is Explicitly Sexual*

Race harassment is explicitly racist. Age harassment is explicitly ageist.

In sexual harassment cases, the behavior must be considered explicitly sexual by a reasonable victim. If the victim is a woman, it's a reasonable woman standard. If the victim is a man, it's a reasonable man standard.[9]

This is an objective standard, not subjective. Just because someone feels harassed, doesn't necessarily mean it's illegal. One still hears today that harassment is "in the eye of the beholder." Not true. If the harassment would not be considered sexual by a reasonable victim, it's not illegal.

If an employee feels harassed, that's a management issue you have to deal with. But the way you handle it may be very different if it's not illegal harassment.

For example, a woman once came to my office about suing her boss for sexual harassment. I said, "What did he do?" She said, "He asked me personal questions." I said, "That can be sexual harassment. What did he ask you?" She said, "He asked me what I was going to do one weekend."

This doesn't sound very sexual, but I asked her, "What was the context?" She said, "A bunch of us were sitting around one Friday afternoon in our department. Everyone said what they were doing that weekend except me. My boss asked me, 'What are you doing this weekend?' I think this is sexual harassment."

I disagreed. A reasonable woman would not say that's explicitly sexual. She didn't have a case.

She was extremely upset. She felt violated. She felt invaded.

Her manager would have to learn to keep his distance. But at least he didn't have to worry about a lawsuit.

Sometimes it seems that an employee complaining of sexual harassment is supersensitive. Everyone else laughs at your jokes. No one else complains about your arm around their shoulders. Anybody else would be thrilled if you asked them to dinner. Everyone knows that's just the way you are, except for this one troublemaker.

Even though you all think the victim is supersensitive, that does not excuse you from the reasonable victim standard. In fact, if the victim can prove you knew he or she was sensitive, you could be held liable for intentionally inflicting emotional distress.[10]

The Reasonable Woman Standard

The only issue is whether a reasonable victim would consider your actions to be sexual harassment. A 1991 landmark case established what is usually called the reasonable woman standard.[11] Ms. Ellison was an employee of the Internal Revenue Service. A male coworker invited her to lunch one day. They went out, and although he didn't do anything particularly inappropriate, she felt uncomfortable. When he asked her to lunch again, she said no. The next day he sent her a short handwritten note. He said he was in constant turmoil and devastated because she rejected him.

She was disturbed by the note but decided to ignore him, hoping he'd go away. He didn't. A few weeks later he sent her a three-page typed, single-spaced letter in which he professed his undying love for her. In one part of the letter he wrote, "I know that you are worth knowing with or without sex . . . . I have enjoyed you so much over these past few months. Watching you. Experiencing you from O so far away."

This man may have thought he was being poetic. But Ms. Ellison had a different reaction. Particularly disturbing was the word "watch." What did that mean? Was he stalking her? Was he following her home? She went to her supervisor and demanded he be disciplined.

The IRS agreed his behavior was inappropriate and told him not to do it again, but they did not treat it like sexual harassment. They did not give him a disciplinary warning. They did not place him on probation. They did not even express strong disapproval.

Even though his harassment stopped, Ms. Ellison felt the IRS had not done enough. She filed suit in federal court and won. The judge said this was sexual harassment. The employer was *required* to take disciplinary action. The judge also said a reasonable man might not consider the letter harassing, but a reasonable woman would. He noted that women are disproportionately victims of rape and sexual assault. Whereas a man might look at language like this in a vacuum, a woman could see it as a prelude to violence.

Thus the court held that if a reasonable woman would consider this behavior to be explicitly sexual, it is sexual harassment.

2. Sexual Harassment Is Repeated or Gross

Harassment by definition is repeated, unless it's so gross that once is enough.[12]

Gross harassment includes touching private parts, a promise or a threat in exchange for sex, and retaliation.

Harassment from a supervisor may be considered more gross than the same harassment from a coworker.

If the harassment is not by a supervisor and is not gross, it must be repeated. But it doesn't need to be repeated by the same person. If one coworker tells dirty jokes, another makes innuendoes, and a third shows obscene cartoons, those actions can be taken together to show the victim was working in a hostile and offensive environment.[13]

3. Sexual Harassment Is Unwelcomed by the Victim

The courts assume that the work place is asexual. People don't talk about, look at, or think about sex when they come to work. This may not be an accurate assumption, but it underlies this requirement. Since the work place is not supposed to be sexual, all sexual behavior is presumed unwelcomed.

When is it welcomed? Welcome means invited or initiated, not passively accepted.[14] For example, I am welcoming when I say to you, "Heard any good dirty jokes lately?" If I tell you a dirty joke, I'm harassing you. But if you tell me one back, I can't complain of harassment. I welcomed it by telling you one first.

What victims wear and talk about is evidence of whether they welcomed harassment.[15] The question to ask is what level of harassment is being welcomed. People who wear provocative clothes may be welcoming comments or stares, but not grabbing.

Occasional swearing or talking about ones personal life does not necessarily mean sexual conduct is welcome. Talking dirty indicates the other person welcomes dirty talk. It doesn't mean he or she welcomes abusive comments or physical assaults.

In the case of gross harassment, a court may assume it was unwelcomed even if the target doesn't say so. But the Equal Employment Opportunity Commission (EEOC) encourages victims to tell harassers it's unwelcome.[16]

practical pointer: Assume it's unwelcomed unless it's clearly invited.

Welcomeness must relate to the accused harasser.[17] I had a case in which the company tried to defend itself by saying my client slept with a lot of men at work. True, but that doesn't mean she welcomed being hounded for dates, locked in a room, and forcibly kissed by this particular man.

Filing Internal Complaints

Victims are not required by law to speak up to harassers, although it is recommended. They may be required to give the company notice that harassment is unwelcome if certain conditions are met:

- The company has a written sexual harassment policy that's been publicized to the victim.

- The company has a grievance procedure for filing complaints of sexual harassment.

- The grievance procedure is not futile.[18]

A grievance procedure is futile if sexual harassment complaints have been ignored in the past, if victims have been retaliated against after filing complaints, or if the only person the victim can complain to is the harasser.

Here is a sample policy and grievance procedure. It should be reviewed by a local attorney to make sure it meets all your state's requirements.

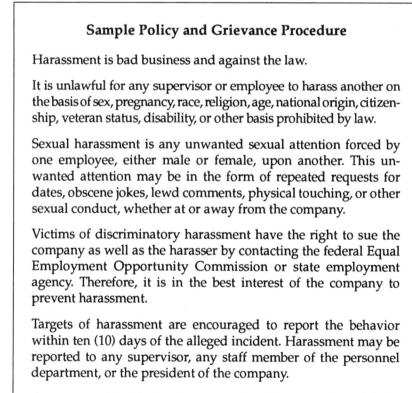

Sample Policy and Grievance Procedure

Harassment is bad business and against the law.

It is unlawful for any supervisor or employee to harass another on the basis of sex, pregnancy, race, religion, age, national origin, citizenship, veteran status, disability, or other basis prohibited by law.

Sexual harassment is any unwanted sexual attention forced by one employee, either male or female, upon another. This unwanted attention may be in the form of repeated requests for dates, obscene jokes, lewd comments, physical touching, or other sexual conduct, whether at or away from the company.

Victims of discriminatory harassment have the right to sue the company as well as the harasser by contacting the federal Equal Employment Opportunity Commission or state employment agency. Therefore, it is in the best interest of the company to prevent harassment.

Targets of harassment are encouraged to report the behavior within ten (10) days of the alleged incident. Harassment may be reported to any supervisor, any staff member of the personnel department, or the president of the company.

Any reported incident of harassment will be investigated fully, and if found to be true, in most cases the harasser will be given a written warning. In the case of a first offense involving gross harassment, threats, or violence, or in the event of a second offense, in most cases the harasser will be terminated.

Even if the company doesn't have a written policy, if the people complaining have participated in the harassment, they must file internal complaints before suing. For example, if an affair between coworkers ends and one begins harassing the other, the target must let the company know the relationship is over and the sexual attention unwanted.

In one case, a woman chemist filed suit complaining about vulgar language, frequent discussions about sex, and sexual teasing. The court found she had participated in and enjoyed this activity. On one occasion she asked her coworkers to stop the crude language, but she herself used the same language after that, so they didn't stop. The court held she couldn't sue for harassment. Since she had participated, she had a duty to make it very clear it was no longer welcomed.[19]

As a practical matter, few attorneys will represent victims if they haven't complained internally first. It's too easy for a harasser to convince a judge and jury the harassment would have stopped if only the victim complained. But even though an attorney won't take a case if the victim didn't complain, a government agency will. The EEOC will investigate any claim of wrongdoing, whether or not the victim complained.

Context Allows Some Conduct

There are some situations where employees expect to be exposed to sexual activity at work and can't claim sexual harassment. By accepting their jobs, they welcomed it.

People who work in topless bars expect to see nudity. Guards in jails and prisons review all magazines and letters that come for inmates to make sure they don't receive contraband. As a result, women and men deputies often are forced to look at pornographic material. They can't complain of sexual harassment in that situation.

But there still is an issue about what level of harassment reasonably was anticipated. For example, Robert Guccione, the publisher of *Penthouse* magazine, was sued for harassment by one of his employees because she was forced to have sex with his business associates.[20] He could not argue that because she worked in an environment where pornography was rampant she welcomed this.

4. *The Company Knew (or Should Have Known) but Did Nothing to Stop It*

The company is held responsible only if it knew or should have known about the harassment and did nothing to stop it. If the company takes immediate and appropriate corrective action, it is not liable.

Let me repeat that. If the company takes immediate and appropriate corrective action, it is not liable. The target of harassment is expected to endure some amount of harassment while the company follows its progressive disciplinary process for the accused.

Top management, directors, and officers are the company. If they harass employees, the company probably will be held liable, even if the harassment was unknown to anyone else.[21]

Whenever a lead, supervisor, or manager harasses a subordinate, the company is likely to be held liable. If these people are given managerial responsibility without close supervision and training to prevent abuses, the company is held responsible.

The company also will be held liable for harassment between coworkers if a manager is told about or sees the harassment and does nothing. If employees harassed others in the past, the company should strictly supervise them in the future. Otherwise, the company is liable for negligent retention (Chapter 5).

If an employee harasses a coworker in complete privacy, the harasser has no history of harassment, and the victim doesn't file an internal complaint, the company shouldn't be held responsible.

The company also is responsible for sexual harassment by outsiders. If a customer, vendor, or contractor comes into your company and sexually harasses your employees, your company is liable if you knew about it and didn't do anything to stop it. If talking to harassing outsiders doesn't work, the only way to protect your company is to ban them from the premises, even if that means you lose customers.[22]

The company may be liable for off-site behavior, if there is a connection with the job. If a supervisor or manager harasses a subordinate, no matter where it is, there is a strong presumption the subordinate's work will be affected.[23] When a coworker harasses a peer, effect on work must be proven.

Intent Is Irrelevant: The Downside of "Just Kidding"

The intent of the harasser is irrelevant. In fact, the federal government study found most harassers did not intend to harass.[24]

I counsel harassers and almost always they say they were teasing, joking, or genuinely in love. Sometimes they say they were nervous and acted without thinking. As one man put it, "My tongue disconnected from my brain."

A woman named Jane once came to my office in tears. She had just started a new job with a prestigious employer. On her second day of work, she made a mistake. When her boss saw it, he said, "Jane, you ignorant slut!" She wanted to sue for sexual harassment.

I said, "Have you ever seen 'Saturday Night Live' on TV?" She said no. I told her this was a running joke on the program. Probably the boss was trying to be funny by making light of her mistake.

But his intent was not important. What was important was the impact this comment would have on a reasonable woman. What would be the reaction of the reasonable woman? Most people have never seen the show, so we assume the reasonable woman has not heard this "joke" before. Even if she had heard it on TV, a reasonable woman would react negatively if her boss said it to her.

HOW TO RECOGNIZE SEXUAL HARASSMENT ON THE JOB

How do you recognize whether particular actions are sexual harassment? We'll cover specific examples in the paragraphs that follow. But there are several general tests.

The "Family Test:" Would this be happening if the harasser's child were standing there? Would it be done if the spouse of the victim was there? Would you want this to be done to your daughter or mother? If not, it may be sexual harassment.

The "Newspaper Test:" Is this something you would like to see in the company newsletter or your local newspaper?

The "Both Sexes Test:" Is this usually done by the accused to members of both sexes? If so, it might not be sexual harassment. This test doesn't work for every form of harassment, though. Telling dirty jokes to men doesn't justify telling them to women, or vice versa. But this test can be useful for other forms of harassment, such as touching.

Here are some examples of sexual harassment and how the courts have ruled on them.

Physical Harassment: The Strike and Neutral Zones

Physical harassment is not uncommon in today's work place. In 1992, a manager at a widely respected company told me, "Last week I was talking with another manager and a secretary. All of a sudden he grabbed her breast!"

To understand physical harassment, I divide the body into two zones. The "strike zone" is just like in baseball: from the chest to the knees is off limits. Any touching in the strike zone probably is going to be considered gross. Once is enough for a harassment case.[25]

An arm around the waist or shoulder may be sexual harassment if unwelcomed, because it's in the strike zone.

In contrast is the neutral zone: hands, arms, and shoulders. This is the area where we touch in our society. We shake hands, touch one another on the arm to get attention, pat someone on the shoulder for a job well done. This is accepted in our society and for the most part would not be considered sexual harassment.[26] Stroking the arm, fondling the hand, or rubbing the shoulders goes over the line into sexual harassment.

Even if a touch is in the neutral zone, it's important to recognize that many of your employees may be uncomfortable about being touched anywhere at all. Many women and men in our country have been abused as children, raped, or battered as spouses. They may feel threatened by touching. Many people who live here are from cultures where touching is taboo. Be sensitive to that and don't touch them, because you don't want to make people feel uncomfortable.

Touchy-Feely: Is It Welcomed or Forced?

Even though there is a sound psychological basis for giving people hugs and backrubs, they easily can be misinterpreted or abused. In the 1970s, I worked in an office committed to creating a touchy-feely environment. We hugged in the morning when we arrived and at night when we left, and gave each other backrubs during the day. This would not be considered sexual harassment because it wasn't explicitly sexual. It also was welcomed by the people involved. If we had employees who didn't want to participate and forced them to do so, it might well be sexual harassment.

The courts consistently have held that unwelcome backrubs are explicitly sexual and illegal harassment.[27] But what if I ask someone to give me a massage and a coworker is forced to watch because we share the same office? Can the coworker object?

In one case the court said if coworkers are forced to watch sexual harassment they are victims too and are entitled to sue, even though they themselves aren't harassed.[28] This is called third-party harassment.

It has not been decided if *welcomed* sexual behavior observed by coworkers is sexual harassment, but why not?

One of my clients had a woman employee who asked a man to rub her neck. Nobody could see them, but her moans could be heard over the cubicle walls. The other employees complained this was sexual harassment. They probably were right.

> *practical pointers:* What if you sometimes hug people at work and now are wondering if it's welcome? Wait for them to ask, "Where's my hug?" Or let them hug you the next few times. If they continue to hug you, the hugging is welcome. If they don't, it's probably been unwelcome all along.

Space Invaders: When You're Too Close for Comfort

Different cultures have different comfortable spaces. People raised in Latin cultures touch each other more in conversation and stand closer to one another than do people from Northern European, North American, and Asian cultures.

If the person invades the space of men and women equally, it's probably cultural and unlikely to be considered sexual harassment. If the person invades the space of only one gender or one person, its more likely to be considered harassment. It usually must be repeated because its not gross.

You should be sensitive to cultural difference in counseling an accused harasser, but it is not a defense in a sexual harassment case. The law is the same for everybody, no matter what their cultural background.

> *practical pointers:* Be aware of invading other's space. If people keep backing away from you, give them more room.

Visual Sexual Harassment

In 1992, one of my corporate clients issued a company calendar. Each month featured a different woman. In one, a woman's breast was revealed.

Pinups, calendars, or computer screens are considered sexual harassment if they are nude, seminude, or sexually explicit.[29] Pictures of women or of men are included. For example, the Chippendale calendars of semi-nude men are just as offensive as pin-ups of semi-nude women.

How explicit does a picture have to be before it is sexual harassment? All the reported cases deal with "pornographic" or "obscene" pictures, but they don't describe them. I would argue that even the *Sports Illustrated* swimsuit calendar could be considered part of a hostile and offensive working environment. It certainly would be evidence in a discrimination case if, for example, a man with such a calendar in his office refused to give a promotion to a qualified woman.

Pinups are dangerous. The company is assumed to know they are posted because they're open and obvious. Sophisticated employees who know what they're doing will complain about a poster. When it's not taken down, they'll rip it off the wall and take it to an attorney's office. Now its not one person's word against another's. Now there's hard evidence. That's Exhibit A.

A boudoir portrait of your spouse also may be offensive to others. To you it's your spouse. To someone else it's just another body.

Pinups should not be allowed anywhere. Employees sometimes claim they have the right to post what they want in their private offices, lockers, and desk drawers. As discussed in the privacy chapter, these aren't private property. They're company property. Company property shouldn't be used for sexual purposes, because it could be seen by others at any time.[30]

> *practical pointers:* Conduct a visual inspection of the entire work
> place and remove all sexually explicit pinups.

Stripping Telegrams

In the 1990s, I've seen corporations use strippers, "bimbos," and sex skits as part of their annual sales meetings. The president, chief executive officer and other top execs were there. If that doesn't send the wrong message from the top, what does?

Bringing in strippers or stripping telegrams can be sexual harassment. They are explicitly sexual. They're gross. Typically, strippers are brought into a big group that hasn't been asked if they welcome it. At least one person in the room probably objects.[31] The company should have known it was happening, because it's so open, especially if the stripper must get past a security checkpoint.

Strippers also may be considered harassment by both men and women on the basis of their religious principles.

Even if it doesn't end up in court, it can end up in the newspapers. That's happened to several employers. Is that the kind of publicity your company wants to have?

Bulletin Boards

Courts expect companies to patrol bulletin boards on the wall.[32] They're open and obvious. Sexually explicit materials, including joke lists and cartoons, are not allowed unless welcomed by everyone.

What about electronic bulletin boards? This is a new area for the courts, and there are no reported cases. But a court probably would analyze them the same as regular bulletin boards. Some companies moderate their networks; others don't. If the company moderates the network, the company has taken on the responsibility. The administrator should eliminate sexual and other harassment. If the company's network is not monitored, it could argue it's unreasonable for a court to force it to do so.

Whatever the legal requirements, electronic bulletin boards are a great place to use peer pressure to prevent sexual and other forms of harassment. When people post messages on the network that other readers consider stupid, the others "flame them." A flame is a nasty electronic message telling people just how stupid they are. The people who are flamed usually lay low for a while in shame before they post more messages, and they don't make that mistake again.

A lawyer in a large computer company told me that "a thousand flames" are common when people post stupid comments on the company's electronic bulletin board. But when dirty jokes or racial slurs appeared, they weren't flamed. Instead, employees complained to personnel. He said, "If everybody flamed the people making these comments, they'd stop a heck of a lot faster than when they get a warning from personnel."

Sexy Clothes

Provocative clothes become an issue in sexual harassment cases in two different ways. An employee can complain that clothing—or lack of it—is sexually harassing.

One of my corporate clients had this situation. A woman came to work wearing a see-through blouse with nothing underneath. Assigned to sit across from her at the assembly table was a man. He went to their supervisor and said, "I'm having a hard time concentrating on my work. This is sexual harassment. And it's probably a safety hazard." The supervisor said, "Go back to work and keep your head down."

The employee made it through that day. A couple weeks later the woman wore the same blouse. Again he complained. This time the supervisor did the right thing. He ordered her to go home and put on some clothes.

For this reason, a written dress code is recommended. See the sample dress code in the box. Even where there is no dress code, employees still can be told to wear appropriate professional attire.

> ### Sample Dress Code
>
> The company requires employees to be dressed appropriately. Supervisors will tell employees how to dress for their particular jobs. Generally, employees may not wear revealing, torn, or dirty clothing. Specifically prohibited are tank tops, halter tops, mesh shirts, crop tops, see-through material, spandex, shorts, miniskirts and T-shirts over leggings.

According to the U.S. Supreme Court, sexy clothes also can excuse sexual harassment.[33] For example, a corporate client had a woman come to work one day wearing a T-shirt that said "Squeeze me" across the chest. Some guy was walking through the office, saw the T-shirt, and squeezed her breasts.

She claimed sexual harassment. I met with her and said, "What do you expect? If you wear an invitation on your chest, people will take you up on it. Don't wear that shirt to work." Then I met with the man and said, "Don't take things so literally."

Provocative clothes may welcome some harassment, but not all. A woman who wears a miniskirt can't complain if a man says, "Nice legs." She welcomed the comment by dressing as she did. The same woman, however, has not welcomed being grabbed, hugged, and kissed. The question is what level of harassment was welcomed. For the most part provocative clothes only welcome comments and staring.

Even then, staring should not get out of hand. A company allowed employees to wear shorts. One woman looked particularly good in shorts. They weren't too tight or too short, they were regular shorts. But every time she wore them, men made it a point to go down her aisle. They'd get tools one at a time and go to the bathroom frequently. We couldn't tell her not to wear shorts, because everybody wore shorts. She had to be treated consistently.

We decided to deal with it as a performance issue. We told the men, "No unnecessary trips down any aisle."

Wandering Eyes

Double-takes, leers, and stares are harassment,[34] but they're tough to prove in court. How can you prove she was staring at you? Maybe she was staring out the window. How can you prove he was staring at your breasts? Maybe he was staring at the floor. How can you prove she was winking? Maybe she had a tic, and if she didn't, she will by the time of trial. These kinds of things aren't necessarily gross, so they will have to be repeated and probably combined with other forms of sexual harassment to win in court.

Quid pro Quo

A promise or a threat in exchange for sex is called "quid pro quo." "Sleep with me and you'll get the job," or "If you don't sleep with me, You're fired." This is the classic form of sexual harassment. It's gross. Only one incident is necessary to have a case. It's presumed to be unwelcomed. And by definition it comes from someone in power, so the company usually is automatically liable.

Dirty Jokes

Dirty jokes have been held to be sexual harassment.[35] "Dumb male" jokes are gender harassment. I think blonde jokes are gender harassment, because they usually refer to women. The only jokes you probably can tell safely are lawyer jokes, doctor jokes, and jokes about other professions.

Propositions

Outright propositions are explicitly sexual by definition. From a manager, or if done in front of others, one proposition is gross. If an employee repeatedly propositions a coworker, the company has a duty to stop it once it's known.

Flirting

If it's sexually explicit, it's harassing. Even if it's subtle, having social conversations with coworkers can be harassment. At the least, it's nonproductive.

Swearing and Obscene Gestures

In some companies, swearing and obscene gestures are an accepted form of corporate communication. In others, they're outrageous. Does corporate culture make a difference?

In 1982, a woman trader on Wall Street filed suit.[36] One of her complaints was that everybody at work swore. She was particularly disgusted by words that were demeaning to women.

She lost her case. In essence, the court said, "Hey, everybody knows traders on Wall Street swear. You knew what you were getting into. You asked for it."

In 1987, two women police officers filed suit against the Philadelphia Police Department alleging that their fellow officers used the same words complained about by the Wall Street trader. The women won. As the court put it, "a police station need not be run like a day care center; it should not, however, have the ambience of a nineteenth-century military barracks."[37]

A specific context may allow swearing. For example, if you swear at your telephone or computer, it is much less likely to be considered sexual harassment than if you swear directly at a person.

Swearing also is objectionable on the basis of religion. Remember, in religious cases, not only must you avoid offensive behavior, you also must reasonably accommodate the religion. I once hired a new receptionist. I told her to put message slips for the attorneys on her desk. Inevitably we would pick up the messages, stand at her desk, and swear at the people who had called us. After a week, she said that listening to the swearing violated her religious principles. I agreed that reasonable accommodation was appropriate and asked everyone to go into their offices to swear at their messages.

Obscene gestures, like swearing, may be accepted in the company. Flipping the third finger at someone you disagree with may be normal. In that situation, it would be difficult to show that it's explicitly sexual. But it shouldn't go too far.

Some gestures that are completely acceptable in the United States are offensive elsewhere. For example, the okay sign and the thumbs up signal have very different meanings in other countries of the world. Using these deliberately to offend could be national origin or sexual harassment.

Overheard Conversations

Overheard conversations are another form of third-party harassment. If what you say would be objectionable to the reasonable person when said directly, it is just as objectionable if it's overheard. Be sure your conversation is acceptable to everyone within earshot, whether you're in the cafeteria, your cubicle, or on the telephone.

Compliments

Sincere compliments about a person's clothing ("nice outfit") generally are not considered sexual harassment. That's socially acceptable. Making comments about how somebody looks in an outfit ("you look sexy in that outfit") or about their body ("nice buns") would be considered harassment.[38]

Even sincere, nonsexual compliments can be harassing if they are repeated over and over, day after day.[39]

No court has said that calling women (or men) "honey," "sweetie," or "babe" is considered sexual harassment. Endearments are presumed to be innocuous to the reasonable victim. But the U.S. Supreme Court has said if you use words to refer to women that you don't use in referring to men, that's evidence of your intent to discriminate.[40] If a woman is denied a promotion, she could point to being called "honey" as evidence of discrimination.

In my experience, the one thing men do that make women mad is calling them "girls," even when the women themselves use the word to describe their friends.

> *practical pointers:* If they're old enough to work, they're old enough to be called women. Young women are just that—young women. Men are men or young men. Personally, I'd like the word "guys" to include everyone, but some women find this insulting.

Requests for Dates with Coworkers and Subordinates

A request for a date should be distinguished from an outright proposition. A request for a date is nice. "Would you like to go out sometime?"

If the request is between two coworkers, they are allowed one free request for a date, because it's not repeated and it's not gross. If the person asked says anything other than "yes," the asker has to say, "Let me know if you change your mind, because I can never ask you again." If coworkers do date, have relationships, live together, or marry, it's important to ensure that their work is not affected.[41]

Repeated unwelcome requests for dates between coworkers are sexual harassment.

A manager, supervisor, or lead should *never* date a subordinate. The dangers of such affairs were dramatized in a 1986 U.S. Supreme Court decision.[42]

In that case, Mechelle Vinson was hired at a bank as a teller-trainee. At the end of her first three months, the branch manager asked her out to dinner. Over dinner, he said he was attracted to her and wanted to have an affair. At first she said no, but later that evening she said yes. For the next four years, they had sex while she was steadily promoted through the ranks to assistant branch manager. After four years she quit her job and sued for sexual harassment. She said she had been forced to have an affair because she was afraid to say no to the boss.

Some people might wonder how anyone could be forced to do anything for four years. Not the Supreme Court. In a unanimous decision, the Court held that if Ms. Vinson did not welcome the first proposition, she could sue for sexual harassment. Some people argue she had a choice to leave the company. But she had a good job. She shouldn't be forced to leave just because her boss was sexually harassing her.[43]

The Court said that Mechelle Vinson would have been sexually harassed even if she had a voluntary affair with the boss. The Court said her eventual agreement to have sex was not important in deciding whether she had been sexually harassed. What was important was whether she welcomed his advances in the first place. In other words, was she giving out signals she was interested? If so, she welcomed his advances and there was no sexual harassment.

This case illustrates the dangers of supervisor-subordinate affairs. Even if you think it's completely voluntary, you could lose later if your ex-lover says it wasn't.

The breakup of an affair leads to other problems. A former lover who's not picked for promotion could claim retaliation.

Lawsuits by other employees sometimes can be filed while the relationship is going on. According to EEOC regulations, it's not illegal for a supervisor to promote a lover instead of another employee who is better qualified. It's not illegal because it doesn't discriminate on the basis of sex: both men and women are excluded from the promotion.

But if the subordinate was forced into the relationship by sexual harassment from the manager, then other employees can claim they are victims of illegal sexual favoritism. And if sexual harassment is so pervasive that virtually the only people promoted and rewarded are sleeping with the boss, that creates a hostile or offensive working environment.[44]

Your state may have a broader interpretation of sexual favoritism. Certainly, employee morale will suffer if the boss is perceived as giving favorable treatment to a lover.

Affairs between managers and employees who do not have direct reporting relationships also are dangerous. The victim still can claim the affair was not voluntary because managers have power to influence each other.

For these reasons, some companies have policies that prohibit supervisor-subordinate relationships. The United Parcel Service (UPS) has a policy that prohibits social relationships between any manager and any nonmanager. UPS fired a manager who had worked for the company for 25 years because he was living with a subordinate. He sued for wrongful termination and lost. The Court said the company had the right to enforce this policy to prevent sexual harassment.[45]

If a relationship is ongoing, what can the company do to protect itself? The reporting relationship should be changed if neither person is disadvantaged as a result. If one person must be disadvantaged, it should be the supervisor, since the supervisor is held to a higher standard than the employee.

If separating the two is not possible, at a minimum you should talk to the subordinate privately to determine if the affair was welcomed. If the subordinate says it is, document it. It may help you defend a lawsuit if one is filed later. Audit decisions made about everyone in the work group to make sure there's no sexual favoritism.

RETALIATING AGAINST A PERSON WHO COMPLAINS ABOUT SEXUAL HARASSMENT

Retaliation against a person who complains about sexual harassment is illegal. Retaliation comes in many forms. It includes giving poor performance appraisals, assigning demeaning tasks, demoting, taking pay away, nit-picking and other adverse actions.

You can't retaliate against a person who complains, even if the complaint is not substantiated. Someone who files an honest but mistaken complaint is protected by the law. In many cases, people have lost their sexual harassment claims, only to win on illegal retaliation.[46]

A person who intentionally files a false complaint within the company may be reprimanded, just as any other person who falsifies company documents.

A person who intentionally files a false complaint with the EEOC can NOT be given a disciplinary warning or terminated. This is considered illegal retaliation because it would have a chilling effect on people who may want to file complaints in the future.[47] Filing a false complaint is defamatory and just as illegal as sexual harassment. However, the courts say the only remedy is for the person who was falsely accused to sue the accuser for defamation. Defamation is covered in Chapter 4.

FIVE FUNDAMENTAL RESPONSIBILITIES OF A COMPANY FOR PREVENTING HARASSMENT

According to EEOC regulations, a company must take *all steps necessary* to prevent harassment.[48] That's a very high standard. It means you have to be proactive. Don't wait for a complaint.

The first step in preventing harassment is to have a written sexual harassment policy as described earlier.

In addition, the EEOC says there are five minimum requirements for preventing harassment:

1. Affirmatively raise the issue.
2. Express strong disapproval of harassment.
3. Develop appropriate penalties for harassers.
4. Inform employees of their right to raise and how to raise the issue.
5. Develop methods to sensitize all employees.

The best way to meet these objectives is to have a formal training program for all managers, supervisors, leads, and employees. In that training program, the issue will be raised. Strong disapproval will be communicated. The penalties for harassment will be expressed. Employees will be informed that harassment is illegal and that they have a right to file complaints. And the training will sensitize employees to the gray areas and fine lines.

Once training has been conducted, don't wait for a complaint. If you see sexual harassment, you have a duty to stop it. As a manager, you are the company.

Listen to what people are talking about. Look at what's on the walls.

Rumors and graffiti can put the company on notice that harassment has occurred. Investigate all leads. Stop all inappropriate behavior.

Managers often object to reporting sexual harassment if the particular incident has been resolved. Earlier I mentioned one manager who saw another grabbing a woman's breast. The manager said he didn't think he should do anything because the offender immediately apologized and the woman "laughed it off." But he must report it to the personnel department. If the other manager is this out of line in front of a witness, its likely he's done it in the past or will do it in the future. The company must stop this gross misconduct from happening ever again.

WHY TARGETS DON'T COMPLAIN

According to the federal government study, most targets of harassment do not file complaints about harassment.[49] They endure it, go along, or quit. Indeed, if a particular manager has a high turnover of employees, it may be evidence that harassment is occurring.

Why don't targets file internal complaints? Many times, they don't know how. Often companies don't have harassment policies, or the personnel department is seen as part of the problem.

Recipients of harassment often blame themselves. They think if only they acted differently, this wouldn't have happened. In my experience, both male and female victims of harassment have this response.

Targets of harassment often are too embarrassed to talk about what happened to them. They are afraid others will laugh at them. When the harassment is from a higher-ranking employee, they're afraid the other person will be believed instead.

Employees don't file complaints because they're afraid of retaliation. They fear they'll lose their jobs, or at least be excluded and isolated by others. In these violent times, many targets fear that complaining will cause the accused to attack them physically.

Finally, victims sometimes don't complain because they don't want to get the accused into trouble. They realize a charge of sexual harassment could hurt the other person's career. They often recognize the many good qualities the individual has. They don't want to be responsible for injuring another person's reputation, especially if they think they can handle it.

How to Handle Complaints from Employees

If employees come to you complaining of sexual harassment, they are trusting you to treat them seriously. Listen. Listen. But don't agree. The worst thing you can do is exclaim, "That's sexual harassment!" That's an admission in court.

Don't sympathize, empathize. "It sounds like you are really upset." At the same time, you don't want to be cold. You want the person to feel relieved they came to you.

Once you've listened to the complaint, ask, "What do you want me to do?" You are not asking to find out what you should do. You are asking to find out how serious the victim is. If the victim says, "I just want it to stop," you are going to have a different reaction than if the victim says, "I want this person fired now."

If the victim wants the harasser fired, you need to counsel that immediate termination is rarely justified. Harassers almost always should receive at least one warning. But having asked the question, now you know the person complaining is more likely to go to a lawyer than someone who just wants it to stop.

Sometimes victims will say, "I don't want you to do anything about this. I want to let you know, just in case." If victims describe something that's not sexual harassment, they can be allowed to resolve it themselves. But if it's sexual harassment, you can't ignore it. You are the company. If it happens again, the employee could complain, "I told my boss and nothing happened."

Your response might be, "The employee told me not to take action." But at trial the attorney representing the employee will ask you, "Since when do you do what employees want? If an employee ran in and said someone was brandishing a gun in the lobby, wouldn't you do something?" As a manager, you have to use your own good judgment.

When receiving a complaint, don't bring up confidentiality. That's a negative. If asked, don't make a blanket promise of confidentiality. You will keep the situation confidential to the extent possible. Only people with a need to know will be informed. And you will attempt to keep the victim's name out of it as much as possible.

Don't promise you will fix the problem. Only promise to investigate and check back. End the session by setting a date and time to meet. Then have that meeting, even if all you can say is that you've done some research and talked to some people, but you still need to do more. Then set another date. If you cancel a follow-up meeting, you will alienate the victim and increase the likelihood that he or she will seek legal action.

Once you receive a complaint, call an expert on sexual harassment. Call your personnel department or employment lawyer immediately. This is a mine field.

Investigating Complaints: Three Parties Who Must Be Questioned

Once an expert gets involved, the complaint must be investigated. Three parties must be questioned. The victim must be asked about specifics: the what, where, when, and why. See sample questions in the box.

Questions to Ask in Sexual Harassment Cases

1. When did you and accused first meet? In what capacity? What was your relationship like at first?

2. When and where did you first experience sexual harassment?

3. What exactly did the harasser do and say? What was your response? What was harasser's response? (and so on for each incident)

4. Were there any witnesses to these incidents? Who? What exactly did they see or hear?

5. Have you told anyone about it? Who? How can I reach them?

6. Have you made any notes or kept a diary? May I see them?

7. Have you confronted harasser? What response?

Second, coworkers must be questioned. They may be victims themselves, or maybe they witnessed the harassment.

Coworkers often can be questioned without bringing in the name of either the complaining victim or the accused harasser. A police chief told me how he investigated a problem in his department. There was only one woman police officer. She complained about a male officer sexually harassing her. The chief knew if he confronted the man, it would be obvious who complained.

So he talked to all the other women who worked with his officers—clerks, bailiffs, secretaries. He asked them, "Have you had any problems of sexual harassment from any of my officers?" The universal response was, "Most of your officers are great. But there's this one guy. . . ."

This investigation was impartial and maintained confidentiality. Now the chief was able to reprimand the officer for harassing 10 women without identifying any of them.

The third party to be questioned is the accused harasser. Harassers have rights too, most important the right not to be wrongfully terminated. Their side of the story must be heard.

What if the accused asks, "Who told you?" In many cases your response should be, "I can't tell you." On the other hand, it may be necessary for the harasser to know who complained in order to respond fully to the charges. Of course the harasser should be warned not to retaliate or even discuss the matter with the person who complained.

Whom Do You Believe?

In sexual harassment cases it's common not to have any witnesses. It's one person's word against another's. As a result, many managers fear that someone could file a false complaint and ruin another's career. Although false complaints are filed, they're rare. Just because it's one person against another doesn't mean the complaint is inherently false. Complaints often are filed with the police and in the courts based on one person's word. Robbery, assault, and oral contracts often involve just two people's stories.

In evaluating a complaint of sexual harassment, look at whether the victim has a motive to lie. For example, if a complaint is filed after the victim has been disciplined, fired, or laid off, there may be a motive to lie.

Sometimes the motive for lying is outside the work place. A personnel director called me one day in a panic. He said a woman employee had come in that morning and said she'd been raped by a coworker in the company parking lot. I was shocked and asked him, "What are you going to do?" He said, "I'm getting his final paycheck ready and calling a security guard. We'll terminate him as soon as he reports to work." I said, "What was his response when you confronted him?" He said, "Oh, I didn't ask him. Its obvious she's telling the truth. She's very sincere. I believe her. There's no reason to contact him."

You know what I said. "You must talk to him!" The accused had the right to have his side of the story heard. I told my client to call back after he talked to him.

When he called back, he said, "I talked to him. He said they've been having an affair for the last 11 months. They've been having sex in her car in the parking lot the entire time. He wants to know which of those times it was rape." Naturally, I was shocked. I said, "Now what are you going to do?" He said, "I'm going to fire the woman. She obviously filed a false complaint. I really believe him. He's very sincere. I think we should terminate her employment."

You know what I said. "You have to go back and confront her with his evidence and get her side of the story."

By the end of the day, the woman admitted they had been having an affair. Her husband found out and, to make it okay with him, she claimed she had been assaulted. If we hadn't conducted a vigorous investigation, we would have made a terrible mistake.

This was an unusual case. Complaints filed internally with your company's personnel department by current employees usually aren't false. That's because most employees believe if they complain to personnel they'll be labeled troublemakers. Maybe they won't be retaliated against, but they won't be considered team players.

Victim's Behavior: Irrational Does Not Mean Untrue

In the course of conducting your investigation, you may discover the victim acted irrationally. That's what happened during the confirmation hearings for U.S. Supreme Court Justice Clarence Thomas. Many of the senators at the time said they did not believe Professor Anita Hill's charges of sexual harassment. They pointed out that she acted irrationally. She said she had been sexual harassed while working with Clarence Thomas at the Department of Education, yet she followed him to work at the EEOC. After she left the EEOC, she saw him twice and talked to him on the phone. And she recommended to the FBI that he be appointed to the Supreme Court.[50]

The senators' reactions: if she had been sexually harassed, she wouldn't have done those things. Therefore, they reasoned, she had not been sexually harassed.

The fact is that victims often do irrational things. They've been traumatized. Other options aren't always obvious to them. Anita Hill may have done what she did because she thought it was best for her health, her self-esteem, and her career. We've all been taught to go along to get along. That doesn't mean the harassment didn't occur.

After the Investigation: How to Take Action

Once you've completed your investigation, you must take immediate and appropriate corrective action.[51] If you take corrective action designed to stop the harassment, you can't be sued by the victim.[52] But if you don't take corrective action and the victim quits, he or she can sue not only for harassment but also for constructive discharge (being forced to quit).[53]

The action you take can range from firing the harasser for gross misconduct, to writing a warning, to verbally counseling for low-level harassment. If what happened was in fact an honest misunderstanding, a meeting between the so-called harasser and the so-called victim may be appropriate.

It also may be appropriate to take action with the person who complained. A victim who is unreasonably sensitive should receive counseling and training, too.

Transfers are appropriate in some circumstances. Harassers should be transferred if possible after a written warning. Targets of harassment should never be transferred against their will. They can be informed of other job possibilities, but should not be encouraged or discouraged from applying.

It's often difficult for managers to take appropriate action when the evidence is one person's word against the other's. They're tempted to throw up their hands and say, There's no evidence so I can't do anything. Even if you have only one person's word, that's evidence. That's enough for a jury to decide that sexual harassment occurred, so that's enough for you.

Many managers find themselves faced with the same situation as the senators in the Clarence Thomas hearings. Several senators said they voted for him because they weren't convinced beyond a reasonable doubt that harassment occurred. "Beyond a reasonable doubt" is not the correct standard of proof. That's the standard in criminal cases. In sexual harassment cases, the standard of proof is "preponderance of the evidence."

What's the difference between "beyond a reasonable doubt" and "preponderance of the evidence?" To use a football analogy, beyond a reasonable doubt is a touchdown. Preponderance of the evidence is any forward movement. A foot is preponderance of evidence.

Or, to change the analogy, if you have the scales of justice before you, they need to tip only a little bit in favor of one person as opposed to the other in order for a court to decide, and for you to decide, whether sexual harassment occurred.

When to Follow Up

If disciplinary action is taken against an accused, the victim should be informed that "corrective action has been taken." To protect the confidentiality of the harasser, don't reveal what level of discipline was given. Require the complainant to keep it confidential, too.

After a complaint of harassment has been resolved, you have a duty to follow up. Check back with the victim two weeks, four weeks and six weeks later. Do this privately.

In one of my cases, the personnel representative went up to my client in front of other employees, and asked her, "Are you having any more problems?" Of course she said no then. She intended to go to personnel during her break to report that the harassment had not stopped. But as soon as the personnel rep heard there were no more problems, he put through the paperwork to have the harasser promoted to be supervisor of my client. That's when she quit and sued.

After six weeks of follow-up, say to the victim, "Let me know if you have any more problems." Even if your personnel department has taken over the entire matter, you, as the manager, want to encourage your employees to come back to you if they're not happy.

What Victims Can Do to Stop Harassment

Managers can't be victims of harassment from their subordinates, because they have the power to stop it by disciplining and firing them. If higher management prevents you from firing a subordinate for harassment, that could be grounds for you to sue the company.

Since managers also may be victims of harassment from their managers or coworkers, it's appropriate to say a few words here about what you can do to stop harassment if you are the target. The EEOC and the courts highly encourage victims to file internal complaints. But as a practical matter, the more you do informally, before talking to the personnel department, the better results you will have.

If you are uncomfortable about sexual behavior, be direct. One approach is to use nonjudgmental phrases to ask people to stop: "I know you don't mean to be offensive, but comments like that make me feel uncomfortable."

"I'm sure you don't realize it, but I find that kind of language offensive."

"I'm not the kind of person who likes dirty jokes."

If these phrases don't work, you can write a demand letter. Demand letters are written by attorneys for their clients, but they're just as effective coming from you.

The demand letter is addressed to the harasser. It has three paragraphs:

1. In the first paragraph, list the behavior you find harassing. Give times, dates, places, and details. At the end of this paragraph, write the sentence, "I consider these actions to be illegal sexual harassment."

2. In the second paragraph, list the effects of the harassment. You can't concentrate on your work. You worry when you get home. You can't sleep. You're depressed. You have an eating disorder, migraine headaches, ulcers. All the physical and emotional effects of the harassment should be listed, but don't exaggerate.

3. In the last paragraph, make your demand. In most cases, you want the harassment to stop. "I demand that you stop this and any other harassment. If you don't stop, I will show a copy of this letter to the personnel department. If you do stop, this matter will not go beyond us. I look forward to developing a good working relationship with you."

Give the letter to the harasser. In most cases, seeing their actions on paper causes harassers to stop. If they don't, you can take the letter to the personnel department, where the matter should be taken very seriously since you've documented the problem and given the harasser an opportunity to improve.

MEN, WOMEN, AND MIXED MESSAGES

Sexual harassment is the most emotional topic in employment law. At least half of the women managers in my courses have experienced sexual harassment. Some have filed complaints, but most just ignore it. It's the price you pay to be a woman in business.

About 90% of the managers who take my courses are men. Many of them are openly hostile to the law. Even though it protects men as well as women from harassment, in fact most cases are brought by women against men. And that's the way they see it: women against men.

Some men have said, "I'm not going to worry about sexual harassment. I just wont hire any women." My response, "Why don't we stop harassment by not hiring any men?" But then I deal with the real issue, which is the fear and powerlessness they feel.

Women and men live in close proximity. For this reason sexual harassment is very different from racial or other types of harassment. A dedicated bigot can construct his or her life to live in a segregated society. It's hard to avoid the opposite sex in life. Men sometimes feel surrounded and outnumbered.

Many men don't know where the line is. They're confused. Things that were tolerated 20 years ago are illegal today. Our society gives us mixed messages. Sexual innuendo is common on television sitcoms. Advertising blatantly uses sex to sell. Pornography is readily available.

Sex permeates our society outside of work. In this context, men (and women) wonder: Why do we have a law that prohibits even talking about sex at work? The answer is that the sexual harassment law is the result of a unique consensus in U.S. society. It embodies norms shared by many diverse cultures and religions. It crosses virtually all party and ideological lines.

The term "sexual harassment" originally was coined and outlawed by a federal judge liberally interpreting the general sex discrimination law. A few years later, during the Carter administration, feminists convinced the EEOC to adopt regulations prohibiting sexual harassment. They became law in 1980.

In 1986 the U.S. Supreme Court heard its first sexual harassment case. By that time, the court included several Reagan appointees and was considered conservative. Many observers, myself included, assumed the Court would gut the regulations. To my surprise, the unanimous opinion praised the law of sexual harassment and gave it an expansive reading.

Why would the conservative court approve a feminist law? Because conservatives and feminists agree when it comes to sex. Both groups have opposed pornography, obscene music lyrics, and other sexual activities considered disrespectful toward women. They haven't been able to do much about sex in society because of the First Amendment. But the sexual harassment law has given them a tool to restrict sex in at least one sector of our lives.

Most sexual harassment is verbal or visual. Prohibiting it directly conflicts with freedom of speech for the accused. Is the sexual harassment law unconstitutional? The American Civil Liberties Union is representing a man accused of harassment arguing just that. Thus today in the law we have two conflicting trends: conservatives and feminists pushing to expand the law of sexual harassment, and liberals trying to restrict it. No wonder we all are confused!

GUIDELINES FOR INTERACTING WITH THE OPPOSITE SEX

In my courses, people at some point begin worrying they will never be able to talk to a member of the opposite sex again. I would hate to see that happen. But since most harassment is unintentional, it's important for all of us to think about how we should act so we don't unintentionally harass someone.

Through the years I've collected guidelines for interacting with the opposite sex. One of my favorites came from a cop who said, "I've found the best way to avoid harassment is not to talk to women." I said, "You really can't do that. That's sex discrimination." He said, "Nope. Its not sex discrimination, because I don't talk to men either!" This is not the answer.

Another guideline came from a man who said, "In my forty years of working, I found the best advice is to treat every woman like your mother. That way you don't get into trouble." I thought that was a great guideline until I tried it in another class. A man asked if he could scratch himself in front of women. I said, "Would you do that in front of your mother?" He said, "The woman gave me birth! I'll do what I have to."

I was in Atlanta and a manager said his secretary told him, "Pay me like a man, but treat me like a lady." I tried that out in California, and several women said they didn't want to be treated like ladies.

A lawyer who worked for me had this idea. She said, "If men want to get along with women, just say, 'Yes Ma'am!'" Talk about sexist!

A manager in one class suggested, "How about the Golden Rule? Treat others as you want to be treated." That sounded like a good idea until another man stood up and said, Okay, Rita, "I'd like to be harassed by you. Does that mean I get to harass you now?" So the Golden Rule didn't work.

practical pointers: The best guideline for behavior is the Platinum Rule: "Treat others as they want to be treated." In any large work place, you will find people who range in tolerance of sexual behavior from Mother Theresa to Madonna. Observe. Listen. Be perceptive. Treat people the way they are telling you they want to be treated.

You can always ask, "Would you like to hear a dirty joke?" "Do you mind if I swear?" If others accept your behavior, then you don't have to worry. Asking also means you have to respect "no."

The final guideline is, when in doubt, don't. Especially as a manager, you need to be aware of what you're saying and how You're saying it, so there is no question about your behavior.

The Value of Keeping Sex Out of the Workplace

Ultimately, it makes good business sense to keep sex out of work. We work with people of diverse religions, sexual orientations, and cultural values. No one should impose their values on others at work, where we all have to go to make a living.

I was talking about values in class one day when a Japanese woman said, "In Japan, it's so different. There the female body is seen as something beautiful to be admired."

One of the American salesmen in the group said, "Yeah! That's what I think!" Another woman manager said, "The body is beautiful only if it belongs to a beautiful person. Pictures just turn women's bodies into sex objects."

Another man said, "It's against my religion to have lustful thoughts. I can't stop them when I see pinups."

What struck me about these reactions was that everyone agreed they would be distracted by a pinup. They wouldn't be working. And that's not good for business.

The law of sexual harassment gives you the opportunity to show you value the diversity of the work force, respect the dignity of individuals, and provide a good place to work for all.

Chapter 7

LIFE AND DEATH ON THE JOB

OSHA, Worker's Compensation, and Stress

One of my clients was a real estate office. There were 11 agents and employees. A husband and wife owned the brokerage.

One day I got a telephone message from them. I had been in court all morning. I was busy and behind in my work. The message said, "Employee broke his leg. What should we do?"

I thought, "Do I have to hold everyone's hand? Call a doctor!"

I put the message on the bottom of the stack and dealt with all the others. A couple hours later I got another message. "Employee died. Now what do we do?"

I called back immediately. An employee had fallen off a stepladder while stacking some reports. They had taken him to the hospital. While setting the leg, a bone chip was released. It went to his heart and caused cardiac arrest.

The owners were devastated. Both this employee and his brother had worked at the firm for many years. His family socialized with the owners. He had two young children, another one on the way.

It was difficult for the owners to deal with the death emotionally. Then the legal system got involved and made it worse.

Unlike other laws covered in this book, the safety laws are literally a matter of life and death. I learned from this experience that even though an accident sounds minor, it can become a tragedy.

PART ONE: FOUR KINDS OF LAWS THAT IMPACT SAFETY AT WORK

Workplace safety is simply a matter of valuing human life. Nationally in 1989, 10,400 employees died on the job, and over 1,700,000 had disabling injuries or illnesses.[1]

The purpose of the safety laws is to prevent these deaths, injuries, and illnesses. When they aren't prevented, the employer is required to pay benefits to the injured employee, the company may be fined, and the manager may be imprisoned.

Or to look at it in a more positive light, the safety rules set by law reduce workplace injuries, thus decreasing your worker's compensation and other costs.

There are four kinds of laws that impact safety: safety laws, environmental regulations, criminal sanctions, and worker's compensation. Those laws will be covered in this part. In the next part, seven hot safety topics will be covered: repetitive strain injuries (like carpal tunnel syndrome), injuries from using computers, AIDS in the workplace, serving alcohol at work, secondhand cigarette smoke, indoor air pollution, and stress claims, including constructive discharge.

SAFETY LAWS AND THE OCCUPATIONAL SAFETY AND HEALTH ACT

The Occupational Safety and Health Act (OSHA) sets the minimum requirements every employer must meet to have a safe workplace. The act was passed by Congress in 1970.[2] There are also state OSHAs which have their own requirements. The term "OSHA" generally is used for both the law and the agency it created.

OSHA mandates minimum requirements for two areas: safety and health. Safety violations usually lead to one-time injuries: slips, trips, falls, and burns. For example, if an OSHA inspector goes to a construction site and finds a broken ladder in use, that's a safety violation because it could lead to a fall.

Health relates to illnesses from toxic fumes; fibers like asbestos, cotton, and dust; and cumulative trauma such as carpal tunnel syndrome. In the health area, OSHA can't keep up with the changes in technology. There are over 8.5 million chemicals registered with the American Chemical Society. Every year, 25,000 new chemicals are developed. OSHA has regulations on less than 1,000 chemicals. It is able to regulate only 9 or 10 new chemicals a year.[3]

States That Have OSHAs

The following states have their own OSHAs. Their requirements are at least as strict as federal OSHA, and in most cases, more so. Also, federal OSHA sometimes exempts employers with fewer than 10 employees, but state OSHAs may apply to small companies. Check with your local OSHA office.

Alaska	New Mexico
Arizona	New York
California	(public employees only)
Connecticut	North Carolina
(public employees only)	Oregon
Hawaii	South Carolina
Indiana	Tennessee
Iowa	Utah
Kentucky	Vermont
Maryland	Virginia
Michigan	Washington
Minnesota	Wyoming
Nevada	

The Five Main Requirements Under OSHA

Under OSHA, employers are required to

1. Provide a safe workplace.

2. Train employees about potential hazards.

3. Keep records of injuries and illnesses.

4. Post warnings and notices.

5. Notify OSHA of major accidents.

1. Providing a Safe Workplace

The most important requirement of OSHA is called the "general duty" rule. It's the fundamental duty of an employer to provide a safe workplace. "Safe" means free of dangers that could cause serious physical harm to employees.[4]

OSHA's standards generally are recognized as bare minimums. Even if there is no OSHA standard, you have a duty to provide a safe workplace.

One court said the precautions you should take are those a conscientious safety expert would recommend.[5]

There are two major ways to make a workplace safe. The first is through engineering. Design the environment to be safe. When that's not possible, the second choice is to provide employees with protective gear.

Some jobs are inherently dangerous, like capping flaming oil wells, cleaning nuclear reactors, and handling hazardous waste. The employer must make those jobs as safe as possible.

2. Training Employees About Potential Hazards

The second major OSHA requirement is to train employees to perform their jobs safely. Of critical importance is a "hazard communication program." Employees must be educated about the hazards of chemicals used or produced at work. OSHA requires every company, no matter how small, to have a hazardous communication program.

Hazardous chemicals include any substance that damages skin, eyes, or lungs, including combustibles, compressed gas, explosives, carcinogens, corrosives, and sensitizers.[6]

If you use hazardous chemicals, your safety program must have three features:

1. Material Safety Data Sheets

2. Written hazardous communication program

3. Training for all workers

Material Safety Data Sheets (MSDS) are required to be kept at the worksite and available to all workers. The MSDS is provided by the manufacturer of the chemical. If you use hazardous substances, the MSDS should come with the first shipment. If you produce them, you also must write an MSDS and send it to your customers.[7]

You may be surprised at what is considered a hazardous substance for which an MSDS must be kept. One of my clients makes a device which contains an ordinary AA battery. The firm is required to keep an MSDS on hand for their employees who store, ship, or insert the batteries. They also must provide an MSDS for the batteries to their own customers.

The MSDS must include the following information:

Physical hazards, like flammability and reactivity

Health hazards, including symptoms of exposure and medical conditions aggravated by exposure

The primary *routes of entry*

The recommended *exposure limits*

Whether it is a *carcinogen*

How to handle safely

Control measures such as protective gear required

First aid and *emergency procedures*[8]

The second requirement for every company that uses hazardous chemicals is to have a written hazardous communication program. You must keep a list of all chemicals used in the plant. You also must have a procedure for labeling every container and pipe that contains hazardous chemicals.

Finally, training is required. Employees must receive training when they're hired, when they're assigned to work with a new chemical, or when a new chemical is brought into production. Training should include everything covered in the MSDS.[9]

Even if you don't use hazardous substances, your state OSHA may require routine safety training. California requires employees to be trained when hired, when new processes are introduced, and periodically thereafter.

3. Keeping Records of Injuries and Illnesses

In addition to a safe workplace, OSHA also requires extensive record keeping. There is a $70,000 maximum fine *every* time you don't log an injury or illness.

Only two kinds of employers are exempt from record keeping. Employers in low-hazard industries like retail trade, banking, insurance, real estate, and law don't have to keep extensive records. Companies with fewer than 10 employees also are exempt from some record keeping. But even these companies may be covered by state OSHA requirements.

OSHA Form 200 is the key document. It is a log of all workplace injuries and illnesses that resulted in medical treatment, work restrictions, or death. This log must be posted every year for at least a month. It's kept for five years and is available to employees.

"Medical treatment" means more than first aid. Guideline: If the employee had to leave the worksite for treatment, that's more than first aid. A second visit to the company medical department for the same injury usually counts as medical treatment, too.

Even if an injury doesn't result in medical treatment, it must be logged if the employee is placed on work restrictions or transferred to another job. If employees can't do portions of their regular jobs, they should be logged as injuries. Employees do not have to be on official "light duty" to be considered restricted. Even if you accommodate them only informally for a day, it counts.

You should have a policy requiring employees to report every injury, no matter how minor. Supervisors should fill out accident reports for every injury. Since second visits require injuries to be logged, you should have a procedure for following up on all injured employees.

Exposure and Medical Records. If you have any records showing what hazards your employees have been exposed to, you have to keep them for 30 years. The purpose of this requirement is to allow employees to go back and prove that conditions with long latency periods like cancer, asbestosis, and black lung disease are work related.

The most important document to keep is the Material Safety Data Sheet. Any tests or reports of monitoring in the workplace also must be kept.

Employee records made by the company's medical staff must be kept under this rule. Also included are preemployment medical tests, reports of first aid, and employees' medical complaints.[10]

Exposure records must be given without cost to employees within 15 days of requesting them. Only employees' own medical records can be shown to them, unless there is a court order.

Management attorneys advise employers to avoid collecting more records than required by OSHA. For example, OSHA does not require companies to give medical exams. But once given, the records must be available to employees and kept for 30 years.

4. Posting Warnings and Notices

A notice entitled "Job Safety & Health Protection" must be posted in every language spoken by at least 10% of the employees. Call your local OSHA office for a copy. Your state OSHA also may have posting requirements.

Every February the company must post the OSHA Form 200 log of injuries and illnesses from the previous year.

Citations received from OSHA also must be posted.

5. Notifying OSHA of Major Accidents

If an employee dies on the job, or if 5 or more employees are hospitalized, every company, no matter how small, has 48 hours in which to notify the nearest OSHA office.[11]

When to Expect OSHA Inspections

To enforce its requirements, OSHA conducts unannounced inspections of the workplace. A company representative is allowed to accompany the OSHA inspector.

The company's consent is required before an investigation can be conducted. If you don't consent to an inspection, OSHA is required to get a search warrant. You can fight an inspection if there is no good cause for a search, or you may be able to limit the scope of the inspection. But according to James E Sharp, a former inspector, "Believe me, we'll get a search warrant. And when we come back, we'll be mad."[12]

There are three types of inspections. *Random* inspections are conducted regularly, particularly of businesses engaged in high-risk occupations. These include construction, mining, and chemical manufacturing. You also will be inspected whenever there is a major *accident* or death, and when a *complaint* is filed by an employee.

How to Deal with Employee Complaints

You can't discriminate against an employee who complains to OSHA.[13] Discrimination in the form of denial of pay increase, loss of promotion, negative performance review, harassment, or termination is illegal. This antidiscrimination provision is interpreted broadly by the courts. It covers not only complaints filed with OSHA, but also informal complaints made to the company.[14]

In one case, a complaint made to the media was protected.[15] A newspaper received an anonymous tip that asbestos dust was being blown into the air from uncovered trucks hauling debris from a remodeling site. A reporter went to the job site and interviewed an employee, who allowed his name to be used in the story. After the article appeared, a supervisor asked the employee if in fact he had spoken to the reporter. He said yes and was fired.

The employee sued for discrimination under OSHA and won. The court said the purpose of OSHA would be undermined if companies were allowed to fire employees who brought safety violations to the attention of *anybody*.

An employee can refuse to work if it is unsafe. The employee must have a reasonable good faith belief that there is an immediate risk of serious injury or death.[16] In one case, two construction workers were working three stories up, using gondolas that continually malfunctioned.[17] For example, pushing the "up" switch caused the gondola to go down.

They complained to the foreman. He was able to get the gondolas running again and ordered the employees back up. They refused to work until the machines were properly inspected by a mechanic. The foreman refused to call a mechanic and fired them. They sued for discrimination.

The court held the employees had a reasonable and good faith belief the gondolas were hazardous, because they had malfunctioned in the past. And the court found that the employer's attitude toward safety was "at best cavalier, and at the worst, reprehensible." The project supervisor expected workers to do their assigned tasks "despite safety concerns." The employees won the case.

If two or more employees come together complaining about lack of safety, they also are protected by the labor union laws, even if they aren't members of any union. See Chapter 8.

OSHA Penalties

The penalties for violating OSHA requirements are a minimum of $5,000, up to a maximum of $70,000 per willful violation.

In December 1990, Arco Chemical Company agreed to pay $3.48 million in penalties for safety violations to OSHA. The penalty was the largest in the agency's history at that time.[18]

Even if you meet all the OSHA requirements, you still can get an environmental claim, worker's compensation case, or criminal violation. That's because OSHA doesn't set all the standards.

Environmental Regulations That Affect Companies

In addition to OSHA, various environmental laws impose requirements on business. The U.S. Environmental Protection Agency (EPA) enforces laws that regulate hazardous materials. Some states have their own laws controlling substances used in companies. Local ordinances may apply to the transportation and storage of toxics.

These requirements apply to companies not only to protect their employees, but also the general public in the community. If a company dumps toxic chemicals into the sewer without a permit, that's a violation of the Clean Water Act. It's a violation of the rights of the employees doing the dumping, because they're exposed to hazardous substances and forced to break the law. It violates the rights of the downstream neighbors affected by the fumes, and ultimately the entire community whose drinking water, food supply, and air quality are threatened.

There are four major U.S. environmental laws that affect companies, and by extension their employees:

Clean Air Act

Clean Water Act

Solid Waste Disposal Act

CERCLA (Superfund)

Clean Air and Water Acts

The Clean Air[19] and Clean Water[20] acts do not prohibit pollution. They simply require your company to get a permit to pollute. Permits are given depending on the overall air or water quality. The more polluted the air and water, the fewer permits are given.

The Clean Air Act requires permits for both continuing and one-time emissions. One-time emissions include remodeling buildings, demolition or new construction. These activities may require permits to regulate the release of asbestos into the air. The Clean Air Act also covers vinyl chloride, benzene, beryllium, arsenic, mercury, and radionuclides.

The Clean Water Act protects rivers, channels and lakes from both direct and indirect sources of pollution. Dumping toxins down drains, gutters, or sewers may indirectly pollute navigable waters and violate the act.

Companies are strictly liable for spills of oil and other hazardous substances into water. Strict liability means the company that owns the chemicals must pay for the cleanup, whether or not it was at fault for the spill.

What are pollutants? Besides the usual hazardous materials, dredged soil, heat, wrecked equipment, rock, and sand can't be dumped in water without a permit.

Clean Land: The Solid Waste Disposal Act

The Solid Waste Disposal Act[21] controls the storage, treatment, and disposal of waste and garbage if it is ignitable, corrosive, reactive, toxic, or hazardous. If your company generates any hazardous waste and stores it for at least 90 days, the company must have a storage facility permit.

The Solid Waste Disposal Act has extensive requirements for underground storage tanks. Many cities and counties do as well. That's why you may see your local gas station digging up its tanks: to comply with underground toxic storage ordinances.

The act has a manifest or log system that tracks hazardous waste "from cradle to grave." The log must be signed by a responsible person at the company, certifying that all EPA requirements are met. This requirement can lead to employee lawsuits. If employees refuse to sign the log because the company doesn't comply with the law, they are protected from discrimination and retaliation.[22]

The Superfund Law for Cleaning Up Existing Pollution

The three acts just discussed are designed to prevent air, water, and land pollution. The Superfund law is for cleaning up existing pollution. Officially it's known as the Comprehensive Environmental Response, Compensation and Liability Act (CERCLA).[23]

Superfund was passed by Congress in 1980 after families of Love Canal in New York discovered they were living on a toxic waste dump. In those days, people were outraged that such a chemical brew could be buried and turned into a housing development. Far from being an isolated occurrence, there are now over 800 sites in the United States targeted for eventual cleanup by Superfund.

Superfund holds everyone responsible for cleaning up pollution:

Past and present owners of the polluted land

The companies that operated there

The carriers that transported chemicals or waste to the site

Liability is on a no-fault, strict liability basis. There are exceptions for "innocent" site owners and a few others, but it's difficult to qualify for them.[24]

The EPA can order one or more companies to clean up a site or the government can do it and assess the responsible parties. Superfund taxes the sales of hazardous chemicals to fund government cleanups.

Reporting Spills and Releases

You are required to report spills and releases so EPA will know when cleanup is required. Spills over a certain amount must be reported within 24 hours to the National Response Center (800-424-8802). Local authorities, especially fire departments, also must be notified.

Superfund has a community right-to-know provision. Companies are required to reveal their inventories of toxic substances to the public as well as to employees. Even employees who don't work with chemicals must be informed if they are on site. To do this, companies that use 10,000 pounds of chemicals per year must submit all MSDSs to local or state environmental agencies and to local fire departments. There they become public record.

One purpose of this requirement is to assist firefighters in adequately responding to emergencies. Since they must respond to fires everywhere, they have a need to know which chemicals are located where. In recent years, firefighters have had to educate themselves about how to handle chemical emergencies, with a corresponding increase in the level of their professionalism. Firefighters are some of the real heroes of our chemical society.

Employee Claims

The Clean Air[25] and Water[26] Acts, the Solid Waste Disposal Act,[27] and Superfund[28] all prohibit firing or in any other way discriminating against employees. All these acts specify that employees can't be discriminated against for filing a complaint under the acts or for testifying on behalf of another employee.

Like the similar provision under OSHA, these sections have been broadly interpreted to cover even informal complaints. For example, in one case a gas station attendant refused to put leaded gas in a car labeled "unleaded gas only." He said doing so would pollute the air. He was fired, sued for wrongful termination under the Clean Air Act, and won.[29]

Employees who have been discriminated against under any of these laws must file a complaint with the U.S. Department of Labor (DOL) within 30 days of the discrimination.[30] The DOL will investigate, and if the charges are found to be true, the company will be sued by the department.

The general public also can sue when companies violate these acts. However, citizens are not entitled to any money damages. They only can force the company to comply with the law.

CRIMINAL SANCTIONS FOR FAILING TO MEET SAFETY STANDARDS

OSHA, the EPA, and various state agencies set the minimum requirements all companies must meet. What happens if you don't meet these standards? Worst case, you could go to jail.

In Chicago, three managers ordered an employee to work with toxic chemicals. The barrels were labeled in English and Spanish, but he could not read either language. The managers knew that, but did not inform him of the danger. The employee died. The managers were convicted of murder.[31]

The Clean Air and Water Acts, and the Solid Waste Disposal Act, have criminal fines and penalties. Felony convictions can result in jail time. Under the Clean Air Act, unlike most criminal laws, a felony conviction can be based on negligence, without showing intent.

Under a doctrine known as the "responsible corporate officer," a manager may be convicted of a crime even if he or she had no direct knowledge that the law was violated.[32]

WORKER'S COMPENSATION

Even if you meet all the standards, employees still will get injured and become ill at work. That's where worker's compensation comes in. Worker's compensation gives benefits to all employees who become injured or ill on the job.

By law, worker's compensation is liberally interpreted in favor of the employee. That's because if a worker is injured, it is in the service of the employer. The injury would not have happened but for the job.

When does an employee become disabled? Anyone considered disabled under the Americans with Disabilities Act (ADA) also would be covered by worker's compensation (see Chapter 2). In addition, employees are covered even if they are not permanently disabled and even if disabled only from doing their particular jobs.

For example, an employee with a bad back may be disabled from working some jobs but not others. That employee would be entitled to worker's compensation even if not disabled from working in other jobs.

Any injury that occurs on the job is covered.

> *practical pointers:* Injuries that require more than first aid, where an employee is sent to a clinic or doctor, should be reported to your worker's compensation carrier immediately. An injury report form should be given to the employee within one working day of the accident.

An employee who has a preexisting condition that's aggravated while working for you is still covered by your worker's compensation. If the preexisting condition was caused by other employment, the payments are prorated with the other employers. If a pre-existing disability was not caused by other employment, benefits are "apportioned" between the two injuries. You pay benefits only for the new disability.

The "eggshell employee" is covered, too. Someone who is medically diagnosed as supersensitive to cigarette smoke, toxic chemicals, or anything else at work will be compensated. An industrial hygienist can come into the building, take samples, and say, "I can't measure any amount of toxics." If employees can't work because of their sensitivity to the atmosphere, they may be entitled to worker's compensation.

I know a woman who is hypersensitive to fluorescent lights. The flickering gave her seizures. Obviously, this is a severe disability. She can work in very few places, because fluorescent lights are everywhere. If she can prove the seizures are caused by working, she is entitled to benefits.

Types of Injuries Covered

Virtually all injuries are covered by worker's compensation. For example:

Off-site: Employees are covered by worker's comp if they were on company business when they were injured. Employees who have car accidents while driving on company business are covered, unless they ran personal errands at the same time. That's called an "unauthorized departure."

Parking lot injuries: If the employer provides, pays for, or suggests using a particular lot, employees are covered from the time they turn into the driveway until they drive out. They're covered for injuries to and from the lot, even if it's three blocks away.

Commercial travelers: Overnight business trips are covered by worker's comp from beginning to end, including nights and weekends, for reasonably foreseeable injuries like slipping in the tub. If the injury was a result of "personal frolic" such as going to the beach, it is not covered.

Coming and going rule: Employees usually are not covered coming to and going from work. They may be covered if

They make a detour for the company, like a drop-off at the post office.

They occasionally are held over late or called in early.

They ride in company-provided transportation (including van pools, ride sharing and public transportation vouchers).

They are reimbursed for travel or commuting.

practical pointer: To minimize claims, you should consider not reimbursing employees mileage for commuting. Increase their base pay instead.

Exceptions to the No-Fault System

Worker's compensation is a "no-fault" system. No-fault means employees will receive benefits in the vast majority of cases, even if they were injured as a result of their own negligence or carelessness.

Employees are not eligible for worker's comp only in a few situations:

Intoxication: If employees drink or take drugs and then hurt themselves at work, they aren't allowed to claim worker's comp. The rule is different if the company provides the liquor. That's discussed in the hot topics section. You may wish to consider asking employees to take drug and alcohol tests after major accidents (but read Chapter 4 and talk to a local worker's comp attorney first).

Self-inflicted injuries: Employees who deliberately injure themselves are not entitled to compensation. The employer generally is not held responsible for an employee's suicide.

Horseplay: An employee who is an innocent bystander injured by others' horseplay is covered. The employee who initiates the horseplay in some states is not covered. In other states, the initiator is covered if horseplay is routinely tolerated on the job.

Fights: An employee who is the victim in a fight *about* work is covered by worker's comp. The aggressor is covered in a few states. Personal arguments are not the responsibility of the company, unless the company condones them.

Recreational activities: If events are off-duty and voluntary, injuries aren't covered by your worker's comp.

practical pointers: People who play on a company-sponsored team should sign a statement they are participating voluntarily, especially if the captain of the team is their boss. Company-provided basketball courts, showers, and gyms should have legal notices posted that all use is considered voluntary.

Holiday and social activities: If attendance is voluntary, injuries aren't covered by worker's comp. Avoid saying things like "We want 100% participation this year" or even "Everyone is going to be there."

There may be other times when employees' fault will prevent them from winning worker's comp benefits. Check your state's worker's compensation statute.

Exclusive Remedy Rule

So far, we have been talking about no-fault from the employee's side. No-fault also works the other way. Worker's comp applies even if the company was negligent. The company generally will not be penalized for having an inherently dangerous work environment. But there is one exception.

Companies are penalized for serious and willful misconduct. If the employer physically assaults an employee,[33] hides the results of medical exams from employees,[34] or fails to follow general industry safety standards,[35] it will be penalized. Depending on your state, the penalty may be an increase in worker's compensation benefits, or the penalty could be exempting the employee from the "exclusive remedy rule."

What is the exclusive remedy rule? That means worker's compensation is the only remedy for all workplace injuries. Employees cannot choose to sue in court if they are injured. They can get only worker's compensation for their injuries, including death.

But when the lives of employees are deliberately endangered, they aren't limited to worker's compensation benefits. They can sue in court for personal injury damages, which can run into millions of dollars. This is allowed because if worker's compensation was the exclusive remedy in such cases, there would be no disincentive for employers to risk employees lives.

Employees often try to get around the exclusive remedy rule because of the small payments from worker's comp. One way is by filing third-party suits. Rather than suing the employer, the employees sue the manufacturer of the product that injured them at work.

According to newspaper accounts, electronics workers in New Mexico became disabled after being exposed to toxic solvents by their employer. They got worker's compensation. Then they filed a multimillion-dollar third-party suit against the chemical company that made the solvents for failing to warn them adequately of the dangers.[36]

Defending Worker's Comp Cases

Worker's compensation benefits are paid by the employer through insurance. Like other forms of insurance, worker's comp premiums skyrocketed in the late 1980s. Many companies now use aggressive cost-cutting techniques to keep down worker's comp costs. This is called "case

management." It means reducing the amounts paid in benefits by thorough-
ly investigating and vigorously defending these cases.

For example, we said earlier that benefits may be increased if an employer
engages in serious and willful misconduct. It works the other way, too. If
employees refuse to use safety equipment, they are engaging in serious and
willful misconduct. You can fight to get their benefits reduced or denied.

Case management is necessary to weed out frivolous claims, but you
may not want to lose sight of the human side. Remember my clients whose
employee died from a broken leg? A few days before, he told coworkers he
wanted to hurt himself so he could get worker's comp.

Clearly his survivors would not be entitled to benefits if he died of a
self-inflicted injury. But my clients did not want to deprive his family of benefits.
They had to decide whether to enforce the letter or the spirit of the law.

Payments and Benefits

Worker's compensation payments are a proportion of the employee's
regular salary. Since they're not taxable, theoretically the employee should
have no salary loss. For example, in California the payments are 60% of the
regular salary. However, the maximum payment is $336 a week. Obviously,
many employees are not fully compensated for their lost salaries.

At some companies, worker's compensation payments are the only
disability payments employees receive. Companies that provide additional
disability benefits may deduct any worker's comp received by employees.

How long the payments last depend upon the "rating." A rating is the
percentage of jobs in the overall work force that a person is excluded from
because of the disability, combined with age, education, experience, and
skills. A 50% permanent disability means the employee will never be able to
do half of the jobs in the work force.

A person who is 100% permanently disabled would receive the maximum benefit. A person less disabled is given a rating to determine how much
money their disability is worth. Worker's compensation lawyers actually
have a book that places a dollar value on each type of disability (for example,
the loss of an eye might be paid $18,000).

If the employee dies and has dependents, there is a death benefit. This
can be paid out at the regular weekly rate or taken as a lump sum.

Worker's comp also pays the employee's medical bills for that injury.
If the employee needs lifetime treatment for a workplace injury, medical bills
are paid for life. If the injury is cured but then flares up again years later,
worker's comp pays for the medical treatment.

Vocational Rehabilitation—Retraining Employees in New Jobs

A new worker's compensation benefit available in some states is vocational rehabilitation—retraining employees in new jobs after they become disabled from their old ones. Voc rehab starts by assessing the employee for current skill level, trainability, and interest in new fields. Employees often require pretraining before they're able to enter a regular program.

The voc rehab program itself may take a couple of years. Throughout that time, the employee will be receiving worker's compensation benefits. All tuition, fees, and books are paid.

> *practical pointers:* Vocational rehabilitation can be expensive, especially when outside services are used. To manage your company's vocational rehabilitation costs, consider bringing the function in-house.

There are stories about hundreds of thousands of dollars being paid out for elaborate programs that turn menial laborers into chief executives. But vocational rehabilitation is not the lottery. Its purpose is not to give people their dreams, but to give them a living—a living comparable to the one they had at the time they were injured.

There may be no legal requirement under your state's worker's compensation to provide jobs to your employees after retraining. But under the ADA, you are required to accommodate disabled employees (see Chapter 2). Your state also may have tax credits, insurance premium rebates, and other incentives for reemploying disabled workers.

When employees are unable to complete vocational rehabilitation, they may be able to return for more assessment, more pretraining, and another training program.

Some employees abuse the system, repeatedly starting and stopping various programs. The company can fight giving more benefits if it can show the employee is malingering.

What to Do Before You Terminate an Employee on Worker's Comp

While employees are out on worker's compensation, you must treat them the same as anyone else with a disability. For example, if the company allows employees disabled away from work to have one-year disability leaves with their jobs guaranteed, then the same rights must be given to employees on worker's compensation.

Generally, you can't discriminate against an employee who files for worker's compensation benefits. In most states, you cannot fire an employee who is on worker's compensation unless you have a legitimate business reason.

There are a few legitimate business reasons. One is if the position was eliminated in a general cutback, although the time off work generally can't count against the injured worker's seniority. You also may be able to dismiss employees who are on worker's compensation if they are unable to return in the foreseeable future after exhausting the company's standard leave policy. If you have no positions available for employees who become permanently disabled, you may be able to refuse to reinstate them.

Check with a worker's comp attorney before terminating an employee who is receiving benefits.

Practical Tips for Creating a Safe Workplace

- Your first responsibility as a manager is to prevent injuries and illnesses. You as manager are responsible for making your area a safe place to work. Prevention is the key.

- Training employees in safe work procedures is critical. More OSHA citations are given for lack of training than for any other cause. As Jim Chung, a CalOSHA inspector says, "Ignorance is the greatest hazard in the workplace."

- The days are gone when safety training is showing a film on how to lift boxes. You need to address the dangers of needless stress, secondhand cigarette smoke, and computer terminals through training, too.

- Encourage employee suggestions and reports. If an employee complains about a hazard, call the safety department or outside industrial hygienist whether or not *you* think there is a problem. You are not an expert.

- If you see any hazards, report them immediately to your company's safety department, personnel, or top management. Let everyone in the area know about them. Post signs and blockade dangerous areas.

- Be prepared for emergencies. Know the evacuation routes. Learn lifesaving techniques (CPR). Have the emergency telephone number listed on all phones, and be sure the complete number is listed, for example, 9-911.

- In the case of an accident, after you call the ambulance, call safety, security, or personnel immediately. See the accompanying box for other people to call in case of accident.

Accidents: Who You Gonna Call?

In case of serious accidents, consider calling these resources:

Police department
Fire department
Local OSHA office
EPA national response line (800-424-8802)
General and worker's comp insurance carriers
Your company's employee assistance program
The media for proactive public relations
Your lawyer

- It is your responsibility as a manager to document accidents. You must be an investigator. Who are the witnesses? Get statements from them that day. Reconstruct the scene. Leave everything where it is. Take pictures or make sketches showing the positions of the victim, witnesses, and equipment.

- Once you have reconstructed the scene, secure any machine or tool involved. Put it in storage or take it out of production until it can be examined by the OSHA investigator or worker's compensation claims adjuster. You must preserve the scene of the "crime," because if you don't, you're tampering with evidence.

SAFETY: THE BOTTOM-LINE BENEFITS

The Boise Cascade Corporation's worker's compensation insurance claims and premiums were rising significantly. Their insurance liability one year was $13 million.

The company decided to do something about it. They instituted safety as a corporate goal. All managers were rated for safety on their performance appraisals. After five years they reduced their liability to $2.4 million.[37]

A safe workplace has bottom-line benefits. But there are more important values than reducing worker's compensation payments. If you can prevent one person from dying, its worth it.

PART TWO: SEVEN HOT ISSUES IN SAFETY LAW TODAY

REPETITIVE STRAIN INJURIES

One hot issue is repetitive strain injuries. These are injuries from repeated motions with a certain part of the body. Many back conditions are a result of cumulative trauma—a lifetime of working at lifting, bending, and stretching.

Repetitive strain injury is the fastest-growing category of job-related disabilities. In 1990, it allegedly caused more injuries—almost half—than any other workplace danger.[38]

According to OSHA, two jobs that have problems with cumulative trauma are meat cutters and retail clerks. Meat cutters are required to separate bones from meat, sometimes by sheer force. This causes injuries to shoulders and backs. Constantly twisting the wrist while cutting around bones and fat also causes injuries.

Retail clerks have shown a significant increase in cumulative trauma injuries since the introduction of price scanners. The motion of running the bar code over the scanning eye, repeated thousands of times a day, has led many to suffer tendinitis and carpal tunnel syndrome. That's why you see so many salesclerks wearing wrist braces. Carpal tunnel syndrome is also a risk to anyone who uses a computer terminal.

What is the carpal tunnel? It's a braceletlike ligament in your wrist that contains nerves, ligaments, and bones. Most important is the median nerve which conducts sensation from the fingers and hand up to the central nervous system.

The tunnel is narrow and crowded to begin with. Repetitive hand movements can make the lubricated lining around the tendons sticky and thick. This puts pressure on the median nerve. As a result, you get numbness in the hand, radiating pain up the arms, or ulnar clawing. This is where the fingers claw up and can't be extended completely.

Carpal tunnel syndrome can impact your ability to work. Writing, holding, and typing may be impossible. Carpal tunnel syndrome can be prevented by specific exercises designed to relieve the pressure (discussed shortly). Once constriction begins, a wrist brace or Rolfing can give relief. In severe cases, surgery is the only answer.

Video Display Terminals

Another hot issue is computer monitors or video display terminals (VDTs). To give you an idea of VDTs' impact, one-third of the editors and reporters at the *Fresno Bee* newspaper claimed they got carpal tunnel syndrome or other repetitive motion injury when new computers were introduced.[39] In addition to claiming worker's comp benefits from the company, some of them filed a third-party suit against the computer maker, alleging an inherently dangerous keyboard design.[40]

To prevent these injuries, some cities and states have adopted or are considering VDT ordinances. Many are modeled on the ANSI standards (the American National Standards Institute).[41] ANSI standards are not law, but recommendations. If you want to avoid injury, you and your employees should follow these standards whenever using a computer or word processor.

A large number of ANSI standards involve ergonomics, the correct design and placement of objects to prevent muscle strain. One of the ANSI standards calls for a detachable keyboard. The keyboard design, the shape of the keys, and the distance between keys can affect hand, wrist, and arm position. No one design is best. Experiment with different keyboard and mouse positions to find the one that is the most comfortable.

There should be a 90-degree angle between the upper arm and lower arm. The lower arm should be even or slightly above the keyboard. The keyboard rest should be adjustable up and down to create the correct angle.

The wrists should be even with the hands. In the days when we used typewriters, we needed to have enough force in our hands to press down the keys. To get that force, we held our arms even or above our wrists. But with computers, we barely have to touch the keys. We tend to get lazy and rest our wrists down below the hands. That puts stress on the carpal tunnel.

> *practical pointer:* One way to prevent this is to use a wrist rest. There's no need to buy a specially designed computer wrist rest. A small, rolled up towel will do. Contrary to its name, a wrist rest is not for resting your wrist. It is simply a guide. Your hands and wrist should float over the wristpad and keyboard.

The back of the chair should adjust so it will fit most comfortably in the small of the back. The chair needs to be adjustable for good posture. When you were growing up did your mother tell you to have good posture? Well, now its an ANSI standard.

The screen must be between eye level and 60 degrees below eye level. The screen also should be adjustable, up and down. The document should be in front instead of at your side. The monitor screen should be 22 inches from the eyes to eliminate eye strain.

The *New England Journal of Medicine* in the March 1991 issue published the results of a study by the National Institute for Occupational Safety and Health (NIOSH) on radiation from monitors. Very-low-frequency (VLF) radiation is emitted by monitors. The question is whether this VLF radiation is dangerous to users.

If VLF radiation is hazardous, we would expect to see it in the miscarriage rate of pregnant users. In the NIOSH study there was no increase in miscarriages among telephone operators who used VDTs as compared to those who didn't. The study is continuing on the rate of birth defects, the effect on the eyes, and other possible hazards.

Although ANSI standards do not address this issue, in Sweden the government has set requirements on the amount of allowable VLF and extremely low frequency (ELF) radiation that may be emitted. Most U.S. computer makers offer models that meet the Swedish standard, although they may not be available readily in the United States.[42]

To prevent eye strain, the ANSI standards suggest reducing glare. The user should be able to position the monitor so it doesn't reflect light or to place antiglare screens over the display. The lighting in the area should be between 200 and 500 lux.

Perhaps the most important ANSI standard is to give a 15-minute task break at least every 2 hours. During this time, the user should get up, get away from the computer, and not do any other close work. Part of the purpose of the break is to refocus the eyes. They should focus on something far away until able to see it clearly.

During this break, the hands, wrists, shoulders, and neck should be exercised. Shaking the hands, stretching the wrists down and back, shrugging the shoulders, and rolling the neck all are helpful.

AIDS IN THE WORKPLACE

AIDS was a hot issue in the early 1980s. In the 1990s, it still is. But the nature of the debate has changed.

When AIDS first appeared, many employers reacted hysterically. At that time, little was known about the disease by the general public. One of the first cases involved a young man who had worked for Raytheon Company for several years. He entered the hospital with pneumonia and was diagnosed as HIV positive. One month later, he was released and attempted to return to work. The company refused to reinstate him. He sued for disability discrimination and won.[43]

Since then, we all have learned that HIV can't be transmitted under most circumstances in most workplaces.

> *practical pointers:* Since HIV is transmitted through blood, you should use universal precautions if employees injure themselves and begin bleeding. Half the people who are HIV positive don't know it. Use latex gloves before treating an employee. Gloves should be standard equipment at all first aid stations.

Hospitals were among the first employers to adopt comprehensive policies about AIDS. Many adopted policies supportive of employees with HIV.

A dentist in Florida changed all that. The case of Dr. David Acer is a sad one. He apparently is responsible for transmitting HIV to at least three patients. Dr. Acer is dead, and so are his victims. The human tragedy is immense. Everyone inside and outside the medical profession agrees that such a tragedy should never happen again.

In response, the U.S. Centers for Disease Control issued guidelines recommending that health care workers who are infected with HIV should not perform exposure-prone procedures such as surgery. Such policies have been upheld by the courts.[44] There is demand in Congress to make these guidelines mandatory, even though other surgeons with AIDS have not transmitted the disease to their patients.

Even if the guidelines are mandatory, some patient rights advocates insist on requiring HIV testing. They say that is the only way patients can be sure doctors are not infected.

Health care givers have rights, too. Most important is their right to make a living, their liberty. Doctors and others fear if they are required to undergo HIV testing, those with HIV will be forced out of their jobs, even if they follow all safety procedures and never pose a risk to patients.

Health care workers also have a right to privacy. HIV tests have been held to be searches of the body. Under the Constitution, searches are allowed only if there is a compelling interest and the method for enforcing this interest is reasonable.

Obviously, the state has a compelling interest in stopping the spread of AIDS.

Is mandatory testing a reasonable method? Everyone would have to be tested, including those who are married, monogamous, and not involved in any high-risk behavior. No one could be trusted to be exempt. Even if testing is required, doctors still will become infected and could transmit it between tests. The only way to be safe is to require blood tests daily. But that's not possible.

Isn't there a less intrusive method for protecting patients that doesn't interfere with health care givers' rights? We can mandate more safety procedures. But the fact is no prevention program will be 100% perfect. Perhaps the best approach is to educate the public about what safety procedures to expect from doctors.

The other side of the equation is protecting employees from customers or patients who are HIV positive. To do that, OSHA issued a new standard in December 1991 for bloodborne diseases. It applies to the estimated 5.6 million workers in health care, public safety, funeral homes, linen services, and other jobs where there is a risk of exposure.

The standard requires those employers to have written infection control plans. Free hepatitis B vaccinations must be given to all employees who are exposed to blood on the job. Free follow-up care must be given to an employee who is infected on the job.

Protective gear such as gowns, gloves, and other equipment must be given to employees. Puncture-resistant containers must be provided for needle disposal.

Employers have the responsibility to prevent the spread of AIDS, while not discriminating against people with the disease.

ALCOHOL AT WORK

Friday afternoon beer busts are a common occurrence in many high-tech Silicon Valley companies. At traditional law firms, the senior partner invites other attorneys into his office for an evening sherry sip. At a construction site, the boss and employees hang around the lot drinking beers after work. The philosophy behind all this drinking is that it benefits the bottom line by encouraging informal networking.

It also creates legal liabilities. If the company provides free booze and drunk employees injure themselves, they are entitled to worker's compensation. Because the drinks were free, the employees are considered involuntarily intoxicated.

If a company party is completely voluntary and the employer charges for drinks, the company is not liable for worker's comp when employees injure themselves. Whether or not the company provides free booze, if a drunk employee injures another employee, that employee can get benefits. And if the drunk employee leaves the party and kills or injures someone else, the company may be held liable the same as any other social host or bartender.

It depends on your state laws. The Idaho Supreme Court held in 1991 that a company was liable for the death of a pedestrian killed by an employee who got drunk at an office party.[45]

> *practical pointers:* Your responsibility as a manager is to prevent accidents. Don't push alcohol on others. Monitor your own and your employees' drinking. Those who seem intoxicated should not be allowed to work or drive. Call a cab if necessary.

SECONDHAND SMOKE

Smoking is another hot issue. As of this writing, there is no U.S. law prohibiting smoking in the workplace. However, NIOSH concluded in 1991 that secondhand smoke causes cancer and possibly heart disease. OSHA is expected to adopt regulations restricting smoking in the workplace.[46]

Many states, cities, and counties have passed laws that allow, even require, companies to create nonsmoking areas. New Jersey, Connecticut, and Minnesota have laws requiring non-smoking areas.[47] Check with your local government to see if any such laws apply to you.

Even if there is not a smoking ordinance in your area, you should be sensitive to the complaints of nonsmokers. That's because employees who become disabled from breathing secondhand smoke at work can file claims for worker's compensation. They also may be able to file complaints with OSHA if the amount of carbon monoxide in the workplace exceeds allowable levels.

In recent years, nonsmoking employees have been successful in making two other types of claims to get more than worker's comp benefits.

The first type of claim is for intentional infliction of emotional distress. Most states have laws that prohibit any person from intentionally acting in an outrageous manner to cause emotional distress. What does this have to do with smoking?

In one case, an employee complained to his supervisor about the smoking of his coworkers. After he complained, the supervisor moved the employee's office into an area with more smokers. His coworkers deliberately sat next to him at meetings and blew smoke in his face. In short, he was retaliated against for complaining. The court said that was outrageous and awarded him damages for intentional infliction of emotional distress.[48]

The second type of claim is for disability discrimination. Employees who are sensitive to cigarette smoke are disabled. Employees who are physically disabled must be accommodated. This means the company must prevent smoke-sensitive employees from being exposed to cigarette smoke.

In a recent case, two women who were sensitive to secondhand smoke complained about the smoking of their coworkers. In response to their complaints, the employer moved them into a smoke-free office, installed smoke filters at the desks of smokers, improved the ventilation system, and requested that employees not smoke near them.

Despite these efforts, the women still were affected by cigarette smoke. The employer refused to do more. The women sued for disability discrimination and won. The court said the employer did not accommodate them to prevent the injuries from occurring. Specifically the court said the employer could ban smoking from the office entirely.[49]

> *practical pointer:* Many employers have nonsmoking buildings and allow employees to go outside to smoke. To maintain the morale of nonsmokers, you should not allow smokers to exceed the usual amount of break time in order to smoke.

What about smokers rights? Some states protect smokers as a group. For example, Kentucky, Oklahoma, and Rhode Island prohibit discrimination against smokers in hiring, promotions, and other employment decisions.[50]

Some smokers are addicted to a drug, nicotine. Why shouldn't they receive the same protections at work as other drug addicts?

The ADA requires companies to accommodate employees with drug addictions only if they are rehabilitated. If an employee enters a nonsmoking program, you might be required to give time off work as needed by the program. You are not required to accommodate the smoking, only the rehabilitation.

There is some debate about whether employers in states that don't have prosmoker laws are allowed to discriminate against smokers. Some argue that smokers are less healthy than nonsmokers. They take more days off work. They are less productive. They are more expensive for insurance coverage.

These all may be valid arguments, but they are assumptions. These "facts" may not be true in a given case. One of my clients refused to hire smokers on the grounds they were unhealthy. But when we looked at actual attendance, the smokers had better records than the nonsmokers! If you perceive smokers as disabled, refusing to hire them could be discrimination on the basis of disability.

More low-income people smoke than middle- or high-income groups.

Since disproportionately more blacks and Hispanics have low incomes, a policy of not hiring smokers could discriminate against them.

A policy against hiring people who smoke is difficult to enforce without invading their privacy. Are you going to follow employees home and look in the windows to see if they're smoking? For these reasons, you should not refuse to hire smokers. Just regulate their smoking at work, and require everyone to meet your attendance and sick leave policies.

INDOOR AIR POLLUTION

Poor air quality always has been an issue for manufacturing, construction and mining employees. Today, it affects office workers, too.

According to the EPA,[51] "sick building syndrome" occurs when a building's occupants have eye, nose, or throat irritation; sensitivity to odors; dizziness; nausea; difficulty in concentrating; fatigue; and headaches. Sound like where you work?

In sick building syndrome, the specific cause of these symptoms is not known. And most of the symptoms disappear shortly after people leave the building. Another condition is "building-related illness." This is where people have coughs, chest tightness, fevers, chills, and muscle aches. These symptoms can be traced to an identifiable cause. For example, Legionnaires disease is caused by heating, ventilation, and air conditioning (HVAC) systems. People who suffer from building-related illnesses don't recover when they leave the building. They may be ill for a long time or die.

A Harvard Medical study found that 27 out of 47 people working in one building were infected with tuberculosis from one employee. By recirculating the air, the HVAC system spread the disease throughout the building.[52]

Radon and asbestos cause long-term diseases which occur years after exposure. They are another source of indoor air pollution. According to the World Health Organization, 30% of new and remodeled buildings worldwide have indoor air pollution.

Sick buildings are caused by poor ventilation, such as

Indoor sources of pollution not properly vented

Outdoor pollution entering

Bacteria contaminating the HVAC system

Indoor sources of pollution are paints, solvents, adhesives, pesticides, carpeting, upholstery, plywood, copy machines, laser printers, cleaning supplies, tobacco smoke, space heaters, woodstoves, and gas stoves.

Another indoor pollution problem is noise. High noise levels are extremely hazardous. Even low levels of noise can cause headaches, irritation, and other symptoms of stress. OSHA has set standards for allowable noise levels.

practical pointers: The most important step in preventing sick people is to have a well-ventilated building.

The EPA recommends companies routinely maintain their HVAC systems. The ventilation system should process 20 cubic feet of air per person per minute. Replace water-stained ceiling tile and carpet. Institute smoking restrictions. Vent rest rooms, copy rooms and print shops.

To prevent sick building syndrome, treat every remodeling job like a chemical spill. Use toxics in well-ventilated areas when the building is empty. Allow time for new building materials to off-gas before returning to work.

JOB STRESS

One of the hottest safety issues today is job stress. Henny Youngman said, "My nephew has an industrial disease: work makes him sick." It used to be a joke, but today sometimes it's fatal.

In Japan, *karoshi*—death from overwork—is recognized as a fatal combination of apoplexy, high blood pressure, and stress. By 1990, an estimated 10,000 people had died according to the National Council for Victims of Karoshi.[53] One man died after working 100 hours a month of overtime for over a year. On the night he died, he had just put in three 15-hour days.[54]

A lot of people in the United States work just as much or more. And they're probably dying, too. We just don't recognize the cause.

Stress kills others besides those who are stressed. It's no longer news to hear of disgruntled employees returning to work and shooting their coworkers. They are victims of stress.

According to the American Institute for Preventive Medicine, stress is responsible for two-thirds of all office visits and plays a role in our two major killers—heart disease and cancer.[55]

Stress is sometimes referred to as a yuppie disease. But according to a study at Carnegie Mellon University, as income increases, stress decreases. The people most likely to be stressed had incomes under $50,000 or were women or minorities.[56]

Stress claims for worker's compensation are increasing. In the 10-year period from 1979 to 1988, the number of stress claims filed in California rose by 700%. During that same time the number of other worker's compensation claims rose by only 25%.

If an employee is stressed and becomes disabled, in about 25 states a claim for worker's compensation can be filed. Its just like any other disability. Hypersensitive victims are covered. If they are disabled by stress, they're entitled to worker's compensation, as long as its job related.

In perhaps the most extreme case, a woman retail clerk felt her boss was harassing her about the job.[57] He rated her too low, she thought. He gave her jobs that weren't as good as the jobs he gave others. As a result, she became stressed, went to a doctor, and was put on medical leave.

She applied for worker's compensation benefits. At trial the company proved she was not harassed. The manager treated her the same as any other employee, the jobs he gave her were the same, and her performance evaluations were accurate.

But the judge said even though she wasn't harassed, by the mere fact she felt harassed, she was stressed, and therefore entitled to worker's compensation insurance.

Remember, it's a no-fault system. Your only defense is that the stress didn't happen because of work, and that's very difficult to prove in most of these cases.[58]

If stressed employees remain on the job, their work may be affected. Stress can lead to absenteeism, mistakes, accidents, low morale, theft, and substance abuse. Stressed employees can be disciplined, up to and including termination, if they don't do the work assigned and obey all company rules.

At the same time, if they are disabled by stress, they must be reasonably accommodated. The ADA may require giving them part-time work schedules.

The ADA also says you should restructure jobs. You can imagine the demands employees could make to eliminate the stressful parts of their jobs. But you don't have to eliminate any essential functions of the job, no matter how stressful they are. If stress is a normal part of the job, someone has to do it.

What if the employee says, "I'm stressed because of my boss, and if you just fire my boss I'll be fine." That may not be required under reasonable accommodation. But transferring the employee to another manager might be reasonable. And if there are a lot of complaints about a particular manager, that manager might be a safety hazard.

Constructive Discharge: Harassing Employees Until They Quit

Stress claims also arise in lawsuits for constructive discharge. In constructive discharge, the manager harasses employees until they are forced to quit. The issue in these cases is whether a reasonable person in the same situation would feel forced to quit.

Courts have found constructive discharge in cases of sexual and racial harassment, or where other laws were broken. An example is a violation of a safety regulation. If employees quit because OSHA standards are violated, that's constructive discharge.

What if managers yell and scream at their subordinates? Is yelling a good reason for the reasonable person to quit? It probably depends more on what is yelled. Yelling alone may not be enough.

Where there hasn't been discriminatory harassment or violation of some other law, where there has been only work-related harassment, the courts have been reluctant to find constructive discharge except in outrageous situations.

Here's an example of this kind of outrageous behavior. Chris Panopulos had a Stanford MBA. He worked as an accountant for Westinghouse for 32 years. One day, without warning, he was permanently relocated. His job title wasn't changed, but he was assigned to work in the archives, stacking 150-pound boxes and retrieving records. Overnight he went from doing paperwork with others in a white-collar environment to performing manual labor alone in a filthy warehouse with no toilets or drinking water. The court said that Chris could sue for constructive discharge if he quit immediately after being assigned to the warehouse.[59]

Can employees sue for work-related harassment if they aren't forced to quit? It depends on your state.

Texas allows suits by employees for intentional infliction of emotional distress. In one case, the employer demoted an employee with 30 years experience as an executive to an entry-level janitorial position. As a result, he suffered severe depression but did not quit. He was able to sue in court for his emotional distress.[60]

Surprisingly, on the other extreme is California. There, if the emotional distress is a result of demoting or promoting the employee, criticizing work, arguing about grievances, or routine termination, the employee's exclusive remedy is worker's compensation.[61] The Texas case probably would be seen by the California Supreme Court as the kind of behavior that "normally occurs in the workplace."

How to Minimize Stress in the Workplace

You have the duty under OSHA to prevent workplace illnesses. Stress is a workplace illness just like carpal tunnel syndrome. Both are the result of minor trauma over and over to the same spot. You wear down, and finally break.

Experts say that most employees who become violent at work show signs of stress long before the shooting starts.

In September 1989, an employee in Louisville, Kentucky, killed seven of his coworkers because he was angry about being put on disability leave. Another employee said, "This guy's been talking about this for a year."

His stress problems may be why he was placed on disability. The employer in this case was in a no-win situation. But perhaps early referral to an employee assistance program (EAP) or outside counselor could have prevented this tragedy.

Most stressed employees don't end this way. In fact, most stressed employees will solve their own problems. But they may solve them by drinking, going out on stress leave, or quitting. These options aren't productive for the company or the employee.

> *practical pointers:* Managers should not create needless stress for employees. But as we've seen, sometimes employees feel stressed even when there is no objective evidence of a stressful environment.

According to a comprehensive study, the primary cause of employee stress is a feeling of a lack of personal power.[62] Personal power is a sense of inner security that you can meet whatever challenges you face. To minimize the amount of stress in the workplace and to develop healthy responses to the stress there is, consider implementing these empowering and stress reduction techniques for you and your employees:

Admit that there is stress

Communicate openly

Use time management techniques

Plan projects

Create paper trails for coworkers

Train employees to be adaptable

Avoid yelling, sniping, sarcasm

Reduce caffeine, sugar, nicotine, and alcohol at work

Encourage employees to work undisturbed when needed

Create a quiet room for escape

Go for a walk around the building

Take deep breaths

Encourage exercise

Celebrate achievements healthily

Bring in community wellness programs

Evaluate managers on stress reduction habits

Even if you create a reasonably stress-free workplace, employees still may feel stress. One way to discover that was developed by David O'Brien, a retired worker's compensation appeals board judge. He suggests giving all employees questionnaires twice a year to determine if they are stressed. His questionnaire is reproduced on the next two pages.[63]

SEMIANNUAL WORK DUTY REVIEW QUESTIONNAIRE[64]

Employee_____ Date_____

To aid the company in determining the need, if any, for modification of your work duties and determine the need, if any, to alter your working environment, please answer the following questions:

1. What is your job classification (job title)?_____

2. Does the attached job description accurately describe your work duties at the present time?   yes   no

   If the attached job description does not correctly describe your work duties at this time, please explain the discrepancy:

   _____

3. How long have you been working in your present job classification?___

4. What is the name of your immediate supervisor?_____

5. Are you usually able to complete your daily work duties in 8 hours? yes   no

   If the answer is no, state approximately how many hours you work overtime, if you do, to complete your work._____

   If you work overtime, where and when is that overtime completed?

   _____

6. Do you find it necessary to take work home to complete on weekends? yes   no

   If the answer is yes, state generally how often, in the course of a month, you take work home on weekends._____

7. Do you receive telephone calls at home in regard to your work? yes   no

If the answer is yes, how often in a month do you receive such calls and who usually calls you? _____

8. Do you find your work meaningful (fulfilling)? yes no

If the answer is no, state how you feel your work duties can be modified to make your work meaningful.

_____

9. In what other ways, if any, would you recommend that your work duties be modified? _____

10. Do you feel that your work, or working environment, is having a detrimental effect on your mental or physical health? yes no

If the answer is yes, explain in what way your health is being affected and what you recommend be done to correct the problem.

_____

11. Do you feel you are under pressure while performing your work duties? yes no

If the answer is yes, explain what brings on the pressure and your recommendations as to how your work duties can be modified to eliminate or reduce the pressure.

_____

12. Are you being sexually harassed by any supervisor or co-employee? yes no

If your answer is yes, please contact the personnel office immediately.

13. Do you experience a pleasant working relationship with all your supervisors and co-employees? yes no

If the answer is no, describe the unpleasantness. (You need not identify the person) _____

14. Do you work in a smoke-free environment? yes no

If your answer is no, would you like to have a smoke free environment and if so, state any recommendations you have to correct the situation.

_____

_____

Employee's signature_____ Date _____

I have reviewed the above statements and discussed them with the employee.

_____   _____

Supervisor's signature   Date

[Employees should be encouraged to return this form to the personnel department with or without the supervisor's signature.]

If employees disclose stress in response to the questionnaire, you have the opportunity to restructure their jobs before they are forced to go out on leave. If they do not reveal stress, the form can be used later as contrary evidence if they file stress claims.

You also should be sensitive to employees' clues about stress off the job. There is a fine line between invading someone's privacy and managing their stress. Your bottom line should be that you don't care why employees are stressed in their private lives. You want them to be happy at home because they will be productive at work.

As a manager, you are limited in what you can do. You can listen sympathetically to small problems (for a while, anyway). Don't give advice. For major problems, the employee should be referred to counseling.

How to Refer Employees for Counseling Without Creating More Problems

How do you make a referral without creating more problems? Joan Holland, an employee assistance therapist in Palo Alto, calls her service the Distinguished Employee Program. Imagine how easy it would be to tell the employee, "I want you to enter our Distinguished Employee Program so you can become successful here." So much better than, "You need a shrink!"

To refer employees, you want to state the *problem*, tell the employee the *manager's role*, ask for *employee's suggestions*, and *make the referral*. Consider these approaches:

Problem: "You seem a little preoccupied." "You don't seem to be focusing on work." "You aren't performing up to your usual high standard."

Manager's role: "It's not my business what happens at home, but I am concerned about your work," "I don't want to get involved in your private life, but I do want to help you."

Employee's suggestions: "Is there anything I can do to help you resolve your situation?" "What can I do to help?" "What would you like me to do?"

Make the referral: "Would you like to talk to someone about it?" "I can give you time off to talk with a counselor if you'd like." "Do you want to use my office to call the EAP program?"

Stressed employees may be inevitable. You can reduce the number and severity of stress claims by being sensitive to the needs of the whole person.

Chapter 8

EVERYTHING ELSE YOU NEED TO KNOW

Independent Contractors, Overtime, Benefits, Unions, and More

*I*n this chapter, we will discuss everything else you need to know: the laws concerning independent contractors, overtime pay, unemployment benefits, the Consolidated Omnibus Budget Reconciliation Act (COBRA), the Employee Retirement Income Security Act (ERISA), posting requirements, labor unions, nonunion arbitration, government employees, trade libel, and antitrust.

INDEPENDENT CONTRACTORS OR EMPLOYEES? HOW TO TELL THE DIFFERENCE

I once represented a dentist who ran an office in association with other dentists. He provided office space, reception and billing services, as well as some patient overflow. The other dentists advertised to attract their own patients, directed their own work, and set their own hours. They paid my client a percentage of their billings as rent. He had them sign standard contracts to confirm their independent contractor status.

My client entered into this arrangement with a woman dentist. Soon they fell in love and got married. She stopped working for a a few years. When she returned to work, they had an oral agreement that she would pay his business a percentage of her fees, although now it was a lower percentage than before.

A year went by, and they decided to divorce. She continued working there after the divorce was final. But one day they had an argument at work, and she quit.

Within two weeks, she (1) filed an amended return with the Internal Revenue Service (IRS) claiming she had been an employee, not an independent contractor, (2) filed with the state Labor Commission saying she should have been paid overtime, and (3) filed for unemployment insurance stating she was an employee and had been forced to quit because of intolerable working conditions.

As an independent contractor, she was responsible for paying self-employment tax; my client was not required to pay the employer contribution. As an independent contractor, she was not entitled to overtime pay. And as an independent contractor, she was not entitled to unemployment insurance. The case was more complex because the definition of independent contractor was different at each agency.

We won all three claims. But it took my client almost a year of time and a lot of money to do it. It would have been cheaper and easier if he had a written contract with her. Although a written contract alone is not enough, it does help prove she was an independent contractor.

Twenty Factors Define Independent Contractors

I've also known many employers who claimed workers were independent contractors when in fact they were employees. One consultant hired a full-time assistant to run his office. The assistant suggested she be paid as an independent contractor rather than as an employee. The consultant agreed, since that saved him the employer contribution to social security, state disability, and worker's compensation.

After two years, the assistant quit and filed for unemployment. She was found to be an employee. Because the consultant had not been making payments into the state unemployment fund, he had to pay her unemployment out of pocket, make all back payments and a penalty of 10%. The unemployment office also notified the state tax board and the Internal Revenue Service (IRS).

The IRS penalty if you misclassify an employee as an independent contractor is payment of all employment taxes for that worker, payment of the worker's income tax and the worker's contribution to social security, and a penalty equal to 100% of these taxes.

It's not up to you or your employees to decide they are independent contractors. For them to be independent contractors, you must show you do not have the right to control their work. Even if in fact you do not control their work, if you have the right to do so, they may be considered employees.

The IRS has identified 20 factors that indicate whether sufficient control is present to establish an employer-employee relationship.[1] How important each factor is depends on the occupation and the context. Not all or even most factors are necessary in order to find employee status. The 20 factors follow:

1. *Instructions:* An employee must obey instructions about when, where, and how to work. Even if no instructions are given, the control factor is present if the employer has the right to give them. Contractors are given specifications instead of instructions.

2. *Training:* An employee is trained to perform services in a particular manner. Independent contractors ordinarily use their own methods and receive no training from the purchasers of their services.

3. *Integration:* An employee's services are integrated into the business operations. They are important to the success or continuation of the business.

4. *Personally Rendered Services:* An employee personally performs the work. This shows that the employer is interested in the methods as well as the results. A contractor can provide a reasonable substitute.

5. *Hiring Assistants:* An employee works for an employer who hires, supervises, and pays assistants. An independent contractor hires, supervises, and pays assistants under a contract that requires him or her to provide materials and labor and to be responsible only for the result.

6. *Continuing Relationship:* An employee has a continuing relationship with an employer. A continuing relationship may exist even when work is performed at frequently recurring although irregular intervals.

7. *Set Hours of Work:* An employee has set hours of work established by an employer. An independent contractor is the master of his or her own time.

8. *Full-Time Work:* An employee normally works full time. An independent contractor can work part time, for one or several companies.

9. *Work Done on Premises:* An employee works on the premises of an employer or works on a route or at a location designated by an employer.

10. *Set Order or Sequence:* An employee must perform services in the order or sequence set by an employer.

11. *Reports:* An employee submits regular reports to an employer. This shows that the employee must account to the employer for his or her actions. Contractors generally report at predetermined milestones and at the end of the project.

12. *Payments:* An employee is paid by the hour, week, or month. An independent contractor is paid by the job or on straight commission.

13. *Expenses:* An employee's business and travel expenses are paid by an employer; contractors pay their own expenses, although they may bill for reimbursement.

14. *Tools and Materials:* An employee is furnished significant tools, materials, and other equipment by an employer.

15. *Investment.* Independent contractors have significant investment in their businesses.

16. *Profit or Loss:* An independent contractor can make a profit or suffer a loss.

17. *Multiple Persons or Firms Serviced:* An independent contractor provides services to two or more unrelated persons or firms at the same time.

18. *Services Available to General Public:* An independent contractor makes his or her services available to the general public.

19. *Right to Fire:* An employee can be fired at will by an employer. An independent contractor cannot be fired so long as he or she produces a result that meets the specifications of the contract.

20. *Right to Quit:* An employee can quit his or her job at any time without incurring liability. An independent contractor usually agrees to complete a specific job and is responsible for its satisfactory completion or is legally obligated to make good for failure to complete it.

In addition to these 20 factors, state agencies may use their own criteria. For example, the unemployment office may consider workers to be employees if

They are not in a distinct trade or occupation.

This type of work usually is done by employees.

The work is not highly skilled or specialized.

They have little or no meaningful discretion over how to do the job.

There is no written contract showing the intent of the parties to create an independent relationship.

practical pointers: The IRS assumes workers are employees unless you prove otherwise. The burden of proof is on you. When in doubt, treat workers as employees, not independent contractors.

If a worker truly is an independent contractor, you should insist they provide you with proof of worker's compensation insurance. Some states provide that if independent contractors do not carry their own worker's compensation coverage, the employer will be liable for their medical expenses and disability if they injure themselves at work.[2]

OVERTIME RULES: EXEMPT VERSUS NONEXEMPT EMPLOYEES

The Fair Labor Standards Act (FLSA) covers overtime pay and the minimum wage.[3] Here we will cover only the overtime provisions. For more information, call the U.S. Department of Labor, Wage and Hour Division. They have offices in every major city.

The FLSA applies to all employees who work in enterprises engaged in interstate commerce. This includes virtually every private employer, as well as state and local governments. There are exceptions for agricultural workers on small farms, babysitters, fishermen, amusement park employees, cab drivers, live-in domestic help, and employees who sell cars.[4] However, these may be covered by your state's overtime rules.

Even if the business itself is not involved in interstate commerce, an employee whose duties involve the movement of goods, persons, or services across state lines is covered. For example, a secretary who regularly sends mail across state lines or uses the telephone to call out of state is considered engaged in interstate commerce.[5]

Once you determine your enterprise or employees are engaged in interstate commerce, the next question is whether a particular employee is "exempt" or "nonexempt" from the overtime law. The FLSA requires employers to pay overtime only to nonexempt employees who work more than 40 hours a week.

The presumption made by the Department of Labor is that all employees are nonexempt and entitled to overtime pay unless proven otherwise. The burden of proof is on you to show they are exempt. Employees are exempt only if they work in executive, administrative, professional, or outside sales jobs.

"Executives" have the primary duty of managing the business or part of it. They regularly direct the work of two or more employees, have the authority to hire, fire, and promote; and regularly exercise discretion. Most important, executives spend at least 80% of their total time on these duties (60% if they are in the retail or service industries).[6] Thus "working leads" or "office managers" who spend most of their time performing routine work are not exempt as executives.

The primary duties of employees in "administrative" jobs are directly related to management policies or general business operations of the company. They regularly spend at least 80% of their time exercising discretion and independent judgment (60% in retail and service industries[7]). And they regularly assist an executive or other administrator, perform specialized technical work, or work only under general supervision.[8]

"Professional" employees usually have graduate degrees and perform work requiring advance knowledge in a specialized field of learning. Doctors, lawyers, and teachers are in this category. Computer programmers and system administrators recently have been deemed to be exempt. Professionals also include employees in recognized fields of artistic endeavor, whose work is original and creative and the result of their invention, imagination, or talent.[9] Professionals consistently exercise discretion and judgment, their work is predominantly intellectual, and they spend at least 80% of their time in the professional capacity. The 60% rule for retail and service establishments does not apply to the professional exemption.

The "outside salesman" exemption applies to employees who regularly work away from the employer's premises making sales, getting orders, or signing contracts. They must spend at least 80% of their time in sales activity, including paperwork, deliveries, and collections.[10]

In addition to meeting the exemption definitions just cited, exempt employees also must be paid on a salary basis. In the last few years, this has become a legal mine field for the unwary employer.

"Salary" means employees receive the same amount of pay every pay period, regardless of the quantity or quality of their work.[11] Several recent cases have held that where employees lose pay because they receive disciplinary suspensions or because they have exhausted sick leave, they are no longer considered to be on salary. Therefore, they are nonexempt and are entitled to overtime.[12]

Assuming employees are entitled to overtime, they must be paid one and a half hours for every hour worked. In lieu of paying overtime, you can give nonexempt employees compensatory time off ("comp time"). Comp time must be given at the same rate as overtime pay. In other words, you have to give one and a half hours off for every hour of overtime worked.[13]

You are not required by law to give exempt employees comp time. If you choose to give it, you can give it at any rate you wish, as long as you are consistent.

What if an employee works overtime without your permission? You must pay overtime even if it was not authorized. You must pay if you "suffer or permit" employees to work overtime. Your company is receiving some benefit as a result of the overtime; therefore, you should pay for it.[14]

Every state except Louisiana has laws on working hours, and 38 states have their own laws about overtime.[15] If the state law is more beneficial to the employee than the FLSA, the state law applies. That's why it's important to get local legal advice on this issue.

> *practical pointer:* Because the burden of proof is on you, it's important to keep accurate and complete records of an employee's working hours. If you don't have good documentation, you won't be able to rebut the employee's claimed overtime.

I've been in numerous hearings where an employee's "best guess" about the number of hours worked was accepted by the judge over incomplete records submitted by the employer.

Although salaried employees often resent keeping time records, it may be worthwhile to require them to do so, just in case later there is a question about their exempt status. But don't pay them based on how many hours they work; otherwise, they're no longer considered salaried.[16]

If nonexempt employees work overtime without your authorization, you must pay them. However, you can discipline them, up to and including termination, if they repeatedly violate your instructions not to work overtime.

How Unemployment Insurance is Determined

Unemployment insurance (UI) is for employees who lose their jobs through no fault of their own. The amount is usually a percentage of the employee's pay, up to a maximum such as $800.00 per month. It generally is available for a limited time only, six months to a year.

Employees can receive unemployment benefits if they are laid off or are fired without good cause or if they quit with good cause. "Fired without good cause" is a term defined by each state's unemployment insurance department. If you fire an employee for bad attendance, stealing, or insubordination, the employee should not receive benefits because you had good cause to fire.[17]

On the other hand, employees who can't do the job because they are merely incompetent usually are entitled to benefits, because it's not their fault.[18]

When an employee quits with good cause, benefits also are paid.[19] Good cause to quit includes being sexually harassed, having one's pay or hours cut significantly, and experiencing undue stress on the job. In some states it is not good cause to quit if the employee must move out of the area because his or her spouse has been relocated,[20] in other states it is.[21]

When the employee files for UI benefits, the company can agree the benefits should be paid, or disagree. For example, the employee might state on the UI form that she quit because she had been sexually harassed, but she told you she was quitting because she wanted to spend more time with her family. If the UI department believes you, she will not get benefits. If the department believes her, she will receive benefits. At that point, you can appeal, and a hearing will be held before an administrative law judge or hearing officer.

In some cases, much more is at stake than mere unemployment benefits. In this example, the employee claiming sexual harassment may have an attorney even though no lawsuit has been filed yet. Her attorney may subpoena witnesses for the UI hearing and will have a chance to cross-examine them. The UI hearing is an opportunity for the employee's lawyer to pin down the company's witnesses before they've talked to the company's attorney.

If a former employee makes claims on a form for UI benefits that you believe are outrageous or untrue, check with your lawyer immediately.

> *practical pointers*: If you have good cause to terminate an employee, make sure it's well documented, as discussed in the chapter on wrongful termination. Good documentation will convince the department to rule in your favor without going to a hearing.

If a hearing is scheduled, relax. It's fairly informal. In many cases, the manager who made the decision to fire the employee is capable of representing the company. Most personnel managers handle UI hearings themselves, except for big cases. Then it's time for a lawyer.

Whoever represents the company, it's essential to have all major witnesses present. If the person was fired for fighting, you should have someone there who saw the fight. A supervisor can't testify about what witnesses said. That's hearsay and may not be admissible. Without eyewitnesses, you don't have any evidence. And administrative law judges are notoriously unwilling to reschedule hearings just because you aren't prepared.

Bring all relevant documents to the hearing, including the personnel file. In some states, you may be able to bring in sworn statements from minor witnesses as further backup for your position.

CONTINUATION OF BENEFITS (COBRA): FIVE "QUALIFYING EVENTS"

COBRA is an acronym for a federal law about insurance benefits, the Consolidated Omnibus Budget Reconciliation Act. The act has six provisions, but the most important one requires employers to allow employees to continue their medical insurance after they are no longer eligible for benefits.[22]

It used to be that insurance coverage for employees ended on their last day of work. This left them without medical insurance until they found jobs or bought their own. The effects of even a short period of time without medical benefit coverage can be devastating.

I represented an engineer who was laid off from his job. His insurance coverage ended the same day. He intended to replace it, but didn't start looking right away. Three weeks after his layoff, he had a stroke. He was completely disabled as a result. He had to buy medical insurance after his stroke. Of course, he had to pay higher premiums for less coverage. His deductible was $2,000 month.

COBRA was passed to prevent this from happening. It allows employees to continue their coverage while unemployed or employed elsewhere without benefits. They can buy continued coverage at their employers cost (plus 2%).

Employers with 20 or more employees are covered by COBRA.[23] All health insurance plans are covered, including medical, dental, vision, and prescription insurance.

There are five situations, called "qualifying events," where COBRA comes into effect:

1. If employees quit, are laid off, retired, or fired, they are entitled to continue their insurance for up to 18 months after the last day of work. You don't have to cover employees who are fired for "gross misconduct." However, it's best to cover them anyway. Since the program has no cost to the employer, there's no benefit in getting into an argument with employees about whether their misconduct was "gross."

2. If you decrease the number of hours employees work, and as a result they lose benefits, they are entitled to continue their insurance coverage.

3. If an employee divorces or dies, the spouse is entitled to continue medical insurance coverage. The spouse can continue coverage for 36 months.

4. When employees divorce or die, their children are covered for 36 months. Even children who are not dependents can purchase insurance coverage.

5. When the employee goes on Medicare, the spouse is entitled to continue coverage.

practical pointers: COBRA requires the employer to send a notice to the employee within 30 days of whenever one of the five situations just outlined occurs. Employees have 60 days in which to inform the employer they wish to continue insurance coverage.[24]

The employee pays the monthly premium directly to the employer. You then send the money to the insurance company.

PENSION PLAN PROTECTION (ERISA)

The Employee Retirement Income Security Act (pronounced uh-riss-uh) governs pension plans, employee benefit plans such as disability and medical insurance, and severance pay.[25]

ERISA originally was passed in 1974 in response to the widespread looting of pension funds by both companies and unions. Many retired people who worked and saved for years were left broke as a result of these abuses. ERISA stands for treating employees fairly when it comes to pension benefits. They must be given complete and accurate information about their benefits, and the company can't arbitrarily discriminate against them in giving benefits.

Every employee is entitled to know exactly what benefits are provided under the pension and insurance plans. The law requires you to give each employee a booklet called a "Summary Plan Description" explaining the benefits.[26] The booklet also must inform the employee where a complete description of the plan is available.

ERISA prohibits discriminating among employees when granting or denying benefits. In one case, the company picked people for layoff so that they couldn't vest in their pension plans. That's illegal under ERISA.[27]

You can't give one employee benefits and deny them to another, unless you have a legitimate reason. For example, severance pay given to laid-off employees should be calculated on the basis of a formula such as one week's pay for every year of service. Then the severance payments should be given strictly in accordance with the formula. However, ERISA allows paying inconsistently if the purpose of a payment is not severance pay, but to settle a pending or threatened lawsuit.

If you give employees benefits, you are subject to ERISA, whether or not you intended to be covered.

DEALING WITH LABOR UNIONS

About 15% of American workers are union members. That compares to the high of 30% in 1946.[28] Union organizing efforts are not as common as they once were, but there are active campaigns among workers in the textile industry, electronics, offices, and health care.

If your company does not have a union, you may wish to keep it that way.[29] Companies are most vulnerable to union organizing when employees feel they can't communicate with management. Although paying competitive wages relieves the economic pressure to bring in unions, employees are more likely to seek help from a union when they believe they are victims of unfairness and favoritism.

No-Solicitation Policy

Company policies that prohibit solicitation of employees can be used to prevent union solicitation.[30] A no-solicitation policy can't be implemented or enforced for the first time after a union campaign begins. It must be in place before. The policy must be enforced consistently. That means employees can't solicit each other for Amway products, tickets to church raffles, or candy for a school fundraiser.

A no-solicitation policy must conform with many limitations. It cannot prohibit nonemployee solicitation in parking lots, cafeterias and other places open to the public. It can't prohibit employees from soliciting on their own time at work.[31] The sample no-solicitation policy outlined in the box must be reviewed with a labor attorney before adopting it, as the legal requirements constantly are changing.

No-Solicitation Policy

Nonemployees cannot solicit employees on company property for any reason. Employees cannot solicit other employees during working time. Employees cannot distribute literature in work areas during working time.

Once a union campaign begins, there are restrictions on what you can do in response.[32] You can talk to employees individually or in small groups, but the conversation should be in a public area, not a management office. You can call a meeting of employees on work time, as long as the meeting is not during the last 24 hours before an election.

During these meetings, you can make truthful, factual statements about the union to the employees. For example, you can point out that the union charges its members an initiation fee and annual dues. You can point out how employees can be forced to go out on strike, whether or not they support it, and the economic burden this might put on them and their families.

Examples of Unfair Labor Practices

You can't threaten to take away employee benefits if the union is elected, predict the company will close down, or lie about the union. These are called unfair labor practices. Other things you can't do are

- Promise a pay increase or other benefit if employees vote against the union.
- Spy on union meetings or watch employees as they are campaigning.
- Discriminate against your employees who are union organizers.
- Refuse to allow posting of prounion notices in the same area where antiunion notices are posted.

- Ask employees to wear antiunion buttons or prohibit prounion buttons.

- Visit employees' homes to campaign against the union.

- Ask employees what they think of the union or how they intend to vote.

- Say the company will never deal with the union.

If the company does any of these things, the union can call a strike. This is called an unfair labor practice strike.

The union can't threaten either.[33] But it can make promises, even if the promises aren't true. For example, the union can promise to get a 10% wage increase, even if it knows this is highly unlikely. Unions are allowed to lie because the courts believe that employees know this is propaganda and inherently unbelievable.[34] Supposedly, everyone knows it is not in the union's power to get a wage increase without the company's agreement.

During a union campaign, the organizers will distribute authorization cards. When employees sign the cards, they are either authorizing the union to represent them or merely authorizing an election. Once the union has signed cards from 30% of the employees, it can petition the National Labor Relations Board for an election. As a practical matter, unions usually don't seek elections unless 65% of the employees have signed cards.

If the union gets cards from over half of the employees, and if the company acknowledges the union has majority support, no election is needed. A low-level supervisor who says to a union rep, "It looks like you have a majority," has voluntarily recognized the union and eliminated the need for an election.

> *practical pointers:* Supervisors should be trained by a labor consultant if your company is being organized. There are innumerable restrictions on what they can and can't do.

Collective Bargaining in Good Faith

Once the union is elected, management and labor sit down to negotiate a union contract. This is called meet and confer. During this time, the company should not change any terms or conditions of employment.[35] For example, the company should not give everyone pay raises or take away any benefits, including such things as giving away turkeys to employees during the holidays. There should be no change in any employment term, condition, or benefit during this time.

Both sides are supposed to bargain in good faith.[36] I remember when my father was representing management in a negotiating session. As he was leaving one morning, he said, "I'm off to fight the dragons." Based on my teenaged experience of negotiating with him, I was sure the union rep was probably saying a lot worse things to his family about my dad.

The duty to bargain in good faith prohibits any of these actions:

Refusing to meet at all

Refusing to sign a written contract after an oral agreement has been reached

Refusing to provide information to the union

Using delay tactics during negotiating sessions

Making negotiating conditional on the union stopping the strike first

Repudiating a concession made earlier in the bargaining process

Abruptly changing position for no reason

Raising new demands after apparent agreement has been reached

You can't start the negotiations with a proposal and say, "Take it or leave it." Each side must make some moves, give reasons for positions, and make counterproposals. But if you've done all that and you still can't agree, you've bargained to an impasse. At that point, the union can go on strike. This is called an economic strike.

During an economic strike, the company has the right to hire temporary or "permanent" employees to replace the strikers.[37] Temporary replacements are laid off as soon as the strike is over. Permanent replacements remain employed after the strike is over. The employees who went on strike have the right to be considered for jobs only as openings occur.

If you call replacements "permanent" and then fire them for any reason, you may be vulnerable to a wrongful termination lawsuit as described in Chapter 3.

Rights and Limitations in a Union Contract

The company and union can agree to give employees more rights than the law gives other workers. For example, the law does not require that employees get paid holidays, but union contracts frequently call for employees to be paid double time for holiday work.

The contract also can limit the rights of union employees. Usually, if union employees are fired, they cannot sue in court for wrongful termination. Their exclusive remedy is to file a grievance. If management denies the grievance, it can be appealed to a higher level. Eventually, the employee can request arbitration with an outside arbitrator.

The union contract usually limits what an arbitrator can award to back pay and reinstatement. It is not unusual to see an arbitrator give a fired employee reinstatement but not back pay. This type of decision makes both sides equally unhappy.

Arbitration is not the exclusive remedy for violations of a union employee's fundamental rights. These are rights that aren't mentioned in the union contract, the same rights as all other employees have. For example, union employees do have the right to sue in court for discrimination, sexual harassment, and other claims, as long as they don't involve interpretation of the union contract.[38]

The Union's Duty of Fair Representation

Once elected, the union is the exclusive representative of the employees.[39] The majority rules. There can be no such things as a minority union or side deals with individual employees. The union has the right to be present at any discussion of complaints or grievances between any employee and any supervisor.

Because the union is the exclusive representative of employees, it has the duty to represent all of them fairly. The union can't act arbitrarily, discriminatorily, or in bad faith. For example, the union can't agree with the employer to drop the grievance of one employee in favor of another employee, unless the union already has decided that the one grievance is without merit.

A union can refuse to take a grievance through arbitration for legitimate reasons. Unions have limited resources. Some union employees deserve to be fired. The union has the right to spend its resources on worthy cases.

If the union doesn't take an employee's grievance to arbitration, the employee cannot sue the company directly. Instead, the employee must sue the union for its failure to meet its duty of fair representation. The employee can win only if the union didn't pursue the grievance because of discrimination, personal animosity, or other arbitrary reason.

Union Strategies Today

In recent years, traditional union campaigns have not been successful. As a result, unions are changing their tactics and strategies.

Unions today are getting communities involved in their causes. Cesar Chavez of the United Farm Workers was the first organizer to use widespread consumer boycotts to put pressure on employers to negotiate with his union. His model has been followed since by many others, who have called for boycotts of everything from beer to sheets.

Another recent innovation is called the corporate campaign. A nationwide movement called Justice for Janitors is using this tactic. Organizing janitors has been difficult, because many of them are not legally entitled to work in the United States. They are afraid to sign authorization cards for fear of losing their jobs or being reported to the Immigration and Naturalization Service.

In the Justice for Janitors campaign, instead of getting employees to sign authorization cards, the unions publicize their alleged poor working conditions and low wages. They investigate the owners of the janitorial companies and reveal the kinds of cars they drive, the investment property they own, or the kinds of houses they live in.

The unions put pressure on the companies that hire the janitorial companies by holding demonstrations and press conferences. Often these demonstrations include Democratic officeholders, priests and ministers from activist churches, and other community groups. The tactic is designed to force the company to cancel its contract with the nonunion janitorial service and hire a union one.

These tactics have been successful in some instances and unsuccessful in others. They can backfire, too. One chief executive officer was urging his employees to vote against the union when an employee stood up. She said, "I'm going to vote for the union because you're greedy." He said, "What makes you think I'm greedy?" She said, "You drive a BMW. I can't afford a car like that."

The CEO said, "I drive a five-year-old Chevy. What makes you think I drive a BMW?" The woman said, "It's been in the parking lot every time we have one of these meetings." The CEO looked over at his lawyers. All of them shook their heads. He looked over at the union people. Finally, the union's attorney admitted the car was his.

The union lost.

NONUNION ARBITRATION: THE TREND IN EMPLOYMENT LAW

A new trend in employment law was launched by the U.S. Supreme Court in 1991 when it approved mandatory arbitration for nonunion employees.[40]

In that case, a stockbroker was fired and sued for age discrimination. Like most stockbrokers, when he was hired he was required to sign a contract requiring mandatory arbitration of his disputes with his employer. Traditionally, arbitration has not been the exclusive remedy for discrimination cases. Even union members have been allowed to sue in court for discrimination.

But in this case, the Court said the stockbroker could be forced to arbitrate his claim for discrimination. The Court's language strongly indicated other employment contracts with mandatory arbitration clauses also would be enforced.

The advantage of mandatory arbitration is that arbitrators tend to award less money than juries. The disadvantage is that every termination will go through arbitration, whereas few cases go before juries. The cost per case may be less in arbitration, but the number of cases could more than make up for it.

With the increasing emphasis on alternative dispute resolution, mandated arbitration may be the wave of the future.

DUE PROCESS RIGHTS FOR GOVERNMENT EMPLOYEES

Some government employees are unionized, so they have the same rights as union members. But generally their exclusive remedy is not limited to the union contract.

Government employees also have a property interest in their jobs. Their jobs belong to them. For their property to be taken away, they must receive due process. This is the right to a hearing, and good cause for demotion, termination, pay decrease, or other job loss.

Due process rights generally are contained in civil service or merit system rules. These usually provide for a hearing process that begins with the immediate supervisor and ends with a top executive. If the top decision goes against the employee, the next step depends on the civil service rules and your state's law.

In some cases, employees must go to arbitration. In other instances, they can go to court for a full trial on the issues. Sometimes, they don't get a trial but instead the decision is reviewed by a court. The court will look at a transcript of the hearing, read briefs from each side, and simply decide if the decision was arrived at fairly.

The due process hearing that's required doesn't necessarily have to happen before the employee is terminated.[41] For example, you don't need a hearing before you remove an employee who is a danger to others. The hearing must occur only within a reasonable time. If the hearing officer decides the termination was improper, the employee must be reinstated.

Even when they sue in court, government employees can't get as much in damages as private employees. By law, punitive damages can't be awarded against a governmental entity.[42]

There often are special state laws that give government employees more rights than others. For example, a California law protects police officers who are under investigation for misconduct.[43] Other special rights of government employees are covered in the privacy chapter.

Government employees sometimes have fewer rights than others. Employees of the U.S. government have only 30 days in which to file complaints of discrimination, as compared to the 180–300 days other employees have. U.S., state, and local government employees can be forced to take lie detector tests before hiring, while most private employees can refuse.

HIRING ALIENS: THE IMMIGRATION REFORM AND CONTROL ACT (IRCA)

The purpose of the Immigration Reform and Control Act (IRCA) is to preserve jobs for people legally entitled to work. It accomplishes this by punishing employers who hire illegal aliens. IRCA also prohibits discrimination against aliens who are legally allowed to work in the United States.[44]

IRCA requires you to verify that every new employee you hire has the legal right to work in the United States. This is done by filling out a form called the I-9. A copy of the form is in the appendix.

Every new employee is required to fill out the I-9. Employees must prove they are eligible to work in this country through one of two ways:

1. By showing a valid work authorization card from the Immigration and Naturalization Service.

2. By proving citizenship

A common misconception is that only aliens with green cards are allowed to work. That is not true. Political refugees and aliens with labor certifications are also eligible to work in the United States, as well as aliens with F-1, H-1, J-1, and L-1 cards.

Employees can prove they are citizens by showing a U.S. passport (even if it is expired) or a certificate of naturalization. A birth certificate also can be used. If you do accept a birth certificate, make sure it is a certified copy. It should have an official government stamp, either in purple ink or embossed.

New employees have three days in which to fill out the I-9 forms. If they have lost the documents needed to prove eligibility, they have 18 days to obtain duplicates. But if the copy doesn't arrive within that time, you must fire the employee. To avoid this problem, it is best not to bring on a new employee until the I-9 is complete.

Many employers send the I-9 forms to new employees along with their offer letters. The offer letter should state, "This offer is contingent upon your proof of eligibility to work in this country. Enclosed is a form I-9 for this purpose. Please fill out the form and bring the originals of the requested documents on your first day of work."

The I-9 form must be kept at the site where the employee works. It's a good idea to keep all the I-9s in one file. That way, if you are audited by the government, you will have the forms in one place and won't expose the private information in employees' personnel files to the government auditor.

The I-9 must be kept as long as the employee works for the company. After the employee leaves, the company must keep the form either for three years after the employee's date of hire or one year after the employee's date of termination, whichever is longer.

You must fill out an I-9 form for all new employees—even if you have known them your whole life and know they were born in the United States. If you require only "obvious foreigners" to fill out the form, you can be found guilty of discrimination.

IRCA also prohibits discrimination in hiring. All things being equal, an employer is allowed to choose an American citizen over a noncitizen. But if the noncitizen is objectively more qualified for the job, he or she must be hired.

Some employers have a legitimate business reason for hiring citizens only. For example, if a Department of Defense security clearance is necessary for the job, the government may require citizenship. In most cases, however, you cannot discriminate on the basis of citizenship.

STATE AND FEDERAL POSTING REQUIREMENTS

Many federal and state laws require employers to post notices. The FLSA requires companies to post a minimum wage notice. OSHA requires a safety notice. The polygraph law must be posted, and the EEOC requires an antidiscrimination poster.

Your state may have additional requirements. You may need to post notices about unemployment insurance, state disability insurance, worker's compensation, your state's minimum wage, safety laws, and more.

> *practical pointers:* How do you know what must be posted? Contact every government agency you can think of and ask. Some industry associations, lobbying organizations, or particular state agencies may provide a clearinghouse for this type of information.

TRADE LIBEL: BE CAREFUL WHAT YOU SAY ABOUT A PRODUCT

In the hiring chapter, the issue of giving references for former employees was covered. What if you are asked to give a reference for a product?

Trade libel is an intentional disparagement of the quality of a product which results in a financial loss to its producer. It is a false statement of fact or a dishonest expression of opinion.[45] You could be sued for trade libel if you lie to a potential buyer about a product and if, as a result of your lie, the buyer doesn't purchase it.

An example of a false statement of fact is saying the product does not have a particular feature when it does. A dishonest expression of opinion is where you have a positive opinion about the product, but you give a negative reference for a malicious reason, such as trying to drive out of business the company selling the product.

Trade libel has the same privileges as general defamation. In other words, you are privileged and allowed to give false information in some cases.

You have a privilege for giving untrue statements of fact if you are asked for your opinion by someone who shares your interest in the product. That's just like the privilege for giving negative references on employees who want to transfer within the company. You and other managers of the company share the interest in having a productive work environment. Your opinion about products to be purchased by the company are privileged, because we want to encourage you to state your opinions vigorously without fear of being sued.

Making false statements of fact to other potential buyers may or may not be privileged. As long as you are asked for your opinion, and give it as honestly as you can, it appears there is no liability if you make a mistake.

Exaggerated claims and dishonest expressions of opinion are also privileged if made by a competitor. You can say almost anything you want about a product made by a competitor, as long as you don't imply fraudulent business practices For example, "the reason our competitor's product is so cheap is they take old stuff, refurbish it, and sell it as new," is trade libel unless you can prove it's true. But "our competitor's product is junk" is not libelous. That's healthy competition.

If you were to be sued for trade libel, there is a question about whether your company would be required to represent you. If you were giving the reference in the course and scope of your employment, then you probably would be covered, as when you are asked for your opinion by another manager in your company. But if you are asked by an outsider, then representation would depend on whether your giving an opinion about the product was part of your job.

ANTITRUST LAWS: AN OVERVIEW

After my second year of law school, I worked in the legal department of a major corporation. One day, the boss called me into his office for a new research assignment.

He said, "This is a big one. We're really in trouble." I said, "What happened?" He said, "We have a manufacturing plant up north that uses a lot of electricity. Recently their electric rates were raised. Our plant manager got together with a bunch of other major customers, and they convinced the public utility to reduce the rates!" He hit his desk in frustration.

I asked, "What's wrong with that?" He yelled, "What's wrong? That's price fixing! Haven't you taken antitrust law yet?"

Needless to say, I hadn't. I spent the rest of the summer trying to learn it. I never did. What follows is a very sketchy description of the basic law. If you have any questions about your company's practices, contact an antitrust attorney.

Antitrust laws are not specifically related to employment. But if you instruct employees to engage in antitrust, they may refuse, report the violation, quit in protest, or call the media. In some instances, an employee can sue just as any other third person denied the benefits of a competitive market.

The Sherman Antitrust Act was passed back in 1890.[46] It was Congress's response to popular criticism of the "robber barons" in steel, oil, and railroads. The Antitrust Act prohibits companies from restraining trade by creating monopolies. To do that, antitrust prohibits competitors from working together.

Two Types of Antitrust Violations

There are two types of antitrust violations: horizontal and vertical. *Horizontal* restraints are agreements between competitors to divide the market between them, by price, territories, or customers. An example of a horizontal restraint is price fixing—agreeing with a competitor on what each of you will charge. That's illegal. That's why you should never discuss price with a competitor. But the law specifically allows you to reduce your price to meet a competitor's.

Vertical restraints involve sellers forcing buyers to engage in unfair competition. Vertical price fixing means setting the prices at which resellers may sell the manufacturer's goods. Suggested retail price is not illegal. It is only unlawful to set prices by force or agreement.

Cozy relationships with purchasers are also prohibited under the Clayton Act of 1914.[47] This law prohibits tying and exclusive dealing provisions between seller and buyer.

"Tying" means a seller refusing to sell one product without another product or service, for the purpose of freezing out competition.

"Exclusive dealing" means prohibiting buyers from doing business with competitors of the seller.

Price Discrimination

"Price discrimination" is prohibited under the Robinson-Patman Act.[48] Price discrimination is charging different prices to different buyers, but it is illegal only if it tends to create a monopoly or substantially lessen competition with either the seller or the buyer.

Unlike antitrust, price discrimination does not usually involve agreements between managers from different companies. In fact, if a particular buyer negotiates a cheaper price from the seller, that is *not* illegal price discrimination.

The law originally was passed to prevent large buyers such as chain stores from gaining price preferences based on sheer economic power. Price differences can be based on differences in the grade, quality, or quantity of the item sold or in the costs of selling or transportation.[49]

You can give quantity discounts and otherwise pass along cost savings to customers. But you can't do what our plant manager did: force the utility to give him a rate decrease solely because we were a big account.

The law also prohibits charging some buyers more than others if your purpose is to drive them out of business. Price discrimination is illegal only if it lessens competition in the market.

"Dumping" is the practice of selling goods for less than cost. It is an unfair practice because it drives out competitors.

OTHER BUSINESS LAWS

There are numerous laws which affect business. If employees are asked to violate them and they refuse, the employees cannot be retaliated against. See the section on whistleblowers, in Chapter 3, on wrongful termination.

YOUR RIGHTS AS A MANAGER

And Employee Responsibilities

I once represented a small fashion company in southern California. The entire work force was the owner, his wife, their daughter, and two employees.

One day, they received a letter from a woman in New York. She wanted to move to California and was writing to all the fashion houses here to inquire about jobs. Her resume was impressive.

The owner called her. He said, "With your skill, we could create a position that would be highly profitable. But I don't know anything about your area of expertise. I'd be relying on you to pull it off." The woman confirmed she could do all that was on her resume and more.

The owner flew to New York for an interview. Then he flew her out for another. They agreed on the job. She moved to California. The company laid off an employee to make room for her.

Within a week, it was obvious she had lied. She didn't have the skills she claimed. After two weeks, she stopped coming into work. She would arrive late, leave early, and take long breaks away from the company. She never told anyone where she was, where she was going, or when she would be back.

We gave her a warning. When she didn't improve, we terminated her employment. She was allowed to receive unemployment (after all, she was "merely incompetent"). But when she hired a lawyer to threaten a wrongful termination lawsuit, we threatened a countersuit.

She had breached her duties as an employee. She had committed resume fraud.[1] She had lied in order to get a job in California.

With all that's been said about employees' rights, we sometimes forget that employees have responsibilities, too. These employee duties have been handed down by the courts in both England and the United States, and are contained in a set of books called the *Restatement of Laws*.[2]

Although they receive less media attention than employees' rights, these duties have been cited successfully by employers to win wrongful termination cases. Employees cannot win their lawsuits if they violate their common law duties.

The Employment Relationship: Unfair, but Not Necessarily Illegal

In the chapter on wrongful termination, we talked about how the law of employment originally developed from the law of master and servant. The law of master and servant is part of agency law.[3]

Not every agent is an employee. Not every employee is an agent for the purpose of representing the employer. But every employee is bound by agency principles when dealing with the employer.

An employee's most basic duty is to show up for work. Employees can be dismissed for excessive absenteeism. If they are unable to perform their jobs, even if due to physical or mental disability, their employment can be terminated.[4] Sometimes, we forget that.

A woman once asked me to represent her because she had been fired for excessive absences. She said it wasn't fair.

We got copies of her attendance record. In the previous two years, she had worked less than six months.

First, she was in a car accident. After eight months, she returned to work for a couple of weeks. Then she was diagnosed with cancer and had to undergo surgery. She was out for several more months. She returned for a few weeks, then she injured her back at home. She had been out this time for three months, and her doctor didn't know when she would be able to return.

I was sad for her. She had suffered so much. Firing her was cruel and heartless. But the company had the right to do it. The employer can't be forced to keep someone on the books who can't work.

Not everything that is unfair is illegal.

Using Reasonable Care: Employees' Fiduciary Duty

An agent is a *fiduciary*.[5] A fiduciary is like a trustee. That means employees must treat the company's interests better than their own. They should treat the company's business, equipment, and money as if holding them in trust.

Employees must tell the employer about all important information they learn concerning the employer's business.[6]

Agents and employees must use reasonable care, diligence, and skill while working.[7] They must use the care and skill that are standard for that kind of work. If employees say they have special knowledge or expertise, they must have it and use it.

The duty of care doesn't mean employees have to be perfect. But if they don't use reasonable care, and as a result the employer is injured, they are liable to the company for the damage.

In one case, Mr. Wilcox was hired to build, manage, and maintain a low-income housing development.[8] As the project manager, he was responsible for the smooth running of the operation. But after seven years of employment, he left a "chronicle of failures."

Among other things, his hands-off management style resulted in thefts by high-ranking employees, illegal accounting practices, violations of government regulations, failure to collect rent, vandalism, and poor construction resulting in leaking roofs, backed-up sewers, and no electric or water service.

Mr. Wilcox was fired for mismanagement. He sued for the management fees still owed him. The court refused to require his former employer to pay. The court said Wilcox had failed to meet the standards of reasonable skill or care. Mr. Wilcox brought disrepute upon his employer because of his shoddy management.

Personal Life Versus Work: Employees' Duty of Loyalty

Employees must give their undivided loyalty to the employer during their employment.[9] They must give a good day's work for a good day's pay.

A friend in Texas called me one Monday morning. He said he had hired an employee whose first day of work had been Friday. She worked well that day, he said, but . . .

"This morning she showed up a half-hour late, looking like hell. She laid her head on the desk and started moaning she had a hangover. With the time difference, I couldn't wait until your office opened. Now I'm calling to see if I did the right thing."

I said, "What did you do?" He said, "I fired her ass! What should I have done?" I said, "Fire her ass!"

Employees can't allow their personal lives to affect their jobs.

Love affairs and divorces often disrupt job performance. As discussed in Chapter 7, on safety, you should reasonably accommodate an employee's stress, no matter what the source. But if it's not job-related, after a reasonable amount of time the employee must be counseled, warned, and ultimately terminated if performance standards aren't met.

Employees can't hold second jobs or run their own businesses if they interfere with job performance. Many companies have conflict of interest policies to remind employees of this responsibility.

You can't assume all second jobs will interfere with employees' performance. You must be able to prove it—the employee falls asleep at work, receives phone calls from the other job, or is not available during working hours (including normal overtime and on call).

Employees must put the company's interest ahead of their own, even at their own expense.[10]

BRINGING DISCREDIT TO THE COMPANY: EMPLOYEES' DUTY OF GOOD CONDUCT

Depending upon their positions, employees must not do anything in their private lives that bring disrepute upon the employer.[11]

As discussed in the chapter on privacy, an employer shouldn't pry into the personal lives of employees. But where the employee's private life becomes public, either voluntarily or involuntarily, the employer can protect its own reputation.

The book *Cyberpunk* has an example of a termination under this rule.[12] It's the story of Kevin Mitnick, a notorious hacker who broke into computer systems during the 1980s. At the same time he was breaking into other computer systems, Kevin was hired by Security Pacific Bank to work as a computer security consultant in its electronic funds transfer section. As soon as the bank learned of his past illegal activities, it terminated his employment.

The bank was allowed to fire him to protect its funds. But what if he never went after the bank's money? He had been covered by the media as a result of his arrests. If the public had the perception he was dishonest, he still could be terminated because his employment would bring discredit to the bank's reputation for financial integrity.

Obnoxious or Antisocial Workers

The duty of good conduct also requires employees to work well with others, especially you, the manager. As the *Restatement* of common law puts it, the employee "need not render cheerful obedience, but he must not be insubordinate" in speech or otherwise.[13] If an employee addresses you in highly abusive language, that is grounds for discharge for breach of the duty of good conduct.

Some employees say, "You can't fire me as long as I do a good job." They think they can be obnoxious, withdrawn, or mean to their coworkers. Wrong! It's hard enough to run a productive organization when everyone gets along. If employees are so antisocial they disrupt the workplace, they can be counseled, warned, and ultimately terminated.

Back in the days when I would represent *anybody* (for money), a young man came to my office. He wanted to sue a mom-and-pop hardware store for wrongful termination. He had worked there eight years, first as a salesman and then as office manager. He received yearly increases. A few performance appraisals had been completed over the years. In most categories, they showed above-average to excellent ratings.

He had been terminated for disrupting the workplace. His personnel file was full of documentation. For years, he had made rude remarks about the owners, made faces behind their backs, and called them names. In his role as office manager, he pitted one employee against the other. Finally, the owners had enough, gave him three warnings, and fired him.

I told the potential client I could not take his case on a contingent-fee basis, because I didn't think we could win. The employer had a right to terminate him. He clearly was a disruptive influence in the office. Particularly in his position as office manager, he should support management, not sabotage it.

He insisted he would win and put his money where his mouth was. He lost. (I never lost a case. But my clients did!)

"LOOSE LIPS:" EMPLOYEES' DUTY OF CONFIDENCE

Agents and employees have the duty not to disclose information given to them in confidence by the employer.[14] This duty goes beyond protecting trade secrets (discussed in the next section). As long as the information is not generally known and would injure the employer if known, the employee can't reveal it. This duty applies both to employees and former employees.

The reason for the rule is simple. The relation of employer and employee requires freedom of communication and trust. If employees could tell competitors, potential investors, and customers what they learned at work, employers would be reluctant to reveal any information. Work would slow to a standstill.

The duty applies not only to information labeled confidential but also to any information which the employee *should know* is confidential.

Employees may reveal information to people, like family members, who won't use it to injure the employer. The duty is to protect the company from unfair competition, not to prevent all disclosures. But don't forget: "Loose lips sink ships."

Once I was eating lunch with one of the supervisors in that day's class. We were talking about traveling. I mentioned my recent trip to India. He said, "I was just in Thailand to check out the company's new state-of-the-art facility there. It's a great country, but I tell you—they've been saying that facility is going to be the key to the company's future. If that's the key, we're in big trouble."

He then went on to tell me in great detail about all the problems at the plant. Finally, I asked him who else he had told. "Besides my boss, just a few friends here at the company and my wife."

Employees of the company and spouses are the safest people to tell confidential information. If you do, ask them not to tell others. Imagine how damaging this information would be to the company if it got out to investors or competitors.

But if other people don't have a need to know, don't tell them. If you can't keep your duty of confidence, how can others—who have no duty—be expected to keep it quiet?

EMPLOYEES' DUTY NOT TO REVEAL TRADE SECRETS

The Uniform Trade Secrets Act has been adopted in 37 states.[15] Most of the states that have not adopted the uniform act still apply the common law, on which the act is based.[16] Although it is not identical in every state, the law generally prohibits any person, including employees and former employees, from obtaining trade secrets through improper means.

A "trade secret" is information, including a formula, pattern, compilation, program, device, method, technique, or process, that has value because it is not generally known to competitors.

Examples of trade secrets are

- Salary information
- Product specifications
- Inventions
- Customer lists
- Vendor lists
- Unpublished works
- Software
- Sales and marketing plans
- Pricing information

A trade secret does not have to be novel to be protected. Even "know-how" trade secrets are protected. These are procedures, methods, and expertise that do not rise to the level of a patent. Know-how secrets include new applications of known skills or processes.

How to Protect Customer Lists

When employees leave your company, they may want to take your customers with them. Can the company prohibit that by claiming the customer list is a trade secret?

A customer list is protected to some extent in a few instances. The names of customers usually aren't protected, unless those names would not be known or accessible to any competitor in the market. To determine that, courts ask these questions:

- Is the information available from public sources?
- Was the list easy to compile?
- Did the employee have personal relationships with customers?
- Do the customers purchase from more than one supplier?

If the answer to any of these questions is yes, the names of customers probably will not be protected.

If a customer list contains specialized information like the names of contacts, expiration dates of contracts, previous price quotations, or product preferences, it may be protectable.[17] Even if a customer list is a trade secret, it still may be used by a former employee to announce a new business. But your former employee can't use it to solicit your customers for a new business.

What's the difference between announcing and soliciting? Announcing is advertising, which is basic to everyone's right to engage in fair competition. Soliciting is personally asking a particular customer for business.[18]

In one case, some accountants took a card file from the office and sent out announcements for their new business.[19] The court said the customer information was not a secret, because the employees only sent announcements to clients who they knew personally (through their employment, of course!)

The court said taking the information from the card file "merely saved them from the minor inconvenience of obtaining the desired addresses through generally available resources." If the customers had not been known to the employees (say, the employees had been in the payroll department), then it could be a breach of trade secret.

Fifteen Tips for Keeping a Trade Secret

A trade secret is the opposite of a patent. A patent is made public. A trade secret is kept secret. A trade secret has no term of life like a patent. It's protected as long as it gives the company a competitive edge in the industry and the company attempts to keep it secret.

To keep a trade secret, you must make reasonable efforts of secrecy. What are reasonable efforts? As one attorney said, "Treat a trade secret like money: don't leave it lying around so someone can walk off with it."

If former employees walk out with a trade secret, you can prevent them from using it only if you can prove you treated it as a trade secret. Whether or not the secret was kept secret is the most commonly litigated issue. Here are some things a court may expect you to do to keep your trade secrets:

1. Treat trade secrets as private and confidential.
2. Have written procedures for handling trade secrets.
3. Reveal trade secrets only to employees with the need to know. Give them complete training on their duty of confidentiality.
4. Give employees only portions of trade secrets. Minimize the number with complete information.
5. Don't disclose secrets outside the company. If necessary to reveal trade secrets to vendors, customers, and contractors, require them to sign confidentiality agreements.
6. Mark the information as "company confidential," "secret," and so on. Don't mark things secret that aren't.
7. Keep trade secrets in a secure place, with check-in and check-out procedures. Keep a log of everyone who has access to trade secrets. Conduct a regular audit or inventory.

8. Establish a system of physical plant security, such as badges, entrance guards, briefcase inspections, not allowing cameras on premises, and card-key or locked security doors into sensitive areas. Don't allow employees to "tailgate" into locked facilities; employees must use their own keys to get in.

9. Control visitors by keeping a visitor log, issuing visitor ID tags, and not allowing unescorted visitors on company premises.

10. Do not maintain trade secrets on computers without security measures such as encryption. Avoid placing them on networked machines. Discipline employees who breach any computer security.

11. Control access to photocopy machines.

12. Destroy or shred waste materials containing trade secrets.

13. Require written employee confidentiality agreements.

14. Conduct new hire and exit interviews emphasizing legal duty to maintain secrecy.

15. Pay competitively and treat employees fairly to remove their motivation to steal trade secrets.[20]

Not all these steps are required in every case. But the more you take, the more likely you are to win.[21]

Protecting Against Competitors

Trade secrets are protected from disclosure only by improper means, such as using physical force, lying to induce someone to disclose them, and spying on competitors.[22] Reverse engineering alone is not considered improper means.

A competitor can't induce your employees or former employees to breach their duty to maintain secrecy. In fact, you should enlist the aid of competitors to ensure your former employees don't reveal trade secrets.

When key employees leave, write letters to their new employers. Your letter should inform the company of the general nature of the trade secrets known by the employee and request the company to confirm in writing that the employee will not be allowed to use any of the secret information.

If your competitor refuses to cooperate, you may be able to get an injunction. That's what IBM did in January 1992. The company got a court order prohibiting a former employee from using or disclosing IBM technology to his new employer. The injunction also prohibited him from working on his new employer's version of the same technology.[23]

WRITTEN CONFIDENTIALITY AGREEMENTS

Written confidentiality agreements don't necessarily give you any more protection than common law. But experts recommend you have them anyway.

They are evidence that you treat trade secrets with the appropriate secrecy and that employees know of their duty to maintain confidentiality. Employees can't later claim ownership of trade secrets specifically mentioned in the agreement. And just by signing an agreement, employees may take their responsibility more seriously.

There is a form confidentiality agreement in the box.

Confidentiality Agreement[24]

As a condition of employment, Employee specifically agrees that Employee will not at any time, during or after Employee's employment by Employer, in any manner, either directly or indirectly, use, divulge, disclose, or communicate to any person, firm, or corporation, any confidential information of any kind, nature, or description concerning any matters affecting or relating to the business of Employer (hereinafter referred to as "Confidential Information").

Confidential Information includes but is not limited to: [specify trade secrets] and to the names, buying habits, or practices of any of Employer's customers; Employer's marketing methods and related data; the names of any of Employer's vendors or suppliers; costs of materials; the prices Employer obtains or has obtained or at which it sells or has sold its products or services; manufacturing and sales costs; lists or other written records used in Employer's business; compensation paid to Employees and other terms of employment; manufacturing processes; scientific studies or analyses; details of training methods, new products or new uses for old products, merchandising or sales techniques, contracts and licenses, business systems, computer programs, or any other confidential information of, about, or concerning the business of Employer; its manner of operation, or other confidential data of any kind, nature, or description.

Employee and Employer agree that, as between them, Confidential Information is important, material, and trade secret and affects the successful conduct of Employer's business and its goodwill.

From time to time during the term of this Agreement, additional Confidential Information may be developed or obtained. Employee specifically agrees that all such additional Confidential Information shall be included within the terms of this Agreement.

Prior to employment, Employee had knowledge of the following information which is specifically excluded from this Agreement: [specify]

All equipment, notebooks, documents, memoranda, reports, files, sample books, correspondence, lists, other written and graphic records, and the like, affecting or relating to the business of Employer, which Employee shall prepare, use, construct, possess, or control is Employer's sole property.

If any Confidential Information or other matter described in this Agreement is sought by legal process, Employee will promptly notify Employer and will cooperate with Employer in preserving its confidentiality.

DATE: Signature of Employee:

EMPLOYEES' DUTY NOT TO COMPETE WITH THEIR EMPLOYERS

While employed, an employee cannot compete with the employer, either by starting a competing business or working for a competitor. Your employees can't solicit customers for a rival business while employed by you.

I once met a telephone installer who started his own business while still working for Pacific Bell. He was sent by his employer to a customer site, and whenever the customer requested additional work, he would say, "If you hire my company, I'll come back tonight and do it for half the Pac Bell rate." That violated his duty not to compete. The company was justified in terminating his employment.

Generally, employees are allowed to agree among themselves to leave and go into competition.[25] But they can't actively solicit their coworkers to leave and work for them or another rival.

Employees don't have to inform you about their plans for competing, unless not revealing those plans would harm your company. While employed, they can take steps preliminary to starting business such as writing announcements, leasing office space, and forming a corporation.

Your employees may be hired away by your competitors as long as no deceptive or unfair methods are used. For example, a competitor cannot hire away all your employees with the intent to shut down your company.

In addition to this common law prohibition on employees competing, a company can have written noncompete agreements that are more extensive. See the box for a model that suggests how far an employer can go.

Sample Noncompete Agreement

While Employee is employed by Employer, Employee agrees not to, directly or indirectly, own an interest in, operate, join, control, or participate in, or be connected as an officer, employee, agent, independent contractor, partner, shareholder, or principal of any corporation, partnership, proprietorship, firm, association, person or other entity producing, designing, providing, soliciting orders for, selling, distributing, or marketing products, goods, equipment, or services that directly or indirectly compete with Employer's products or Employer's business.[26]

Some employers have agreements that cover not only current employees but also members of their households. They prohibit a spouse, for example, from working for a competitor. Such agreements have been upheld.[27]

Noncompete Contracts with Former Employees

Generally speaking, you can't prohibit former employees from working in a competing business after leaving your employment. That is a restraint of trade and unfair competition.[28]

But if necessary to protect the company, you can place reasonable restrictions on former employees if the restrictions don't cause them undue hardship.[29] The liberty of employees to work where they want must be balanced against both the business interests of the employer and the public's interest in a competitive market.

To be held valid, noncompete agreements must be reasonably limited by locality. Traditionally, noncompete agreements are upheld only if they prohibit competition in the same town or county. In today's world, many markets are global. I wonder if an agreement not to compete nationally will be held valid some day. Noncompete agreements also must be limited in time. Typically, six months to a year is held to be reasonable.

These restrictions don't apply to noncompete agreements between the former owners of a business and its buyers. For example, when Ross Perot sold EDS to General Motors, he agreed not to compete nationally for three years. That was bargained for as part of the purchase price.

Unfair Competition: Interference with Contract

It is illegal for any person, including a former employee, to try to take away your business with another company or person.[30] When the relationship currently exists, this is called interference with contract. If the contract is anticipated for the future, the same principle applies, and it is called interference with prospective economic advantage. Interference with contract is unfair competition—intentionally using improper means to take away business from a competitor.

The cases turn on the employee's motive or purpose, and whether improper means were used to accomplish it. "Improper means" include fraud, violence, intimidation, defamation, blackmail, extortion, and other crimes.

For example, Mr. Carlson was a certified public accountant who worked for Ernst & Ernst. He was fired because he disagreed with some legitimate, if aggressive, tax advice given by the firm to one of its clients, Cubic Corporation.

After he was fired, Mr. Carlson applied for a job with Cubic. When he wasn't hired, he bought 100 shares of stock and began a campaign to force it to amend its tax returns. He called the corporation's attorneys and threatened to bring a shareholder's suit. He wrote letters to the corporate officers. He brought it up at a stockholders' meeting in front of the press. He reported it to the SEC and the IRS.

Ernst & Ernst sued for an injunction to stop him. The court granted it, holding that Carlson had interfered with the contract between Ernst & Ernst and Cubic Corporation by attempting to destroy the client's confidence in its accountants.[31]

Mr. Carlson did more than interfere with the contract. He also breached his duty as an employee by revealing confidential information about Ernst & Ernst. And he violated his duty of confidence as an accountant to his client, Cubic Corporation.

When Employees Threaten to Sue

Through the years, many potential clients came to my office and described terminations which were completely legal. Some of them said, "And I told my boss, 'You can't do that! I'm going to sue.'"

I'd ask, "Did you talk to a lawyer before you said that?" They'd say, "No. I don't have to. I know my rights." I always took a perverse pleasure in telling these people they didn't have a case. I don't like bullies, especially ignorant ones.

> *practical pointers:* If someone threatens to sue, you should say in a calm manner, "I believe I'm right. I'll be glad to consider an outside opinion if you want to get one. Until then, I expect you to follow my instructions."

If an employee does present you with an opinion letter from an attorney, check with your attorney to make sure your decision was right.

When Employees Threaten Violence

One day I got a call from the owner of a jeans shop at the mall. He said, "An employee came in yesterday and threatened to kill me. I called my business lawyer, and he said we can't fire her until something happens. What do you think?"

I started ranting and raving. "Wait for something to happen?!?!? You have good cause to fire anyone who threatens you bodily harm."

But I did agree with the corporate lawyer on one thing—we had to go slow. It had to be a managed termination. It had to be managed both legally and psychologically.

We contacted a psychologist who specializes in "extracting" threatening employees from the workplace.[32] He spent several days interviewing everybody at work who knew the employee to learn everything about her.

On the last day, he spent four hours with the employee to prepare her for her termination, determine how she would respond to it, and establish psychological domination. We got her final paycheck and paperwork ready. The owner terminated her in a 20-minute meeting. We had plainsclothes security guards outside the office. Her supervisor helped her pack up. She was walked out. We posted uniformed guards for a few days, but she didn't come back. Later we heard she got herself together and was working again.

As a manager, you must protect yourself.

YOUR RIGHTS AS A MANAGER

I like to joke in class that this is the shortest section. People laugh because they don't believe managers have *any* rights. But you do.

Like employee responsibilities, managers' rights are derived from the common law of agency and master-servant. You have the right to have employees obey you.[33] Employees must follow all reasonable directions from management.

The duty to obey is the essence of the employment relationship. By definition, an employee is someone who agrees to work under the control of the employer. Once the employee withholds the agreement to be under your control, the relationship is ended.

If employees were told when hired that they would not be required to do something, you can order them to do it. They must follow your instructions. Of course, you can't ask them to do anything illegal or unethical.

If an employee refuses an order, no matter how trivial, that is insubordination. Insubordination is a deliberate and willful disregard for authority. According to the common law authorities, insubordination always is grounds for immediate termination, because the employee is rejecting the employment relationship itself.[34]

A 1981 case illustrates this principle. Carl Bracale was the general manager of an Anchorage television station. The Board of Directors, his bosses, ordered him to fire one of his salesmen for excessive drinking. Bracale admitted the salesman drank heavily. But he refused to terminate the salesman because he said the drinking didn't interfere with his work.

After several warnings, the Board terminated Bracale for insubordination. He sued for wrongful termination. He said he couldn't be fired because the order he violated was trivial.

The Alaska Supreme Court disagreed and he lost.[35] The Court said it doesn't matter if the order is trivial as long as it is not illegal or unethical. What's important is the relationship. If the employee refuses to recognize authority, he or she can be terminated.

If you decide not to terminate an employee for a terminable offense like insubordination, you can't come back later and terminate for the same offense, unless new facts have come to light. But if the employee later commits an offense that itself does not justify termination, the previous misconduct can be used so that the two incidents, taken together, may justify termination.[36]

YOUR RIGHT TO REQUIRE EXCELLENCE

You have the right to set standards and expectations. You may have different expectations from your employees' previous managers. As long as you tell them in advance and give them reasonable opportunities to achieve, you can appraise their performance against new standards.

You can change the job duties of subordinates for legitimate business reasons. In most cases, you don't have to change the formal job description.

I've heard employees say, "You can't make me do that—it's not in my job description." The correct answer is, "It is now. Are you refusing a direct order from your superior?" If they are, that's insubordination.

You have the right to require excellence. I said this at one company and the personnel manager said, "That's not true here! We force managers to rank on a bell-shaped curve. By definition, most employees aren't excellent."

I don't agree with that method of employee motivation, but it doesn't matter. It's just semantics. You can set the bar wherever you wish.

Your right to require excellence may be the most important right of all. It's one right that all employers have, including supervisors of unionized and government employees. It's a right that managers in many other countries *don't* have. For example, in Japan, companies that employ for life and promote based strictly on seniority keep nonproductive employees filling seats. In Germany, employees can be hired and fired only at certain times of the year.

The right of employers to require excellence gives U.S.-based companies a competitive edge. We all know the competitive costs of our legal system. But there are some benefits, too, and this is one.

If you consistently apply your standard of excellence to everyone, including yourself, you will be fulfilling your highest duty of loyalty to the company.

WHEN THE ISSUES AREN'T CLEAR CUT

The emphasis in this book has been on the law. The law sets the legal minimum for how employees should be treated in a few specific situations. In the vast majority of situations, the law is not clear. It can be interpreted different ways.

Where the law is not clear, other considerations can be taken into account. One is what impact a decision will have on the business of the company. Business considerations may justify action if the law is unclear.

Even if a firing is illegal, top management might decide to risk it, because the costs of not firing are higher than the cost of any lawsuit. A CEO called me and said he wanted to fire the vice president of sales for poor performance. There was no documentation in the file.

I said, "You can't fire someone without any documentation!" He said, "This guy is costing me a half million dollars a month in lost sales. How much would it cost me if he sued?" I had to admit he would make up the cost of a lawsuit very quickly. The CEO decided to fire him, and the vice president never sued. That decision made business sense.

Where the legal and business issues aren't clear cut, the bottom line is fairness. What is the most fair thing to do for the most people? Consider not only the employee to be disciplined, but also their coworkers and you. Yes, you the manager have the right to be treated fairly, too.

JUSTICE AT WORK: A DELICATE BALANCE

The ancient Greek goddess of Justice (Themis) symbolizes the essence of employment law. The *scales* of Justice represent fairness. Employees' rights must be balanced with employers' rights, so that the result is fair to both sides.

The *sword* of Justice represents consequences. If employees' rights are violated, the consequences are lawsuits. In this book, we've outlined employees' rights so that you don't suffer the consequences.

But the sword of Justice works in favor of the employer, too. When the company's rights are violated by an employee, the consequence is termination of employment.

Your job as a manager is the delicate one of balancing the rights of employees and of the company. I hope this book helps you do that now and in the future, to create a good working environment for everyone.

GLOSSARY

AA Affirmative Action, which see.

AAP Affirmative Action plan, which see.

actionable Not everything that is unfair is illegal; only certain conduct can be the subject of a lawsuit or legal action.

ADA Americans with Disabilities Act, which see.

ADEA Age Discrimination in Employment Act, which see.

admissible In a trial, only admissible evidence is allowed to come before the jury.

admission A statement made out of court (hearsay) that is admissible because it goes against the interest of the person who said it ("Oops, we goofed!").

Affirmative Action The practice of recruiting, hiring, and promoting certain groups that otherwise would be underrepresented in the work force (Chapter 2).

Affirmative Action plan The written document that implements Affirmative Action (Chapter 2).

Age Discrimination in Employment Act Legislation that prohibits discrimination against people over 40 (Chapter 2).

Americans with Disabilities Act Legislation that prohibits discrimination against people with disabilities (Chapter 2).

burden of proof Which side must convince the judge it is right; the employee usually has the burden of proof.

class action A lawsuit brought by a few employees on behalf of themselves and all other similar employees; for example, a class action sex discrimination suit would include all women employees (and perhaps applicants) of the company.

COBRA Consolidated Omnibus Budget Reconciliation Act, which see.

Consolidated Omnibus Budget Reconciliation Act Legislation that allows employees to continue insurance benefits after termination (Chapter 8).

court of appeals The first court to review a judge or jury decision to ensure it complies with the law; court of appeals decisions are precedent only for the district in which the court sits. However, different courts often influence others by their opinions.

damages The amount of money awarded to the successful party in a lawsuit (Chapter 1).

defendant The side being sued, usually the company or manager in an employment case.

Department of Labor Government agency that enforces the overtime rules and minimum wage law (Chapter 8).

deposition Pretrial testimony under oath in front of a court reporter but no judge; usually one side's attorney calls witnesses from the other side and questions them about their testimony; the process can last from a few hours to many days.

discovery The process during a lawsuit before trial where each side asks the other to answer written questions (interrogatories) and provide copies of relevant documents.

DFWA Drug-Free Workplace Act, which see.

DOL Department of Labor, which see.

Drug-Free Workplace Act Legislation that requires antidrug policy (Chapter 4).

EAP Employee Assistance Program, which see.

EEO Equal employment opportunity or nondiscrimination.

EEOC Equal Employment Opportunity Commission, which see.

Employee Assistance Program A program provided by some employers voluntarily to counsel employees with personal problems including substance abuse.

Employee Retirement Income Security Act Legistlation that concerns employee pensions and benefits (Chapter 8).

Environmental Protection Agency Government agency that enforces the Clean Air and Water Acts (Chapter 7).

EPA Environmental Protection Agency, which see.

Equal Employment Opportunity Commission Government agency that enforces the U.S. laws prohibiting discrimination on the basis of sex, age, race, color, national origin, religion, citizenship, and disability (Chapter 2).

ERISA Employee Retirement Income Security Act, which see.

exclusive remedy For certain wrongs, an employee cannot sue in court because their exclusive remedy is restricted to rights under a particular law; for example, worker's compensation is the exclusive remedy for employees injured at work.

Executive Order 11246 Presidential order which established Affirmative Action (Chapter 2).

Fair Labor Standards Act Federal overtime and minimum wage law (Chapter 8).

filed How a lawsuit begins; the legal complaint is filed in court.

FLSA Fair Labor Standards Act, which see.

holding The actual decision by the court, which is legally binding as precedent; when a court states an opinion that is not part of the holding, that part of the opinion is dicta.

I-9 Form required to be given to all new hires to prove they legally are entitled to work in the United States (Chapter 8).

Immigration Reform and Control Act The law that prohibits employers from hiring people not legally entitled to work in the United States (Chapter 8).

indemnify Where one person pays the legal expenses of another because the first person caused the injury or expense.

Internal Revenue Service The agency that enforces the law on independent contractors and other tax matters.

IRCA Immigration Reform and Control Act, which see.

IRS Internal Revenue Service, which see.

liable (or held liable) Legally responsible.

National Institute of Occupational Safety and Health A government agency which performs and analyzes measures of workplace safety.

National Labor Relations Act The law concerning labor unions (Chapter 8).

National Labor Relations Board The agency that enforces the labor laws (Chapter 8).

NIOSH National Institute of Occupational Safety and Health, which see.

NLRA National Labor Relations Act, which see.

NLRB   National Labor Relations Board, which see.

Occupational Safety and Health Act   Law requiring employers to provide a safe workplace (Chapter 7).

OSHA   Occupational Safety and Health Act, which see.

plaintiff   The side that files the lawsuit, usually the employee.

precedent   A case that must be followed by other courts.

standard of proof   The amount of evidence that must be proven in court to win a case.

Statute of limitations   The length of time a person has to file a lawsuit; can range from 30 days to 4 years, depending on the type of claim.

Supreme Court   The highest court in each state (except New York), and the highest court in the United States. All state supreme court decisions are precedent and binding on the lower courts in that state and may influence courts in other states. U.S. Supreme Court cases are binding on all courts.

Title VII of the U.S. Civil Rights Act of 1964   The law that prohibits discrimination on the basis of sex, race, color, national origin, religion, (Chapter 2).

trial court   The court where a judge or jury will listen to all witnesses and decide who wins how much.

verdict   The decision of the jury.

THE AFFIRMATIVE ACTION PLAN PROCESS

*T*he affirmative action plan (AAP) consists of five parts: the work force analysis, the availability analysis, the underutilization analysis, goals, and timetables.

WORK FORCE ANALYSIS

The work force analysis shows the number of women and minorities currently working at the company in every job classification. See Table 1 below for a sample work force analysis. In this sample, we will be focusing on job group 19, "electrical engineers." These are listed in three separate categories in Table 1, but are combined later, as you will see in Table 3.

				Male				Female				
Job Title	Job Grp	Tot All	Mal	Fem	Blk	Hsp	Am Ind	Asn	Blk	Hsp	Am Ind	Asn	Total Minor
Associate Electr. Eng.	19	2	2	0	0	0	0	0	0	0	0	0	0
Electronic Engineer	19	64	58	6	1	0	0	2	0	0	0	0	3
Sr. Electr. Eng.	19	47	43	4	1	0	0	0	0	0	0	0	1

Table 1
Work Force Analysis
As of December 31, 19XX

Blk - Black
Hsp - Hispanic
Am Ind - American Indian
Asn - Asian

The work force analysis shows that there are 2 associate systems engineers, both white males. There are 64 systems engineers, 58 men and 6 women, and 3 minority men. There are 47 senior systems engineers, 43 men, 4 women, 1 black male. In total, there are 113 engineers, including 4 minorities and 10 women. This is a snapshot of the work force on December 31.

AVAILABILITY ANALYSIS

The next step in the affirmative action plan is calculating the number of women and minority employees who are qualified as electrical engineers and available for employment. This is done by analyzing the percentage of women and minorities in the work force in the local community.

Eight different factors are evaluated in order to get a total picture of the number of minority and women engineers in the local area. Table 2 shows the eight factors in the far left-hand column.

1. The first factor is the percentage of women and minorities in the population at large. This information comes from the U.S. Census Bureau. In the second column of Table 2, you see "Value Weight." This is a number assigned by the company to the likelihood that this statistic is relevant in determining the number of women and minority engineers in the work force. Since the vast majority of people are not electronic engineers, this factor should be given no weight. In contrast, if you were hiring for an entry-level janitor job, you would probably give this factor weight close to 1.00 (100%).

2. The second factor is the overall unemployment rate in the community. Again, overall unemployment is not relevant to filling an electronic engineers position, so this factor is given no weight in our example.

3. The third factor, again, is a general population statistic. The numbers here are the result of multiplying factor 1 (number of minorities and women) times factor 2 (unemployment rates for minorities and women).

4. The fourth factor is one that is very important in our example, and as a result, it is weighted 40%. The percentage of minorities or women "with the requisite skills" in the local area is obtained from the state employment office. Here, it is determined that 10% of the local engineers are minority and 5% are women.

Table 2
Availability Factor Composition Form
EEO-1 Category: Professionals
Job Group: 19. Electrical/Electronic Engineers

	Value Weight	Raw Statistics						Weighted Factor						Source
		Min.	Fem.	Blk.	Hsp.	Am Ind.	Asian	Min.	Fem.	Blk.	Hsp.	Am Ind.	Asian	
1. Percentage of population in the specific labor or recruitment area.	.00	20.1	51.4	11.5	6.4	0.6	1.6	0.00	0.00	0.00	0.00	0.00	0.00	Population by Race/Sex (A)
2. Percentage of unemployment in the specific labor or recruitment area.	.00	28.5	42.4	18.3	7.9	1.1	1.2	0.00	0.00	0.00	0.00	0.00	0.00	Unemployed Population by Race/Sex (A)
3. Percentage of minorities or women in total work force in specific labor area.	.00	17.8	42.6	10.0	5.7	0.5	1.6	0.00	0.00	0.00	0.00	0.00	0.00	Civilian Labor Force (A)
4. Percentage of availability of minorities or women with the requisite skills in the specified labor area.	.40	10.0	5.0	2.9	2.4	0.2	4.5	4.00	2.00	1.16	0.96	0.08	1.80	Electrical/ Electronic Engineers (A)
5. The availability of minorities or women having requisite skills in an area in which the contractor can reasonably recruit.	.00	0.0	0.0	0.0	0.0	0.0	0.0	0.00	0.00	0.00	0.00	0.00	0.00	
6. Percentage of minorities or women promotable and transferable within the contractor's organization in the specified labor area.	.15	2.0	2.5	0.4	0.8	0.0	0.8	0.30	0.38	0.06	0.12	0.00	0.12	Job Group #31
7. Estimate of existence of training institutions for the requisite skills required for minorities or women	.40	10.0	5.0	2.9	2.4	0.2	4.5	4.00	2.00	1.16	0.96	0.08	1.80	Electrical/ Electronic Engineers (A)
8. Estimate of training efforts the contractor is reasonably able to undertake to make the job group available to minorities or women.	.05	2.0	2.5	0.4	0.8	0.0	0.8	0.10	0.13	0.02	0.04	0.00	0.04	Job Group #31
Estimated Availability	///	///	///	///	///	///	///	8.40	4.5	2.40	2.08	0.16	3.76	///

Labor Force Essentials, 1980 Census, San Mateo/Santa Clara Counties Averaged

287

5. The fifth factor is the number of minorities and women with skills, who live outside the local area, but in an area the company can reasonably recruit in. For example, to get good electronic engineers, a company might reasonably expect to recruit nationally. Here, though, the company has decided there are enough engineers in its locality, so it gives no weight to national recruiting.

6. The sixth factor is the percentage of women and minorities who can be transferred into the job of electronic engineer. Here, the company has identified job group 31, "technicians," as a group from which some employees could transfer. The company assigned 15% value to this factor.

7. The seventh factor is the percentage of women and minorities who are graduating from engineering schools in the local area. This is a very important factor, so it is weighted 40%. The percentage of women and minority students studying electrical engineering comes from the local universities.

8. The last factor is the effect of training programs the company could institute to make employees transferrable. The company gave this a 5% weight.

After the eight factors are weighted, the weights are multiplied by the raw statistics. For example, since 10% of the local engineers are minorities, and since we are giving that factor 40% weight in factor 4, the weighted value is 4%. The same is true for factor 7. Factors 6 and 8 are also weighted. When the weighted values are added, they add up to 8.4%. In other words, considering the number of minority engineers locally, and the number of minority technicians in the company who are transferrable now, or who would be with training, we should have about 8.4% minority engineers.

Doing the same analysis for women, we would expect to have about 4.5% female engineers.

UTILIZATION ANALYSIS

The third step in the AAP process is simple: compare the work force analysis with the availability analysis to see if the company has "utilized" as many women and minority engineers as expected.

In Table 3, you see the comparison. For job group 19, electronic engineers, 3.5% of the current employees are minorities. But 8.4% of the local engineers are minorities. So the company is "underutilized" for minority engineers.

	Table 3 Utilization Analysis Minority					
	Job Group	Total Incumbent	Minority #	%	% Availablity	Under utilization
19	Electronic Engs.	113	4	3.5	8.4	Yes

In contrast, in Table 4, we see that the company employs 8.8% women engineers, but only 4.5% of the local engineers are female. So the company is "overutilized" in women engineers.

	Table 4 Utlization Analysis Female					
	Job Group	Total Incumbent	Female #	%	% Availablity	Under utilization
19	Electronic Engs.	113	10	8.8	4.5	No

GOALS AND TIMETABLES

After the company completes this third step, the utilization analysis, it sets goals and timetables for curing areas of underutilization. For example, this company might plan on hiring 10 electronic engineers in the next two years. They could set a goal of hiring two minorities among them. That would be 20% of the new hires and increase minority representation by one-third, but still be only 5.3% of the engineers. The company would then have to set new goals and timetables to continue to increase minority representation.

EMPLOYMENT ELIGIBILITY VERIFICATION (Form I-9)

1 **EMPLOYEE INFORMATION AND VERIFICATION:** (To be completed and signed by employee.)

Name: (Print or Type) Last	First	Middle	Birth Name

Address: Street Name and Number	City	State	ZIP Code

Date of Birth (Month/Day/Year)	Social Security Number

I attest, under penalty of perjury, that I am (check a box):

☐ 1. A citizen or national of the United States.

☐ 2. An alien lawfully admitted for permanent residence (Alien Number A _____).

☐ 3. An alien authorized by the Immigration and Naturalization Service to work in the United States (Alien Number A _____ ,

or Admission Number _____ ,   expiration of employment authorization, if any _____).

I attest, under penalty of perjury, the documents that I have presented as evidence of identity and employment eligibility are genuine and relate to me. I am aware that federal law provides for imprisonment and/or fine for any false statements or use of false documents in connection with this certificate.

Signature	Date (Month/Day/Year)

PREPARER/TRANSLATOR CERTIFICATION (To be completed if prepared by person other than the employee). I attest, under penalty of perjury, that the above was prepared by me at the request of the named individual and is based on all information of which I have any knowledge.

Signature	Name (Print or Type)		
Address (Street Name and Number)	City	State	Zip Code

2 **EMPLOYER REVIEW AND VERIFICATION:** (To be completed and signed by employer.)

Instructions:

Examine one document from List A and check the appropriate box, **OR** examine one document from List B **and** one from List C and check the appropriate boxes.
Provide the *Document Identification Number* and *Expiration Date* for the document checked.

List A Documents that Establish Identity and Employment Eligibility	List B Documents that Establish Identity	**and**	List C Documents that Establish Employment Eligibility
☐ 1. United States Passport	☐ 1. A State-issued driver's license or a State-issued I.D. card with a photograph, or information, including name, sex, date of birth, height, weight, and color of eyes. (Specify State_____)		☐ 1. Original Social Security Number Card (other than a card stating it is not valid for employment)
☐ 2. Certificate of United States Citizenship			☐ 2. A birth certificate issued by State, county, or municipal authority bearing a seal or other certification
☐ 3. Certificate of Naturalization	☐ 2. U.S. Military Card		
☐ 4. Unexpired foreign passport with attached Employment Authorization	☐ 3. Other (Specify document and issuing authority)		☐ 3. Unexpired INS Employment Authorization Specify form # _____
☐ 5. Alien Registration Card with photograph	_____		
Document Identification # _____	*Document Identification* # _____		*Document Identification* # _____
Expiration Date (if any) _____	*Expiration Date (if any)* _____		*Expiration Date (if any)* _____

CERTIFICATION: I attest, under penalty of perjury, that I have examined the documents presented by the above individual, that they appear to be genuine and to relate to the individual named, and that the individual, to the best of my knowledge, is eligible to work in the United States.

Signature	Name (Print or Type)	Title
Employer Name	Address	Date

Form I-9 (05/07/87)
OMB No. 1115-0136

U.S. Department of Justice
Immigration and Naturalization Service

290

Employment Eligibility Verification

NOTICE: Authority for collecting the information on this form is in Title 8, United States Code, Section 1324A, which requires employers to verify employment eligibility of individuals on a form approved by the Attorney General. This form will be used to verify the individual's eligibility for employment in the United States. Failure to present this form for inspection to officers of the Immigration and Naturalization Service or Department of Labor within the time period specified by regulation, or improper completion or retention of this form, may be a violation of the above law and may result in a civil money penalty.

Section 1. Instructions to Employee/Preparer for completing this form

Instructions for the employee.

All employees, upon being hired, must complete Section 1 of this form. Any person hired after November 6, 1986 must complete this form. (For the purpose of completion of this form the term "hired" applies to those employed, recruited or referred for a fee.)

All employees must print or type their complete name, address, date of birth, and Social Security Number. The block which correctly indicates the employee's immigration status must be checked. If the second block is checked, the employee's Alien Registration Number must be provided. If the third block is checked, the employee's Alien Registration Number *or* Admission Number must be provided, as well as the date of expiration of that status, if it expires.

All employees whose present names differ from birth names, because of marriage or other reasons, must print or type their birth names in the appropriate space of Section 1. Also, employees whose names change after employment verification should report these changes to their employer.

All employees must sign and date the form.

Instructions for the preparer of the form, if not the employee.

If a person assists the employee with completing this form, the preparer must certify the form by signing it and printing or typing his or her complete name and address.

Section 2. Instructions to Employer for completing this form

(For the purpose of completion of this form, the term "employer" applies to employers and those who recruit or refer for a fee.)

Employers must complete this section by examining evidence of identity and employment eligibility, and:
- checking the appropriate box in List A *or* boxes in both Lists B and C;
- recording the document identification number and expiration date (if any);
- recording the type of form if not specifically identified in the list;
- signing the certification section.

NOTE: Employers are responsible for reverifying employment eligibility of employees whose employment eligibility documents carry an expiration date.

Copies of documentation presented by an individual for the purpose of establishing identity and employment eligibility may be copied and retained for the purpose of complying with the requirements of this form and no other purpose. Any copies of documentation made for this purpose should be maintained with this form.

Name changes of employees which occur after preparation of this form should be recorded on the form by lining through the old name, printing the new name and the reason (such as marriage), and dating and initialing the changes. Employers should not attempt to delete or erase the old name in any fashion.

RETENTION OF RECORDS.

The completed form must be retained by the employer for:
- three years after the date of hiring; or
- one year after the date the employment is terminated, whichever is later.

Employers may photocopy or reprint this form as necessary.

U.S. Department of Justice
Immigration and Naturalization Service

OMB #1115-0136
Form I-9 (05/07/87)

ENDNOTES

CHAPTER 1: MANAGING IN A MINE FIELD

Footnotes to legal citations follow official format. The first number listed is the volume, then the name of the reporter service, followed by the page number. To find any of the cases cited, go to your local county law library or federal court and ask for assistance from the reference librarian.

1. *Without Just Cause: An Employer's Practical and Legal Guide on Wrongful Discharge* (Rockville, MD: Bureau of National Affairs, 1988).

2. *Wrongful Discharge Report*, 1375 Peachtree Street, Atlanta, GA.

3. *Without Just Cause* (Rockville, MD).

4. This amount was overturned by the trial judge and now is on appeal. *San Jose Mercury News*, January 20, 1992, p. 1E.

5. Civil Rights Act of 1991, 42 U.S.C. 1981(b3).

6. *United States* v. *Basic Construction Co.*, 711 F.2d 570, 573 (4th Cir. 1983).

7. *San Jose Mercury News*, April 28, 1992, p. 1A.

8. Veterans Preference Act of 1944, 5 U.S.C. 2108.

9. Speech by Mark Sanborn, National Speakers Association, 1991 Los Angeles Winter Workshop.

CHAPTER 2: THE VALUE OF DIVERSITY

1. Civil Rights Act of 1991, §109, amending 42 U.S.C. 2000e(f) and 42 U.S.C. 12111(4).

2. Uniform Guidelines for Employee Selection Procedures, 41 C.F.R. 60-3.

3. 42 U.S.C. 2000e et seq.

4. For a fascinating account of the political battle to pass the bill, see Charles and Barbara Whalen, *The Longest Debate*, (Seven Locks Press, 1985).

5. For a case reporting similar statements, see *Robinson* v. *Hewlett-Packard* 183 Cal.App.3d 1108 (1986).

6. *Vaughn* v. *Edel*, 918 F.2d 517 (5th Cir. 1990).

7. *Watson* v. *Ft. Worth Bank & Trust*, 101 L.Ed.2d 827 (1988).

8. See Chapter 6, Harassment.

9. *Fragrante* v. *City & County of Honolulu*, 699 F.Supp. 1429 (D. Haw. 1987), *aff'd*, 51 F.E.P. 190 (9th Cir. 1989), *cert. den'd*, 110 S.Ct. 1811, 108 L.Ed.2d 942 (1990).

10. Immigration Reform and Control Act of 1986, Pub. L. 99.603 Nov. 1986, 100 Stat. 3359, in amended form 8 U.S.C. 1101 et seq.

11. Title VII, 42 U.S.C. 2000e et seq.

12. 42 U.S.C. 2000e et seq.

13. 29 U.S.C. 621d et seq.

14. *Kouba* v. *Allstate Insurance Co.*, 691 F.2d 873 (9th Cir. 1982).

15. Diane Crispell, "Women's Earnings Gap is Closing—Slowly," *American Demographics*, Vol. 13, No. 2, (February 1991), p. 14.

16. Norman D. Willis & Assocs., Santa Clara County Pay Equity Study, (Santa Clara, CA: Author, 1987).

17. *Price Waterhouse* v. *Hopkins*, 490 U.S. 228 (1989).

18. *San Jose Mercury News*, August 9, 1991, p. 1A.

19. John Naisbitt and Patricia Aburdene. *Megatrends 2000* (New York: Avon Books, 1990).

20. 42 U.S.C. 2000e (K).

21. California prohibits discrimination on the basis of pregnancy, just like the U.S. law. But California goes further. Even if your company has no temporary disability leave policy, you still must give pregnant employees in California up to four months leave if they are disabled as a result of pregnancy or childbirth. In addition, you must guarantee they can return to their same jobs or jobs substantially similar. Several California companies claimed this law was discriminatory against men, because it requires employers to treat pregnant employees better then men who are temporarily disabled. They took their argument all the way to the U.S. Supreme Court—and lost. The law was upheld. *Ca. Fed. Savings & Loan Ass.* v. *Guerra*, 479 U.S. 272 (1987).

22. *International Union, United Automobile, Aerospace and Agricultural Implement Workers of America* v. *Johnson Controls*, 111 S.Ct. 1196 (1991).

23. See Chapter 7, Safety.

24. Age Discrimination in Employment Act, 29 U.S.C. 621 et seq.

25. 29 C.F.R. 1625.1 et seq.

26. Arguably, there doesn't have to be five years difference if (1) the younger person is outside the protected group (under 40); (2) the older person is age 65 (courts give more protection to this age group, which historically has been forced into retirement); or (3) the person who wasn't hired looks older than the person who got the job. That's an image issue.

27. *Taggart v. Time Inc.* 924 F.2d 43 (2d Cir. 1991).

28. *Metz v. Transit Mix,* 828 F.2d 1202 (7th Cir. 1987).

29. *Ewing v. Gill,* 3 Cal.App.4th 601 (1992).

30. For more on constructive discharge, see Chapter 7, Safety.

31. *Guthrie v. Tifco Industries,* 56 F.E.P. 1438 (5th Cir. 1991).

32. Bona fide executives or high-level policymakers may be forced to retire once they reach age 65 if in the two years before retirement they have served in that capacity, and if upon retirement they are immediately entitled to a pension or other benefit worth at least $44,000. 29 U.S.C. 631. Tenured professors can be forced to retire at age 70.

33. Older Workers Benefit Protection Act, P.L. 101-433, October 1990, 104 Stat. 978, amending 29 U.S.C. 623, 626 and 630.

34. Ken Dychtwald, *Age Wave* (New York: St. Martin's Press, 1989).

35. Charles Handy, *The Age of Unreason* (Boston: Harvard Business School Press, 1989).

36. Americans with Disabilities Act, P.L. 101-336, July 1990, 104 Stat. 327, amending 42 U.S.C. 2000e et seq.

37. *Dept. of Labor v. Texas Industries,* 40 F.E.P. 118, 782 F.2d 547 (1986).

38. Internal Revenue Code, §190.

39. Executive Order 11246, 41 C.F.R. 60.

40. *Johnson v. Transportation Agency, County of Santa Clara,* 480 U.S. 616, 107 S.Ct. 1442, 94 L.Ed.2d 615 (1987). In contrast to its ruling on executive order Affirmative Action, the Court generally has disfavored affirmative action plans written by various courts and imposed on employers for punishment. *Martin v. Wilks,* 490 U.S. 755, 109 S.Ct. 2180, 104 L.Ed.2d 835. Court-ordered Affirmative Action applies to public employers, not private industry.

41. A federal government contractor or subcontractor is defined as someone with at least 50 employees and at least $50,000 annually in federal contracts or subcontracts (including purchase orders). If you sell to a company that uses your product in providing goods or services to the U.S. government, you're

covered. If your billings are at least $10,000 annually but less than $50,000, you have to have an Affirmative Action statement in your contracts, but you are not required to have a written Affirmative Action plan. Some states require state contractors to adopt Affirmative Action. See, for example, Alaska Statutes 36.30.115.

42. Cynthia Taeuber, ed., *Statistical Handbook of Women in America*, (Phoenix, AZ: Onyx Press, 1991).

43. Rehabilitation Act of 1973, (§§ 501, 503, 504) 29 U.S.C. 791b.

44. The Vietnam Era Veterans Readjustment Assistance Act of 1974, P.L. 93-508, S1, December 1974, 88 Stat. 1578 (adding and amending numerous sections in Title 38 U.S.C. beginning at §219)

CHAPTER 3: THE RIGHT WAY TO FIRE EMPLOYEES

1. *Rulon-Miller* v. *IBM*, 162 Cal.App.3d 241 (1984).

2. Bureau of National Affairs, Individual Employment Rights Manual *(IERM)*, August 1989, 505:51.

3. Ibid.

4. *Cleary* v. *American Airlines*, 111 Cal.App.3d 443, 168 Cal.Rptr. 722 (1980).

5. *Beales* v. *Hillhaven*, 108 Nev. 96, 825 P.2d 212 (1992).

6. *Hoffman Specialty Co.* v. *Pelouze*, 164 S.E. 397, 158 Va. 586 (Va. Sup. Ct., 1932).

7. *Pugh* v. *See's Candies*, 116 Cal.App.3d 311 (1981).

8. *Foley* v. *Interactive Data Corp.*, 47 Cal.3d 654 (1988).

9. *Cleary* v. *American Airlines*, 111 Cal.App.3d 443, 168 Cal.Rptr. 722 (1980).

10. *Seaman's Direct Buying Service* v. *Standard Oil*, 36 Cal.3d 752, 206 Cal.Rptr. 354, 686 P.2d 1158 (1984) (commercial contract); *Egan* v. *Mutual of Omaha Insurance Co.*, 24 Cal.3d 809, 169 Cal.Rptr. 691 (1979) (insurance contract), but see *Moradi-Shalal* v. *Fireman's Fund*, 46 Cal.3d 287, 758 P.2d 58 (1988).

11. *Simpson* v. *Western Graphics Corp.*, 293 Or. 96, 643 P2d 1276 (1982).

12. Al Neuharth, *Confessions of an SOB*, (New York: Penguin Books, 1990) p. 289.

13. Mary Kay Ash, *Mary Kay on People Management*, (New York: Warner Books, 1984) p. 39.

14. Andrew S. Grove, *One on One with Andy Grove* (New York: G. P. Putnam's Sons, 1987).

15. Adapted by Rosalind Newton Enright (tel. 415-435-3362).

16. *Khanna* v. *Microdata*, 170 Cal.App.3d 250 (1985).

17. But see Chapter 8. Employees terminated for "mere incompetence" usually are entitled to unemployment insurance.

18. *USAir Magazine* (May 1990) p. 72 .

19. *Dabbs* v. *Cardiopulmonary Management Services*, 188 Cal.App.3d 1437 (1987).

20. *Wagner* v. *City of Globe*, 150 Ariz. 82, 722 P.2d 250 (1986).

21. *Freeman United Coal Mining Co.* v. *Human Rights Cmsn.*, 527 N.E.2d 1289 (App.Ct. Ill., 1988).

22. *Miles* v. *M.N.C. Corporation*, 750 F.2d 867 (11th Cir., 1985).

23. *Metz* v. *Transit Mix*, 828 F.2d 1202 (7th Cir., 1987).

24. See Chapter 2.

25. Under the Worker Adjustment and Retraining Notification Act (WARN) (29 U.S.C. 2101 et seq.), a "plant closing" is a permanent or temporary shutdown of a site or unit. A site is a branch office, stand-alone manufacturing plant, or the like. A unit is a group of employees, for example, the marketing department or an engineering group associated with a particular product. Whenever a site or unit is shut down, you must give 60 days' advance notice, no matter how many employees are affected.

    WARN also applies to mass layoffs. Mass layoffs are defined two ways:
    • 33% of all of your employees are laid off (but at least 50 employees), or
    • 500 employees are laid off.

    For example, if your company has 100 employees and you lay off 33, you are not required to warn because fewer than 50 employees are affected. On the other hand, if your company has 10,000 employees and you lay off 500, you are required to warn even though less than 33% of your work force is laid off.

    If you have two or more layoffs within 90 days of each other, the number of employees are added together to determine whether WARN applies.

26. "Employment at Will State Rulings Chart," *IERM*, 505:51, p. 145. Reprinted with permission from *Labor Relations Reporter—Individual Employment Rights*, pp. 505:51-505:52 (July 1992). Copyright 1992 by the Bureau of National Affairs, Inc. (800-372-1033). This material is frequently updated and readers should consult the up-to-date version in the binder.

CHAPTER 4: NONE OF YOUR BUSINESS?

1. Restatement, Torts, Second, §652A(2)(a).

2. Restatement, Torts, Second, §652A(2)(c).

3. *Jennings* v. *Minco Technology Labs, Inc.*, 765 S.W.2d 497, 500 (Tex. Ct. App. 1989).

4. *Rankin* v. *McPherson*, 107 S.Ct. 2891 (1987).

5. William J. Sonnenstuhl, Harrison M. Trice, William J. Staudenmeir, and Paul Steele, "Employee Assistance and Drug Testing: Fairness and Injustice in the Workplace," 11 Nova L. Rev. 709, 711 (1987).

6. Or as Justice Scalia put it, "There is no reason why [the] determination that a legitimate expectation of privacy exists should be affected by the fact that the government, rather than a private entity, is the employer." *O'Connor* v. *Ortega*, 480 U.S. 709, 730-31 (1987) (Scalia, J. concurring).

7. *Pavesich* v. *New England Life Ins. Co.*, 122 Ga. 190, 50 S.E. 68 (1905).

8. Craig Cornish, "Novel and Emerging Claims," speech at the National Employment Lawyers Association (NELA), June 1991, annual conference and accompanying paper, *Adapting the Common Law Right to Privacy to the American Workplace* available from NELA (San Francisco, CA).

9. *Golden* v. *Board of Education*, 285 SE2d 665 (W. Va, 1981).

10. *Rulon-Miller* v. *IBM*, 162 Cal.App.3d 241, 208 Cal.Rptr. 524 (1984).

11. 48 C.F.R. 223.570.

12. 49 C.F.R. 391.43, 394.7.

13. 14 C.F.R. 61, 63, 65, 121, 61.14, 63.12, 65.23, 14 C.F.R. Pt. 121, App. I.

14. 49 C.F.R. 217.13, 219.301.

15. Study performed at Northwestern University, reported in *San Jose Mercury News*, February 16, 1992, p. 2PC.

16. Statistics according to SmithKline Beecham Clinical Laboratories, reported in *San Jose Mercury News*, February 11, 1992, p. 7E.

17. *Capua* v. *City of Plainfield*, 643 F.Supp. 1507, 1511 (D.N.J. 1986).

18. *Skinner* v. *Railway Labor Executives' Association*, 109 S.Ct. 1402 (1989).

19. *National Treasury Employees Union* v. *Von Raab*, 109 S.Ct. 1384 (1989).

20. Edward M. Chen, Pauline T. Kim, and John M.True, "Common Law Privacy: A Limit on an Employer's Power to Test for Drugs," 12 George Mason L. Rev. 651, 689, fn. 202 (1990).

21. Statistics according to SmithKline Beecham Clinical Laboratories, reported in *San Jose Mercury News*, February 11, 1992, p. 7E.

22. *National Treasury Employees Union* v. *Von Raab*, 109 S.Ct. 1384 at 1399 (Scalia, J., dissenting) (1989).

23. Chen, Kim, and True, "Common Law Privacy," 676-77.

24. *United Paperworkers International Union* v. *Misco, Inc.*, 484 U.S. 29 at 44 (1987).

25. For an exhaustive discussion of accuracy, see Chen, Kim, and True, "Common Law Privacy," 688-90.

26. Performance Factors is located in Alameda, California. Phone 510-769-8300.

27. *Hartness v. Bush*, 919 F.2d 170 (D.C. Cir. 1990)(secret national security clearances); *Bluestein v. Skinner*, 908 F.2d 451 (9th Cir. 1990), *cert. den'd*, 111 S.Ct. 954 (1991)(aviation personnel); *Taylor v. O'Grady*, 888 F.2d 1189 (7th Cir. 1989)(corrections officers); *American Federation of Government Employees v. Skinner*, 885 F.2d 884 (D.C. Cir. 1989), *cert. den'd*, 110 S.Ct. 1960 (1990)(transportation employees); *National Federation of Federal Employees v. Cheney*, 884 F.2d 603 (D.C. Cir. 1989)(Army civilian employees); *Harmon v. Thornburgh*, 878 F.2d 484 (D.C. Cir. 1989), *cert. den'd*, 110 S.Ct. 865 (1990)(top secret clearances of Justice Department employees); *Guiney v. Roache*, 873 F.2d 1557 (1st Cir.) *cert den'd*, 110 S.Ct. 404 (1989)(police officers); *Rushton v. Nebraska Public Power Dist.*, 844 F.2d 562 (8th Cir. 1988)(nuclear power plant employees).

28. *National Treasury Employees Union v. Yeutter* 918 F.2d 968 (D.C.Cir. 1990).

29. *O'Keefe v. Passaic Valley Water Commission*, 253 N.J.Super. 569, 602 A.2d 760 (1992).

30. *Wilkinson v. Times Mirror Corp.*, 215 Cal.App.3d 1034 (1990).

31. *Luck v. Southern Pacific Railroad*, 265 Cal.App.3d 618 (1990).

32. *American Postal Workers Union v. Frank*, 725 F.Supp. 87 (U.S.D.C. Mass. 1989); *Jackson v. Liquid Carbonic Corp.*, 863 F.2d 111 (CA 1st 1988).

33. Me. Rev. Stat. Ann. Tit. 26, §683 et seq. (1989).

34. P.L. 100-690, Tit. V, Subtitle D.

35. 29 U.S.C. 2001 et seq. The law applies to any employer subject to the Fair Labor Standards Act (federal minimum wage).

36. *Stikes v. Chevron USA, Inc.*, 914 F.2d 1265 (9th Cir. 1990).

37. *Morton v. Hartigan*, 495 N.E.2d 1159 (Ill.App. 1986).

38. *American Postal Workers Union v. U.S. Postal Service*, 871 F.2d 556 (6th Cir. 1989).

39. *K-Mart Corp. v. Trotti*, 677 S.W.2d 632 (Tex. Ct. App. 1984).

40. *O'Connor v. Ortega*, 107 S.Ct. 1492 (1987).

41. *Schowengerdt v. General Dynamics Corp.*, 823 F.2d 1328 (9th Cir. 1987).

42. *O'Donnell v. CBS, Inc.*, 782 F.2d 1414 (7th Cir. 1986) (applying Illinois law).

43. *Vernars v. Young*, 539 F.2d 966 (3d Cir. 1976).

44. 18 U.S.C. 2510-20.

45. 18 U.S.C. 2510(5)(a)(i).

46. *Watkins* v. *L. M. Berry*, 704 F.2d 577, 583 (11th Cir. 1983).

47. 18 U.S.C. 2511(2)(d).

48. *Simmons* v. *Southwestern Bell Telephone Co.*, 452 F.Supp. 392 (W.D. Okl. 1978), *aff'd*, 611 F.2d 342 (10th Cir. 1979).

49. e.g. California Penal Code §§630-637.

50. *Harkey* v. *Abate*, 131 Mich.App. 177, 346 N.W.2d 74, (1983).

51. *Fayard* v. *Guardsmark, Inc.*, 5 I.E.R. Cases 516 (E.D. La. 1989).

52. *Saldana* v. *Kelsey-Hayes*, 178 Mich.App. 230, 443 N.W.2d 382, 384 (1989).

53. *Deitemann* v. *Time, Inc.*, 449 F.2d 245, 247 (9th Cir. 1971).

54. *Garrity* v. *New Jersey*, 385 U.S. 493, 497 (1967).

55. *Mansfield* v. *AT&T*, 747 F.Supp. 1329, 5 I.E.R. Cases 1383 (D.Ark. 1990).

56. *Ellis* v. *Buckley*, 790 P.2d 875 (Colo.App. 1990).

57. *Crump* v. *P & C Food Markets, Inc.*, 576 A.2d 441 (Vt. 1990).

58. *Semore* v. *Pool*, 266 Cal. Rptr. 280 (1990).

59. *Kessler* v. *Equity Management, Inc.*, 572 A.2d 1144 (Md.Ct.Spec.App. 1990).

60. "Note: Private Abridgement of Speech and the State Constitutions," 90 Yale L.J. 165, 180, n. 79 (1980).

61. Conn. Gen. Stat. Ann. §§31-51q.

62. *Rutan* v. *Republican Party of Illinois*, 110 U.S. 2729, 111 L.Ed.2d 52 (1990).

63. *Novosel* v. *Nationwide Insurance Co.*, 721 F.2d 894 (3d Cir. 1983)(applying Pennsylvania law).

64. *Swenson* v. *United States Postal Services*, 890 F.2d 1075, 1078 (9th Cir. 1989).

65. Office of Personnel Management standard, 5 C.F.R. 731.201 et seq.

66. *Norton* v. *Macy*, 417 F.2d 1161, 1166 (D.C.Cir. 1969).

67. California Labor Code §1102.1, Connecticut Public Act 9158, §3(1); Hawaii Statutes section 378-2; Massahusetts Ch. 516, Acts of 1989; New Jersey statutes 10:5-4 et seq.; Wis. Stat. Ann. 111.321 to 322.

68. N.Y. Comp. Codes R. & Regs. Tit. 4, §28 (1983).

69. adapted from Lex K. Larson, rev. ed., *Employment Discrimination,* (New York: Matthew Bender, 1977), Section 110.30, fn. 25, 26. Copyright © 1992 by Matthew Bender & Co., Inc. reprinted with permission from *Employment Discrimination* by Lex K. Larson. All rights reserved.

70. *Gay Law Students* v. *Pacific Telephone & Telegraph*, 24 Cal.3d 458, 156 Cal.Rptr. 14, 595 P.2d 592 (1979).

71. *Catholic War Veterans* v. *City of New York*, 576 F. Supp. 71 (U.S.D.C., S.D. New York, 1983).

72. *Soroka* v. *Dayton Hudson*, 1 Cal Rptr.2d 77 (1991), review granted 4 Cal Rptr.2d 180 (1992).

73. *Watkins* v. *United States Army*, 837 F.2d 1428 (9th Cir. 1988).

74. *Matlovich* v. *Secretary of the Air Force*, 591 F.2d 852 (D.C. Cir. 1978).

75. *Morrison* v. *State Board of Education*, 1 Cal.3d 214, 82 Cal.Rptr. 175, 461 P.2d 375 (1969).

76. *Jantz* v. *Muci*, 759 F.Supp. 1543 (D.Kan. 1991).

77. *Golden* v. *Board of Education*, 285 S.E.2d 665 (1982).

78. *Rogliano* v. *Fayette County Board of Education*, 347 S.E. 220, 225 (W.Va. 1986).

79. *Cisco* v. *United Parcel Service, Inc.*, 476 A.2d 1340, 1344 (Pa.Super 1984).

80. Restatement, Torts, Second, §652E, comment b.

81. *Zechman* v. *Merrill Lynch*, 742 F.Supp 1359 (1990).

82. Restatement, Torts, Second, §652C.

83. *Staruski* v. *Continental Telephone Company*, 581 A.2d 266 (Vt. 1990).

84. *Child Protection Group* v. *Cline*, 350 S.E.2d 541, 545 (W.Va. 1986).

85. California Confidentiality of Medical Information Act, Cal. Civ. Code D.1, Pt. 2.6.

86. *Eddy* v. *Brown*, 715 P.2d 74, 78 (Okla. 1986).

87. *Miller* v. *Motorola, Inc.*, 202 Ill.App.3d 976, 560 N.E.2d 900 (1990).

88. *Davis* v. *Monsanto Company*, 627 F.Supp. 418 (S.D. W.Va. 1986).

89. *Bratt* v. *IBM Corp.*, 392 Mass. 508, 467 N.E.2d 126, 137 (1984).

90. *Young* v. *Jackson*, 572 So.2d 378 (Miss. 1990).

91. *Harris* v. *Neff*, 6 I.E.R. 615 (D. Kan. 1991).

92. *Bratt* v. *IBM Corp.*, 392 Mass. 508, 467 N.E.2d 126, 137 (1984).

93. *Neal* v. *Corning Glassworks Corporation*, 745 F.Supp. 1294 (S.D. Ohio 1989).

94. *Leggett* v. *First Interstate Bank of Oregon*, 739 P.2d 1083 (Or.App. 1987).

95. *Daury* v. *Smith*, 842 F.2d 9 (1st Cir. 1988).

96. Privacy Act of 1974, 5 U.S.C. 552(a).

97. *Zinda* v. *Louisiana Pacific Corp.*, 440 N.W.2d 548 (Wis. 1989).

98. *Payton* v. *City of Santa Clara*, 132 Cal.App.3d 152, 183 Cal.Rptr. 17 (1982).

99. *Tobin* v. *Michigan Civil Service Commission*, 416 Mich. 661, 331 N.W.2d 184, 189 (1982).

100. *Jordan* v. *Motor Vehicles Division, State of Oregon*, 308 Or. 433, 442, 781 P.2d 1203, 1208 (Or. 1989); accord *Guard Publishing Co.* v. *Lone County School District*, 774 P.2d 494 (Ore. Ct. Appeals 1989); *Clinical-Technical Union* v. *Board of Trustees*, 475 N.W.2d 373 (Mich. Ct. Appeals 1991); *Newsday* v. *Sisc*, 518 N.E.2d 930 (NY Ct. Appeals 1987).

101. *Healey* v. *Teachers Retirement System*, 558 N.E.2d 766 (Ill. App. Ct. 1990).

102. *Phillips* v. *Smalley*, 435 So.2d 705 (Ala. 1983).

103. *F.O.P. Lodge 5* v. *Philadelphia*, 812 F.2d 105, 110 (3d Cir. 1987).

104. *Thorne* v. *City of El Segundo*, 726 F.2d 459, 471 (9th Cir. 1983), *Eastwood* v. *Dept. of Correction*, 846 F.2d 627 (10th Cir. 1988).

105. *Littlejohn* v. *Rose*, 768 F.2d 765, 869-70 (6th Cir. 1985), *cert. den'd*, 475 U.S. 1045, 106 S.Ct. 1260, 89 L.Ed.2d 570 (1986).

106. *Wilson* v. *Taylor*, 733 F.2d 1539, 1543 (11th Cir. 1984).

107. *Thorne* v. *City of El Segundo*, 726 F.2d 459, 471 (9th Cir. 1983).

108. *Briggs* v. *North Muskegon Police Dept.*, 563 F.Supp. 585, 590 (W.D. Mich 1983), *aff'd*, 746 F.2d 1475 (6th Cir. 1984).

109. *Shuman* v. *City of Philadelphia*, 470 F.Supp. 449 (E.D. Pa. 1979).

110. *Shwago* v. *Spradlin*, 701 F.2d 470, 482-83 (5th Cir. 1983), *cert. den'd sub nom*, 465 U.S. 965 (1983).

111. *Murray* v. *Silberstein*, 702 F.Supp. 524 (E.D. Pa. 1988).

112. *McCrory* v. *Rapides Regional Medical Center*, 635 F.Supp. 975 (W.D. La. 1986).

113. *Staats* v. *Ohio National Life Insurance Company*, 620 F.Supp. 118, 120 (W.D. Pa. 1985).

114. *Karren* v. *Far West Federal Savings*, 79 Or.App. 131, 717 P.2d 1271, 1273-74 (Or.App. 1986).

115. But only if both coworkers are disciplined equally. *Zentiska* v. *The Pooler Motel*, 708 F.Supp. 1321 (S.D.Ga. 1988).

116. *Rulon-Miller* v. *IBM*, 162 Cal.App.3d 241, 208 Cal.Rptr. 524 (1984).

117. *Slohoda* v. *United Parcel Service*, 475 A.2d 618, 622 (N.J.App. 1984), *reversed on other grounds*, 207 N.J. Super. 145, 504 A.2d 53 (1986).

118. *Moffett* v. *Gene B. Glick Co, Inc.*, 604 F.Supp. 229, 236 (N.D. Ind. 1984).

119. *Jarrell* v. *Eastern Airlines*, 430 F.Supp. 884 (E.D. Va. 1977), *aff'd per curiam*, 577 F.2d 869 (4th Cir. 1978); see also *Leonard* v. *National Airlines*, 434 F.Supp. 269 (D. Fla. 1977).

120. *Wislocki-Goin* v. *Mears*, 831 F.2d 1374 (7th Cir. 1987), *cert. den'd*, 108 S.Ct. 1113 (1988).

121. *O'Donnell* v. *Burlington Coat Factory Warehouse, Inc.*, 656 F.Supp. 263 (S.D. Ohio 1987).

122. *Lockhart* v. *Louisiana-Pacific Corp.*, 102 Or.App. 593 (1990).

123. *Tardif* v. *Quinn*, 545 F.2d 761 (1st Cir. 1976).

124. *Andre* v. *Bendix Corp.*, 774 F.2d 786 (7th Cir. 1985).

125. *Bellissimo* v. *Westinghouse Electric Company*, 764 F.2d 175 (3rd Cir. 1985), *cert. den'd*, 475 U.S. 1035 (1986).

126. *Price Waterhouse* v. *Hopkins*, 490 U.S. 228 (1989).

127. *Campbell* v. *Beaughler*, 519 F.2d 1307 (9th Cir. 1975).

128. *Rogers* v. *American Airlines, Inc.*, 527 F.Supp. 229 (S.D. N.Y. 1981).

129. *Conard* v. *Goolsby*, 350 F.Supp. 713 (N.D. Miss. 1972).

130. Stan Davis and Bill Davidson, *2020 Vision*, (New York: Simon & Schuster, 1991), p. 16.

131. *Roach* v. *Harper*, 143 W.Va. 869, 105 S.E.2d 564 (1958).

132. *Hamberger* v. *Eastman*, 106 N.H. 107, 206 A.2d 239, 242 (1964).

133. Ira Michael Sheppard, Robert L. Duston, and Karen S. Russell, *Workplace Privacy, Employee Testing, Surveillance, Wrongful Discharge, and Other Areas of Vulnerability (A BNA Special Report)*, (Rockville, MD: Bureau of National Affairs, 1989), 2nd Edition.

134. Christopher D. Cameron, in "Current Comment and CCH Analysis," *Labor Law Reports*, March 25, 1991, p. 60,485. Reproduced with permission from *Labor Law Reports* published and copyrighted by Commerce Clearing House, Inc., 4025 W. Peterson Ave., Chicago, Illinois 60646.

135. Speech by Joseph R. Grodin, *Constitutional Values in the Private Sector Workplace*, Labor & Employment Law Section of the State Bar of California, San Francisco, October 26, 1991.

CHAPTER 5: HOW TO HIRE THE BEST

1. *Diaz* v. *Pan American World Airways, Inc.*, 442 F.2d 385 (5th Cir. 1971), *cert. den'd*, 404 U.S. 950 (1971). *Wilson* v. *Southwest Airlines Co.*, 517 F.Supp. 292 (N.D. Tex. 1981), is an example of an airline explicitly using sex to sell airline tickets. The court held that was illegal sex discrimination.

2. *Kern* v. *Dynalectron Corp.*, 577 F.Supp. 1196 (N.D. Tex. 1983), *aff'd*, 746 F.2d 810 (5th Cir. 1984).

3. *Abrams* v. *Baylor College of Medicine*, 581 F.Supp. 1570 (S.D. Tex. 1984), *aff'd*, 805 F.2d 528 (5th Cir. 1986).

4. *Fortino* v. *Quasar*, 950 F.2d 389 (7th Cir. 1991).

5. 41 C.F.R. Ch. 60.

6. *San Jose Mercury News*, July 30, 1989, p. 1E.

7. *EEOC* v. *Recruit U.S.A. Inc., Interplace/Newsworld Recruit*, 939 F.2d 746 (9th Cir. 1991).

8. *EEOC* v. *Recruit U.S.A. Inc., Interplace/Newsworld Recruit*, 939 F.2d 746 (9th Cir. 1991).

9. Hawaii Revised Statutes, Tit. 21, §378-2.

10. 41 C.F.R. 60-2.12.

11. Rick Smith contributed to this section. He is a principal in Management Development Associates.

12. Thirteenth Amendment to the U.S. Constitution.

13. Equal Pay Act, P.L. 88-38, June 1963, 77 Stat. 56, Tit. 29 U.S.C. 206.

14. *Schulte* v. *Wilson Industries*, 547 F. Supp 324 (D.C., S.D. Texas 1982).

15. *Kouba* v. *Allstate*, 691 F.2d 873 (9th Cir. 1982).

16. *Berger* v. *Security Pacific Information Systems*, 795 P.2d 1380 (Colo.App. 1990).

17. *Telesphere International, Inc.* v. *Scollin*, 489 So.2d 1152 (Fla. 3d DCA 1986).

18. *Workforce 2000: Work and Workers for the 21st Century* (New York: Hudson Institute, 1987).

19. Speech by Lenora Billings-Harris at the National Speakers Association convention in Palm Desert, CA, July, 1991. Dr. Billings-Harris can be reached at 602-963-4540.

20. Interviewing Candidates from Diverse Backgrounds, *Training and Culture Newsletter*, Vol. 3, no. 3 (January 1991).

21. Civil Rights Act of 1991, 42 U.S.C. 2000e-2 (K) (1Ai).

22. Uniform Guidelines for Employee Selection Procedures, 29 C.F.R. 1607 et seq.

23. The seminal cases are *Griggs* v. *Duke Power Co.*, 401 U.S. 424, 91 S.Ct. 849, 28 L.Ed.2d 158, 3 F.E.P. 175 (1971), and *Albemarle Paper Co.* v. *Moody*, 422 U.S. 405, 95 S.Ct. 2362, 45 L.Ed.2d 280, 10 F.E.P. 1181 (1975).

24. *Albemarle Paper Co.* v. *Moody*, 422 U.S. 405, 95 S.Ct. 2362, 45 L.Ed.2d 280, 10 F.E.P. 1181 (1975)..

25. Lewis R. Goldberg, Julia Ramos Grenier, Robert M. Guion, Lee B. Sechrest, and

Hilda Wing, *Questionnaires Used in the Prediction of Trustworthiness in Pre-employment Selection Decisions: An A.P.A. Task Force Report* . One free copy is available on request from APA Science Directorate, 1200 Seventeenth St., N.W., Washington, D.C. 20036.

26. Ibid., p. 26.

27. *Soroka* v. *Dayton Hudson Corp.*, 235 Cal. App. 3d 654, (1991), *review granted*, 822 P.2d 1327 (1992).

28. *InfoWorld*, September 24, 1984, p. 34.

29. Thanks to Iris Holmes Hatfield, a graphologist with HuVista International, Inc., Louisville, KY, for her help with this section. (tel. 502-423-8423)

30. Kathryn K. Sackheim, *Handwriting Analysis and the Employee Selection Process*, (Westport, CT: Quorum Books, 1990), p. xv.

31. To Land a Position in Paris, Penmanship Can Be Paramount, *The Wall Street Journal*, September 3, 1985.

32. Passing the Penmanship Exam, *The New York Times*, February 24, 1985.

33. Sackheim, *Handwriting Analysis*, p. 148.

34. Binet study reported in G. W. Allport, and P. E. Vernon, *Studies in Expressive Movement*, 2nd ed. (New York: Hafner Publishing Co., 1967).

35. E. B. McNeil, and G. S. Blum, "Handwriting and Psychosexual Dimensions of Personality," *Journal of Projective Techniques*, Vol. 16 (1952), pp. 476-84.

36. 15 U.S.C. §1681-1681(t).

37. For example, California Labor Code §432.7(e), (f).

38. Negligent hiring suits usually can't be brought by your employees, because if they are injured, their exclusive remedy is worker's compensation. See Chapter 7.

39. For a complete description of negligent hiring, see James A. Branch, Jr., *Negligent Hiring Practice Manual* (New York: John Wiley & Sons, 1988).

40. Health Care Quality Improvement Act of 1986, 42 U.S.C. 11101-11152.

41. *Vanderhule* v. *Berinstein*, 285 A.D. 290, 136 N.Y.S.2d 95 (1954) *modified*, 284 A.D. 1089, 136 N.Y.S.2d 349 (1954).

42. Quoted in "Points to Ponder," *Reader's Digest* (May 1991) p. 32.

43. *Comeaux* v. *Brown & Williamson Tobacco Co.*, 915 F.2d 1264 (9th Cir. 1990); see also *Filcek* v. *Norris Schmid, Inc.*, 401 N.W.2d 318, 319, 156 Mich.App. 80, 84 (Ct.App. 1986).

44. *Lindahl* v. *Air France*, 930 F.2d 1434 (9th Cir. 1991).

45. Speech by Cliff Palefsky to the Northern California Human Resources Council (San Francisco) on August 13, 1991.

Chapter 6: How Men and Women Can Work Together

1. "The Man in the Street: Why He Harasses," *Ms.*, May 1981, p. 18.

2. *Sexual Harassment in Federal Government: An Update,* (Washington, D.C.: U.S. Merit Systems Protection Board, 1988).

3. EEOC Policy Guidance on Current Issues of Sexual Harassment, N-915-050, March 19, 1990, p. 19.

4. *Whatley* v. *Skaggs Companies, 707* F.2d 1129 (10th Cir., 1983).

5. *Diem* v. *City and County of San Francisco,* 686 F.Supp. 806 (N.D. Cal., 1988).

6. *Henson* v. *City of Dundee,* 682 F.2d 897 (11th Cir. 1982).

7. *Huebschen* v. *Dept. of Health and Soc. Serv.,* 547 F.Supp. 1168 (W.D. Wis. 1982).

8. See Chapter 7, on safety.

9. *Ellison* v. *Brady,* 924 F.2d 872 (9th Cir. 1991).

10. See Chapter 7, on safety.

11. *Ellison* v. *Brady,* 924 F2d 872 (9th Cir. 1991).

12. *Meritor Savings Bank* v. *Vinson,* 106 S.Ct. 2399 (1986), uses the term "severe or pervasive" rather than gross or repeated (at 2405).

13. *Zabkowicz* v. *West Bend Co.,* 589 F.Supp. 780 (E.D. Wis. 1984).

14. EEOC Policy Guidance on Current Issues of Sexual Harassment, p. 7.

15. *Meritor Savings Bank* v. *Vinson,* 106 S.Ct at 2399.

16. EEOC Policy Guidance on Current Issues of Sexual Harassment, p. 7.

17. Ibid., p. 10.

18. *Meritor Savings Bank* v. *Vinson,* 106 S.Ct at 2407.

19. *Loftin-Boggs* v. *City of Meridian, Miss.,* 633 F.Supp. 1323 (S.D. Miss., 1986).

20. *Thoresen* v. *Penthouse International,* 583 N.Y.S.2d 213, 179 A.D.2d 29 (Ct. App. 1992).

21. *Meritor Savings Bank* v. *Vinson,* 106 S.Ct at 2408, 29 C.F.R. 1604.11(c), *Henson* v. *City of Dundee,* 682 F.2d 897 (11th Cir. 1982).

22. *Buffalo Teachers Federation* v. *Arthur,* 34 F.E.P. 1887 (1984).

23. *Henson* v. *City of Dundee,* 682 F.2d 897 (11th Cir. 1982).

24. *Sexual Harassment in Federal Government: An Update.*

25. *Gilardi* v. *Schroeder,* 672 F.Supp. 1043 (1986), *aff'd* 833 F.2d 1226 (7th Cir. 1987).

26. *Weiss* v. *Coca-Cola Bottling Co. of Chicago,* 1992 W.L. 48018 (N.D. Ill. 1992).

27. *Smith* v. *Hennepin,* 1988 W.L. 53400 (D.C. Minn. 1988).

28. *Fisher* v. *San Pedro Hospital*, 214 Cal.App.3d 590 (1989), *review den'd* (1990).

29. *Andrews* v. *City of Philadelphia*, 895 F.2d 1469 (1990).

30. *Arnold* v. *City of Seminole, OK*, 614 F.Supp. 853 (D.C., OK 1985), is a case finding sexual harassment as a result of pinups in employees' lockers.

31. *Trotta* v. *Mobil Oil Corp.*, 788 F.Supp. 1336 (S.D. N.Y. 1992).

32. *Lipsett* v. *University of Puerto Rico*, 864 F.2d 881 (1st Cir. 1988).

33. *Meritor Savings Bank* v. *Vinson*, 106 S.Ct. at 2399.

34. *Stewart* v. *Cartessa*, 771 F. Supp. 876 (S.D. Ohio, 1990).

35. *Robinson* v. *Jacksonville Shipyards*, 760 F.Supp. 1486 (D.C. FLa. 1991).

36. *Halpert* v. *Wertheim*, 65A.D.2d 724, 411 N.Y.S. 2d 11 (Sup. Ct. App. Div., 1978) aff'd 48 NY 2d 681 (Ct. App. NY 1979).

37. *Andrews* v. *City of Philadelphia*, 895 F.2d 1469 at 1485.

38. *Carrington* v. *Ambrose*, 1986 W.L. 5111 (D.C. N.Y. 1986).

39. *Ellison* v. *Brady*, 924 F.2d 872 (9th Cir. 1991).

40. *Hopkins* v. *Price Waterhouse*, 490 U.S. 228 (1989).

41. See Chapter 4, on privacy, for permissible relationship restrictions.

42. *Meritor Savings Bank* v. *Vinson*, 106 S.Ct. at 2399.

43. After the Supreme Court made its decision, the case was sent back down to the trial court for a new trial. Perhaps because her attorneys felt it would be difficult to prove that in fact she was forced to have sex, the case has never gone to trial.

44. EEOC Policy Guidance on Employer Liability under Title VII for Sexual Favoritism, N-915-048, January 1990.

45. *Crosier* v. *United Parcel Service*, 150 Cal.App.3d 1132 (1983). But see the discussion about relationships in Chapter 4, on privacy.

46. *Proulx* v. *Citibank*, 659 F.Supp. 972 (S.D. N.Y. 1987).

47. *Proulx* v. *Citibank*, 659 F.Supp. 972 (S.D.N.Y. 1987).

48. 29 C.F.R. 1604.119f0; EEOC Policy Guidance on Current Issues of Sexual Harassment, N-915-050, March 19, 1990, pp. 28-29.

49. *Sexual Harassment in Federal Government: An Update.*

50. Suzanne Garner, "Why Anita Hill Lost," *Commentary*, January 1992, p. 26.

51. See, for example, *Bennett* v. *NYC Dept of Correction*, 705 F.Supp. 979 (D.C. N.Y. 1989).

52. EEOC Policy Guidance on Current Issues of Sexual Harassment, pp. 23, 28, *Barrett* v. *Omaha National Bank*, 726 F.2d 424 (8th Cir. 1984).

53. *Derr* v. *Gulf Oil Corp.*, 796 F.2d 340 (10th Cir. 1986).

CHAPTER 7: LIFE & DEATH ON THE JOB

1. U.S. Department of Commerce, Bureau of Labor Statistics, *U.S. Statistical Abstract, 1991*, (Washington, D.C.: U.S. Government Printing Office, 1991).

2. 29 U.S.C. 651 et seq. Much of the information in this section on OSHA and environmental laws is based on Lawrence C. Postol, *Legal Guide to Handling Toxic Substances in the Workplace* (Modesto, CA: Business Laws, 1990).

3. *Occupational Health Guidelines for Hazardous Chemicals* added 65 new chemicals between 1981 and 1988. Contact National Institute of Occupational Safety and Health, Department of Health and Human Services.

4. 29 U.S.C. 654(a)(1)

5. *General Dynamics* v. *Occupational Safety & Health Review Commission*, 599 F.2d 453 (1st cir. 1979).

6. 29 C.F.R. 1910.1200(c).

7. 29 C.F.R. 1910.1200(g)(6).

8. 29 C.F.R. 1910.1200(g)(2).

9. 29 C.F.R. 1910.1200(h).

10. 29 C.F.R. 1910.20(c)(6).

11. 29 C.F.R. 1904.8.

12. James E Sharp is the president of Hazard Management Services, a consulting firm. (209-551-2000).

13. 29 U.S.C. 660(c).

14. 29 C.F.R. 1977.9(c).

15. *Donovan* v. *R.D. Andersen Const. Co., Inc.*, 552 F.Supp. 249 (U.S.D.C. Kansas, 1982).

16. 29 C.F.R. 1977.12(2).

17. *Donovan* v. *Hahner, Foreman & Harness, Inc.*, 736 F.2d 1421 (10th cir. 1984).

18. *San Jose Mercury News*, Business Briefs, January 1, 1991.

19. Clean Air Act, 42 U.S.C. 7401 et seq.

20. Clean Water Act, 33 U.S.C. 1251 et seq.

21. 42 U.S.C. 6901 et seq.

22. 42 U.S.C. 6971.

23. 42 U.S.C. section 9601 et seq., including Superfund Amendments Reauthorization Act of 1986 (SARA).

24. Postol, *Legal Guide to Handling Toxic Substances in the Workplace*, p. 3.003.

25. 42 U.S.C. 7622 protects employees; 7604 allows citizen suits.

26. 33 U.S.C. 1367 protects employees; 1365 allows citizen suits.

27. 42 U.S.C. 6971 protects employees; 6972 allows citizen suits.

28. 42 U.S.C. 9610 protects employees; 9659 allows citizen suits.

29. 408 N.W.2d 569 (1987).

30. Procedure for filing complaints under all of these acts is at 29 C.F.R. 24.3.

31. *San Jose Mercury News*, June 15, 1985, p. 1A. The California Corporate Liability Act went into effect in January 1991. This law has been called "Be a manager, go to jail." The law says if a manager conceals a serious danger, he or she can be sent to prison for up to three years, pay up to $1 million in fines, or both. "Serious danger" means there is a likelihood of death or bodily injury. California Penal Code §387.

32. *United States* v. *Park*, 421 U.S. 658 (1975), *United States* v. *Johnson & Towers*, 741 F.2d 662, 670 (3rd Cir. 1984), *United States* v. *Dee*, 912 F.2d 741 (4th Cir. 1990).

33. For example, California Labor Code, 3602(b)(1).

34. *Johns-Mansville* v. *Contra Costa Superior Court*, 612 P.2d 948 (1980).

35. *Handley* v. *Union Carbide Corp.*, 620 F.Supp. 428 (D.C. W.Va. 1985).

36. *San Jose Mercury News*, December 19, 1989, p. 7E.

37. *San Jose Mercury News*, September 1, 1984, p. 15E.

38. *San Jose Mercury News*, January 16, 1991, p. 1E.

39. *San Jose Mercury News*, September 15, 1989, p. 1D.

40. *The San Francisco Recorder*, May 9, 1991, p. 2.

41. American National Standards Institute, Human Factors Engineering of Video Display Terminal Workstations Standards, Standard NC/HFS 100-1988, Washington, D.C.

42. *San Jose Mercury News*, January 6, 1991, p. 1F.

43. *Raytheon Co.* v. *Cal. Fair Employment & Housing Comsn.*, 212 Cal.App.3d 1242 (1989).

44. *Estate of Behringer* v. *Medical Center*, 249 N.J.Super. 597, 592 A.2d 1251, 55 F.E.P. 1145 (1991).

45. *Slade* v. *Smith's Managment Corp.*, 808 P.2d 401 (1991).

46. *San Jose Mercury News*, July 18, 1991, p. 9A.

47. For example, Connecticut Statutes, Tit. 31, Ch. 557, Part II, 31-40q.

48. *Hentzel* v. *Singer*, 138 Cal.App.3d 290 (1982).

49. *County of Fresno* v. *Fair Employment and Housing Commission*, 226 Cal.App.3d 1541, 277 Cal.Rptr. 557 (1991).

50. Kentucky Statutes, 344.040, Tit. XXVII, Ch. 344; Oklahoma Statutes, 40 §500, Tit. 40, Ch. 14; Rhode Island Statues, 23-20.7.1-1.

51. *Indoor Air Facts No. 4*, ANR-445-W, U.S. Environmental Protection Agency (April 1991).

52. *San Jose Mercury News*, October 2, 1991, p. 3D.

53. *Personnel News*, January 1992, p. 2.

54. *San Jose Mercury News*, April 25, 1990, p. 1F.

55. *San Jose Mercury News*, January 1, 1992, p. 3C.

56. *San Jose Mercury News*, September 17, 1989, p. 2PC.

57. *Albertson's* v. *WCAB (Bradley)*, 131 Cal.App.3d 308 (1982).

58. In California, employees now are required to prove at least 10% of their stress was caused by the job. California Labor Code 3208.3.

59. *Panopulos* v. *Westinghouse*, 216 Cal.App.3d 660 (1989). In the actual case, Chris waited for five years before quitting. The court reasoned it was not a constructive discharge because conditions were not so intolerable that a reasonable person would be forced to quit, since Chris himself did not quit. Later cases have criticized this portion of the opinion.

60. *Wilson* v. *Monarch Paper Co.*, 939 F.2d 1138, 6 I.E.R. 1344 (5th Cir., 1991).

61. *Cole* v. *Fair Oaks Fire Protection District*, 43 Cal.3d 148 (1987).

62. Esther Orioli, "The Key to Controlling Your Stress Claims," *Personnel News*, May 1992, p. 16.

63. Recommended in an audiotape aimed at California employers by David O'Brien, 29 Ways to Reduce Employer's Workers' Compensation Costs, Winterbrook Publishing Co., Covina CA.

64. Reprinted with permission from David O'Brien, (personal correspondence, November 26, 1991).

CHAPTER 8: EVERYTHING ELSE YOU NEED TO KNOW

1. IRS Publication 937, "Business Reporting, Employment Taxes, Information Returns." Also see IRS Form SS-8, "Determination of Employee Work Status for Purposes of Federal Employment Taxes and Income Tax Withholding."

2. See, for example, Maine Statutes, Tit. 39, §146.

3. 29 U.S.C. 201 et seq.

4. 29 U.S.C. 213.

5. U.S. Department of Labor Publication W.H. No. 1340.

6. Title 29, Code of Federal Regulations, §541.1.

7. For both the executive and administrative exemptions, the 60% rule does not apply to employees in multiunit retail establishments. Those executives and administrators must meet the 80% standard. Title 29, Code of Federal Regulations, §541.602.

8. Title 29, Code of Federal Regulations, §541.2.

9. Title 29, Code of Federal Regulations, §541.3.

10. Title 29, Code of Federal Regulations, §541.5.

11. Title 29, Code of Federal Regulations, §541.118.

12. *Abshire* v. *County of Kern*, 908 F.2d 483 (9th Cir. 1990), *cert den'd*, 111 S.Ct. 785 (1991); *Pautlitz* v. *Naperville*, 781 F.Supp. 1368 (N.D. Ill., 1992).

13. *BNA Labor Relations Reporter*, Wages & Hours, 94:1007, Administrative Opinion, 1968.

14. *Truslow* v. *Spotsyvania County Sheriff*, 783 F.Supp. 274 (Dis. Ct. Va. 1992), 29 U.S.C. 203g, 29 C.F.R. 785.11.

15. The states that have overtime laws are Alabama, Alaska, Arizona, Arkansas, California, Colorado, Connecticut, Washington, D.C., Florida, Hawaii, Idaho, Illinois, Kansas, Kentucky, Maine, Maryland, Massachusetts, Mississippi, Minnesota, Montana, Nevada, New Hampshire, New Jersey, New Mexico, New York, North Carolina, North Dakota, Ohio, Oklahoma, Oregon, Pennsylvania, Rhode Island, Texas, Vermont, Washington, West Virginia, Wisconsin, and Wyoming.

16. See, for example, *Thomas* v. *County of Fairfax, Vir.*, 758 F.Supp. 353 (Dist. Ct. Va. 1991).

17. *Carter* v. *Michigan Employment Security Commission*, 111 N.W.2d 817 (Supreme Ct. Mich. 1961).

18. *In re Wrzesinski*, 520 N.Y.S.2d 243 (Sup.Ct.App.Div. 1987).

19. *Southwest Wyoming Rehabilitation Center* v. *Employment Security Commission,* 781 P.2d 918 (Sup.Ct. Wyo. 1989).

20. *Wurst* v. *Dept. of Employment Security,* 818 P.2d 1036 (Ct.App. Utah 1991).

21. California Unemployment Insurance Code §§1030, 1328.

22. Consolidated Omnibus Budget Reconciliation Act of 1985, 29 U.S.C. 1161 et seq.

23. 29 U.S.C. 1161(b).

24. 29 U.S.C. 1166.

25. 29 U.S.C. 1001 et seq., 26 U.S.C. 401 et seq.

26. 29 CFR 2520.102-1 et seq.

27. *Gavalik* v. *Continental Can Co.,* 812 F.2d 834 (3rd Cir. 1987).

28. "Beyond Unions, A Revolution in Employee Rights in the Making," *Business Week,* July 8, 1985, p. 72.

29. Thanks to Ellen Lewis, attorney at law, for her invaluable assistance on this section.

30. *Lawson Milk Co.* v. *Retail Clerks Union Local 698,* 394 N.E.2d 312 (Ct.App. Ohio, 1977).

31. *Republic Aviation Corp.* v. *NLRB,* 324 U.S. 793 (1945).

32. National Labor Relations Act, 29 U.S.C. §158(a).

33. National Labor Relations Act, 29 U.S.C. §158(b).

34. *NLRB* v. *Cal. Western Transport,* 870 F.2d 1481 (9th Cir. 1989).

35. Unilateral changes prohibited, *NLRB* v. *Katz,* 369 U.S. 736 (1962).

36. National Labor Relations Act, 29 U.S.C. 158(d).

37. National Labor Relations Act, 29 U.S.C. 158; *NLRB* v. *MacKay Radio & Tel. Co.,* 304 U.S. 333 (1938); *T.W.A.* v. *Independent Federation of Flight Attendants,* 489 U.S. 426 (1989).

38. *Lingle* v. *Norge,* 486 U.S. 399 (1988).

39. National Labor Relations Act, 29 U.S.C. 159(a).

40. *Gilmer* v. *Interstate/Johnson Lane Corp.,* 111 S.Ct. 1647 (1991).

41. For example, Montana Statutes 7-32-108 (police officers).

42. Federal Tort Claims Act, 28 U.S.C. 2674.

43. California Government Code §3300 et seq.

44. Immigration Reform and Control Act of 1986, P. L. 99.603 Nov. 1986, 100 Stat. 3359, in amended form 8 U.S.C. 1101 et seq.

45. Witkin, *Summary of California Law,* Torts §573-576.

46. 15 U.S.C. 1-7.

47. 15 U.S.C. 12-27.

48. 15 U.S.C. 13.

49. *George Van Camp & Sons Co.* v. *American Can Co.*, 278 U.S. 245, 49 S.Ct. 112, 73 L.Ed. 311 (1929).

CHAPTER 9: YOUR RIGHTS AS A MANAGER

1. For a recent case in which resume fraud discovered after termination could be used to defend a discrimination lawsuit, see *Washington* v. *Lake County, Ill.*, 1992 W.L. 158213 (7th Cir. 1992).

2. *Restatement of Laws* (St. Paul, MN: American Law Institute, 1946).

3. Restatement, Agency, Second, §2, comment a.

4. Restatement, Agency, Second, §409(1), comment c.

5. Restatement, Agency, Second, §13.

6. Restatement of Contracts, Second, §161(d).

7. Restatement, Agency, Second, §379.

8. *Wilcox* v. *St. Croix Labor Union Mut. Homes, Inc.*, 567 F.Supp. 924 (D.C. V.I. 1983).

9. *Fowler* v. *Varian Assoc.*, 196 Cal.App.3d 34, 241 Cal.Rptr. 539 (1987).

10. Restatement, Agency, Second, §393, comment b.

11. Restatement, Agency, Second, §380.

12. Katie Hafner and John Markoff, *Cyberpunk: Outlaws and Hackers on the Computer Frontier*, (New York: Simon & Schuster, 1991), p. 101-102.

13. Restatement, Agency, Second, §380, comment b.

14. Restatement, Agency, Second, §395.

15. Uniform Laws Annotated, Vol. 14, Civil Procedure and Remedial Laws, 1990 (updated 1992 Supp.).

16. Restatement, Torts (First) §757.

17. Ed. Browne, *Competitive Business Practices, 2nd. ed.*, (Berkeley, CA, Continuing Education of the Bar, 1991) §4.12–4.18.

18. *American Credit Indemnity Co.* v. *Sacks*, 213 Cal.App.3d 622, 262 Cal.Rptr. 92 (1989).

19. *Moss, Adams & Co.* v. *Shilling*, 179 Cal.App.3d 124, 224 Cal.Rptr. 456. (1986).

20. List adapted from *Protecting Intellectual Property* (Washington, D.C., American

Corporate Counsel Association, 1990) and from Ed. Browne, *Competitive Business Practices*.

21. *Electro-Craft v. Controlled Motion*, 332 N.W.2d 890 (MN 1983).

22. Restatement, Torts (First), §757(a) comment f.

23. *San Jose Mercury News*, January 4, 1992, p. 10E.

24. Agreement liberally adapted from Ed. Browne, *Competitive Business Practices*, p. 117-118

25. Restatement, Agency, Second, §393, comment e.

26. Agreement adapted from Browne, *Competitive Business Practices*, p. 119.

27. *Moore v. Honeywell Information Systems*, 558 F.Supp. 1229 (D. Hi. 1983).

28. Restatement, Agency, Second, §396.

29. Restatement, Contracts, Second, §§186, 187, 188(2).

30. Restatement, Torts, Second, §766 et seq.

31. *Ernst & Ernst v. Carlson*, 247 Cal.App.2d 125, 55 Cal.Rptr. 626 (1966).

32. Steven G. White, Ph.D., San Francisco (415-398-3966).

33. Restatement, Agency, Second, §385.

34. Williston on Contracts, cited in *Central Alaska Broadcasting, Inc. v. Bracale*, 637 P.2d 711, 713 n. 6 (Alaska Sup. Ct. 1981).

35. *Central Alaska Broadcasting, Inc. v. Bracale* 637 P.2d.

36. Restatement, Agency, Second, §409(2), comment g.

FUTURE INFORMATION

This book is just the beginning. You could contribute to the next one. If there is any information you think should be included (or excluded) in the future, please write me a note. Are there topics you would like to see covered that weren't? Is any part of this book inaccurate, impractical, or confusing? What is your experience? Please correspond to

Rita Risser, J.D.
Stay Out of Court
P. O. Box 2146
Santa Cruz, CA 95063
fax 408-458-0181

INDEX